HOW TO DEVELOP

A Strategic Marketing Plan

A STEP-BY-STEP GUIDE

HOW TO DEVELOP

A Strategic Marketing Plan

A STEP-BY-STEP GUIDE

NORTON PALEY

Taylor & Francis
Taylor & Francis Group
Boca Raton   London   New York

CRC is an imprint of the Taylor & Francis Group,
an informa business

Published in 2000 by
CRC Press
Taylor & Francis Group
6000 Broken Sound Parkway NW, Suite 300
Boca Raton, FL 33487-2742

International Standard Book Number-10: 1-57444-269-4 (Hardcover)
International Standard Book Number-13: 978-1-57444-269-4 (Hardcover)
Library of Congress Card Number 99-045098

**The software (disk) mentioned in this book is now available for download on the CRC Web site at:
http://www.crcpress.com/e_products/downloads/default/.asp**

Library of Congress Cataloging-in-Publication Data

Paley, Norton.
    How to develop a strategic marketing plan : a step-by-step guide / Norton Paley.
        p. cm.
    Includes index.
    ISBN 1-57444-269-4 (alk. paper)
    1. Marketing—Decision making. 2. Marketing—Planning. I. Title.
HF5415.135 .P33   1999
658.8'02 21 dc—21   99-045098

Taylor & Francis Group
is the Academic Division of T&F Informa plc.

**The software mentioned in this book is now available for download on the CRC Web site at:
http://www.crcpress.com/e_products/downloads/default.asp**

Visit the Taylor & Francis Web site at
http://www.taylorandfrancis.com

and the CRC Press Web site at
http://www.crcpress.com

DEDICATION

To my family, with love

CONTENTS

PART VI: COMPUTER DISK: HOW TO DEVELOP A SMP — A STEP-BY-STEP GUIDE

YOUR INTRODUCTION TO STRATEGIC MARKETING PLANNING

Two thirds of rapid-growth firms have written business plans, according to the PricewaterhouseCoopers 1998 Trendsetter Barometer survey. The survey also reveals that over the past 2 years, firms with written plans grow faster, achieve a higher proportion of revenues from new products and services, and enable CEOs to manage more critical business functions than those firms whose plans are unwritten. Additionally, growth firms with a written business plan have increased their revenues 69% faster over the past 5 years than those without a written plan.

As further explicit evidence that planning remains the essential duty and responsibility of all managers, consider the stirring headlines from a *Business Week* cover story:*

> *Strategic Planning — It's Back!*
>
> *Reengineering? Cost-cutting? Been there, done that.*
>
> *Now, strategy is king as Corporate America searches for real growth.*

The story cites four key issues related to planning and strategy:

1. Strategy is again a major focus for higher revenues and profits – and to hatch new products, expand existing business, and create new markets.

---

* Excerpts taken from the *Business Week* cover story, August 26, 1996 issue.

2. Business strategy is the single most important management issue and will remain so into the next decade.
3. Democratizing the strategy process is achieved by handing it over to teams of line and staff managers from different disciplines.
4. Creating networks of relationships with customers, suppliers, and rivals is the strategy of choice to gain greater competitive advantage.

With those convincing validations as the underpinnings for this book, *How to Develop a Strategic Marketing Plan: A Step-by-Step Guide*, is intended expressly for those managers, regardless of job function, who contribute in any way to hatching new products, expanding existing businesses, and creating new markets. Assuming such responsibilities come close to describing your current situation, the central aim is to help you grasp the concepts and apply the techniques of modern strategic marketing planning in a competitive environment.

Most important, this book promises to equip you with the meaningful techniques to generate a credible strategic marketing plan (SMP) so your organization can prosper in 21st-century markets.

Bottom line: properly executed, strategic marketing planning can shape a vision of what the future of your organization would look like. It searches the past and measures performance. It examines the culture of an organization and probes the strengths and weaknesses of people, equipment, and systems.

In its broadest dimension strategic marketing planning sets in motion actions that can impact the economy in which you operate and the long-term prosperity of your organization. In its personal dimension, a well-developed plan can positively affect your career prospects.

This book aims to deliver one primary outcome: you will learn how to develop the SMP for use with an individual product, service, and business unit or for your company as a whole.

Specifically, you will be able to:

■ Customize your own SMP by following the guidelines on the enclosed computer disk.
■ Install an ongoing strategic marketing planning system in your organization or refine the one you already use.
■ Identify business-building opportunities by examining, through actual cases, how the best-in-class companies use strategic marketing planning to solve aggravating competitive problems.

PLANNING IN PERSPECTIVE

To set the stage for planning — and more specifically the SMP — let's see how business planning evolved over the past 45 years. Then, you can more accurately identify critical issues impacting the SMP and view the organizational conditions necessary for developing your plan.

Modern business planning developed over a period of 4 decades. The following historical perspective explains the disquieting relationship of planning in an *internal* organizational environment against the often harsh realities of *external* market forces. You will see why strategic marketing planning developed into the preferred planning format for the 1990s, and why it is likely to remain the model for several decades into the 21st century.

The 1950s

The 1950s was a period of overwhelming economic influence by the U.S. throughout most of the world. During that time, corporate planning dominated most of the larger U.S. companies.

Consisting primarily of production plans, this type of planning focused on satisfying an insatiable demand for consumer goods within the U.S. It also responded to a demand for specific industrial products to help those countries ravaged by World War II rebuild their economies and redevelop consumer markets.

At the highest organizational levels, ranking officers developed corporate plans while maintaining a dominant financial focus. Rarely did lower-echelon managers participate in those planning sessions.

In contrast, lower-level managers geared their planning to maximize productivity for the short-term satisfaction of market demand. Marketing as a distinct unifying function enveloping product development, marketing research, advertising, sales promotion, and field selling did not exist at that time.

The 1960s

Strong consumer demand for products characterized the 1960s. Yet serious competition still remained limited. Overall, U.S. companies were able to sell all they produced. And there was no urgency to change procedures, other than to keep the production lines moving efficiently. In general, what was produced was consumed. The business environment was marked by intensified economic growth in most of the industrialized countries.

In addition to domestic markets and those developing markets in European industrialized countries, third-world countries slowly emerged as customers for products to sustain the basic needs of life. Such products included simple machines, some types of agricultural equipment, and basic transportation in the form of buses and bicycles.

Organizations began to look to business planning as a way to involve senior executives who represented the core activities of manufacturing, research and development, sales, and distribution. As part of the longer-term planning process, there was a conscious effort to integrate diverse business functions through a coordinated plan of operations. In spite of this planning breakthrough, however, long-term plans were still kept separate from those short-term plans prepared by middle managers.

The 1970s

This decade triggered a transitional phase in planning. With the post-war rebuilding process about complete, its full effect was about to impact the world. European companies burst onto U.S. markets. It was the Japanese companies, however, that generated the most aggressive and penetrating competition. The full thrust of their competitive assault hit virtually every major industry from machine tools and consumer electronics to automobiles and steel. The new competitive situation ignited the surging movement to marketing planning.

In turn, marketing planning of the 1970s signaled a period of market identification and expansion. In the U.S., customers demanded more varied products and services and they were willing to pay for them. Responding to the continuing population shift out of the cities, businesses followed increasingly affluent customers into the expanding suburban shopping malls.

Executives reshaped their organizations and merged the individual plans of the once scattered activities of merchandising, advertising, sales promotion, publicity, and field selling into a unified plan to identify and satisfy changing market demands. Typically, the marketing plans developed by middle managers covered a 1-year period.

Within those plans, managers emphasized emerging geographic markets, new technology applications, and international markets. They made extensive use of demographic profiles to define markets with greater precision. Beyond demographics, a new approach to market definition emerged that utilized psychographics, a profiling system that described prospects by lifestyle and behavior.

Marketing as an independent business discipline expanded rapidly into undergraduate and graduate degree programs at state and private universities. In keeping with the evolving and changing market conditions, a broad definition of marketing developed:

> *Marketing is a total system of interacting business activities designed to plan, price, promote, and distribute want-satisfying products and services to organizational and household users in a competitive environment at a profit.*

That definition emphasized understanding customer needs and developing comprehensive programs to satisfy the wants of different market segments. Further, a *total system of interacting business activities* called for integrating various business activities, such as manufacturing, research and development, promotion, and distribution. Doing so justified the use of strategy teams consisting of individuals from each of those functions. It also reaffirmed the integration already begun through business planning.

Managers viewed the marketing planning document as a "housing" to contain all of the above functions and activities in a logical and organized format. Then, to encourage clear and precise communications throughout the organization, the plan became the medium to reach all levels of the organization.

By the late 1970s, still another form of planning took hold: Strategic Planning. Strategic Planning aimed to build on to the long-term, financially oriented corporate plans of the 1960s by adding a strategic focus to the process. More precisely:

> *Strategic planning is the managerial process of developing and maintaining a strategic fit between the organization and its changing market opportunities. It relies on developing (1) a mission or strategic direction, (2) objectives and goals, (3) growth strategies, and (4) a business portfolio consisting of markets and products.*

Corporations still use the generalized terms strategic planning, corporate planning, and business planning. And managers consider them part of a common business vocabulary. Regardless of the term used, the intent shows that volatile environmental, economic, industry, customer, and competitive factors require a more expansive and disciplined strategic thought process for effective planning.

No longer could top-down 1950s-style corporate planning driven by a production-orientation plan suffice. The competitive international marketplace of the 1970s required a more precise orientation satisfied by strategic planning and marketing planning. In turn, that planning approach served as a springboard to the next level of planning.

The 1980s

The 1980s spurred the next stage of planning — strategic marketing planning — which merged two planning formats: the long-term strategic plan and the short-term marketing plan.

There are several reasons why the SMP evolved to this stage of the planning cycle:

1. Although strategic planning permitted managers to create a long-term vision of how the organization could grow, for the most part it lacked implementation. A survey conducted by Deloitte Consulting, the large accounting and management consulting firm, indicated that while 97% of the Fortune 500 companies wrote strategic plans, only 15% of that group ever implemented anything that came out of the plan.

2. Marketing planning incorporated the various activities associated with the marketing function into an action-oriented plan. The planning period, however, was usually 1 year. No formalized planning process existed to link the longer-term strategic plan that needed an implementation phase with the shorter-term marketing plan that required a strategic vision.

3. Typically, each plan developed independently within the organization. No procedure unified planning efforts consistent with the marketing definition of *a total system of interacting activities designed to plan, price, promote, and distribute want-satisfying products to organizational and household users in a competitive environment.*

4. The U.S. marketplace experienced turbulent upheavals during the 1980s: a slowing of real growth, changing demographics, changing life-styles, fragmented markets, deregulation of major industries, global competition, rapid technological change, shortened product life cycles, and accelerated product innovations.

Under those mind-boggling conditions, the SMP evolved to create a linkage of the strategic plan with the marketing plan. It linked the internal functions of the organization with the external and volatile changes of a competitive global environment.

The 1990s

As corporations of the 1980s and 1990s reengineered and downsized to create cost-effective and leaner organizations, a further innovation evolved. The middle-level manager was asked to develop the SMP for his or her product, service, or department.

Using the SMP as a hands-on format, the manager could now conceptualize a product with a long-term strategic direction that focused on future customer and market needs. He or she could project what changes would take place in a framework of industry, consumer, competitive, and environmental areas and identify ways in which technologies would change business practices.

The following classic case illustrates the solid linkage of strategic planning issues with market-related considerations. It demonstrates the compelling relationship between internal organizational functions and external market conditions, the foundation upon which SMPs are developed.

CASE EXAMPLE

Heublein Inc. produces Smirnoff vodka, a leading brand with a dominant share of the U.S market. At one point, Smirnoff was attacked on price by another brand, Wolfschmidt, produced by The Seagram Company Ltd. Wolfschmidt was priced at $1.00 a bottle less than Smirnoff and claimed the same quality. The purpose of the price attack was to capture market share from Smirnoff.

Recognizing a real danger of customers switching to Wolfschmidt, Heublein devised a plan to protect its market dominance. The plan called for raising the price of Smirnoff by $1.00 and preserving the premier image the brand already enjoyed.

Next, Heublein introduced a new brand, Relska, and positioned it head-to-head as a fighting brand against the price and market segment of Wolfschmidt. While that holding action was taking place, Heublein introduced still another brand, Popov, at $1.00 less than Wolfschmidt.

By the end of the 1980s, Smirnoff remained number one in cases shipped of all imported and domestic vodka shipped in the U.S., with Popov in the number two position. Wolfschmidt did not achieve its objective of capturing market share. In fact, there was some deterioration in its market share.

This case illustrates both internal and external factors, long- and short-term strategic marketing issues, and points to the major attributes of strategic marketing planning, such as:

- *Competitive marketing strategies.* The primary output of an SMP consists of competitive marketing strategies. For instance, the planning output of Smirnoff was a series of short- and long-term strategies to retain its dominance as a market leader. And short-term actions to reposition Smirnoff upscale through an increase in price, with related trade and consumer promotions, could be accomplished relatively quickly.

  On the other hand, the strategic decision to invest in two new products had long-term considerations, driven by the corporate objective to retain market share leadership. In effect, Heublein mobilized to meet the competitive attack.

■ *Cross-functional strategy development.* Strategies identified in the SMP should incorporate virtually every function of an organization. For Heublein it was product development, manufacturing, distribution, finance, and product management for three brands: the flagship Smirnoff, the fighting brand Relska, and the lower-priced Popov.

■ *Strategic focus.* The SMP should have a long-term strategic focus that attempts to forecast consumer purchase patterns; examine environmental factors; assess the level of competitive intrusion; and evaluate the nature of the industry on such factors as growth, stability, and decline.

As for Heublein managers, they had to examine future consumption patterns of vodka and determine regulatory considerations related to legal and moral issues impacting the product. After determining the magnitude of industry changes, the managers then considered manufacturing efficiencies, cost structures, and emerging technologies. Finally, by assessing what strategies the Seagrams managers would employ for Wolfschmidt, Smirnoff managers evaluated their ability to sustain aggressive efforts.

CRITICAL ISSUES IMPACTING THE STRATEGIC MARKETING PLAN

The 4 decades of planning evolution culminated in the adoption of the SMP as a preferred form of planning. The refinement of this planning approach will undoubtedly increase with the continuing globalization of markets. For example, the big growth engines of the U.S. and Europe will drive growth in numerous markets on both sides of the Atlantic for the foreseeable future.

Attempting to gain a foothold in emerging markets will employ acquisition, joint venture, or other forms of strategic alliances. However, thanks to the movement of Europe to a single currency of the euro, there has been a consolidation of 11 different countries. With the euro, the 9100 public corporations in Europe come close to the 9900 in America to create massive NAFTA and euro zone trading blocs. Thus, new markets will emerge, others will decline. Countries once dormant will awaken. Others once supreme will decline.

What does this mean for you as a manager attempting to develop a realistic plan? Strategic marketing planning permits you to ask pertinent questions in a structured format. It allows a logical thought process to suggest competitive strategies to maneuver, survive, and grow in the long term and the short term.

Let's examine the critical issues that would influence your SMP. These include market-related problems, company orientation, and managerial participation.

Market-Related Problems

As we saw in the Smirnoff case, the Wolfschmidt price attack created an urgent problem that Heublein managers had to address. For Heublein, the strategies that emerged from the plan not only dealt with the initial price attack, but also focused on long-term product development to sustain market share leadership.

Similarly, you should identify which issues affect your business and determine those that are temporary or long lasting. The time you take to assess your market-related problems can influence the quality of your plan. Think about the following categories related to such dilemmas as:

Sales Decline

If you face a sales decline, it may be temporary due to a local market condition. Or it could be a seasonal factor remedied by short-term sales promotion incentives such as coupons or cash rebates. However, if you face a sales decline inconsistent with industry trends and the overall performance of competitors, there is a possibility of a more serious problem.

The problem could also stem from a faulty distribution network, inadequate promotion, deteriorating management/labor relations, poor-quality products — or even incompetent management. The possibilities are extensive and would influence the development of your plan.

Slow Growth

Slow growth typically results from one of the following: mature products and flat sales growth due to the introduction of similar, undifferentiated products by competitors; or it could be the flattening of the economy due to local or national issues.

For example, the personal computer (PC) reached maturity during the 1990s, characterized by clones attacking the market at bargain-basement prices, and the leveling of consumer demand. Then the total computer industry, not just individual product categories, reported in 1999 that sales increases were at single-digit levels compared with historical sales patterns measured in double digits.

Either of these components could drive long-term planning objectives and strategies, as well as short-term objectives and tactics. For instance, the dire planning implications of a mature product might shift your objectives and strategies to differentiating your products based on quality, reliability, durability, or performance. And the SMP might include such value-added services as post-sales technical support and just-in-time delivery to deal with slow market growth.

As for a mature industry, the planning objectives and strategies would focus on market segmentation, with emphasis on identifying emerging, neglected, and poorly served niches. Based on corporate objectives and the culture of the organization, the planning approach could even permit aggressive action to the point of assuming a combative attitude toward competitors. In turn, such an attitude could result in pushing for sales or market share through competitive displacement.

Changing Buying Behavior

Here, the planning issue concerns management's responsiveness (or unresponsiveness) to changing buying behavior. To what extent is management willing to react to changing consumer buying patterns vs. continuing its past practices, regardless of changing market conditions?

For example, a small Texas-based company, Tecnol Medical Products Inc., noted the fears and anxieties of hospital personnel who worried about infection from fatal viruses and bacteria in their workplaces. Recognizing such buying behavior as a valuable opportunity, Tecnol created a line of high-tech surgical masks that protected physicians and nurses against the growing threats of HIV, the increasing number of tuberculosis cases, and the introduction of laser surgical procedures that produce airborne bacteria from cast-off diseased tissue.

Despite the presence of giant competitors such as 3M and Johnson & Johnson, Tecnol has grown its market share to command 50% of the surgical mask market.

Increasing Competition

Competition is a market-related problem of immense impact on the SMP. For example, consider these issues:

■ Why are more and more competitors entering against you and successfully increasing sales and market share vs. your flat or declining performance?

- What did you neglect in product quality, customer service, or distributor relationships that created opportunities for competitors to enter against you?
- While you focused on traditional competitors, what attention did you give to the surprise intrusion of emerging competitors? Which firms are entering against you through acquisition, joint venture, licensing, or other forms of strategic alliances that can unbalance your efforts and even defeat you?
- How would you describe your management's attitudes toward competition? *Passive* or *active?* The passive attitude is expressed by doing nothing; maybe the problem will go away. Or, the active one is demonstrated by such actions as tracking competitors' penetration of the market, assessing their strengths and weaknesses, and evaluating their future strategies.
- Is there a willingness to relinquish control of market segments against the threat of competitor attack? Or is it one of assuming an aggressive stance to protect a market position?

Company Orientation

Another critical issue to consider before you begin creating the SMP is your company's orientation. Here the issues are similar to the above, but the outcome depends on your assessment of the situation and how it is expressed in the aggressiveness or conservativeness of your plan. For instance, consider the level of risk you and your management are willing to assume.

Think, too, about the kind of innovative strategies you come up with in market selection, product modification, promotion creativity, distribution strength, and pricing flexibility — and, most importantly, those you can implement.

Further, company orientation encompasses your attitudes toward both competitors and customers. Take into account the following factors while assessing your company's orientation:

Focus on Product vs. Focus on Customers

"Give them any color they want, as long as it's black," declared Henry Ford. This now-famous comment reflects a company orientation that brought the Ford Motor Company to the brink of bankruptcy in the 1930s. Compare that orientation to the declaration of a senior executive of IBM, who said, "This is the year of the customer."

Each comment reflects an attitude that permeated those organizations and influenced their respective marketing strategies, including the range of products offered. In turn, attitudes translate to expectations about sales volume, share of market, profitability, level of customer satisfaction, and degree of distributor loyalty.

Insignificant Marketing Research vs. Extensive Marketing Research

A company's customer orientation mirrors the thoroughness with which you conduct marketing research and how you apply the findings in making decisions.

For instance, how much would you spend to evaluate the long-term sales potential of market segments, track changing consumer needs, assess competitors' activities, identify new products, and evaluate the competitive advantage of additional services? Where a small company cannot afford formal research, it could obtain reliable feedback by maintaining close relationships with customers and informally observing nuances of market behavior.

For the SMP, the crystal-clear implication is that marketing research provides the documentation that helps management put the puzzle pieces together and clarifies its competitive position on long-term growth and short-term gains.

Product and Service Development: Self-Guided vs. Guided by Marketing

The Henry Ford statement cited above reflects the self-guided engineering or production orientation toward product development. The IBM attitude is the opposite and expresses a more desirable market-driven orientation. Thus, the probing question: what is the orientation of *your* organization?

Expressed differently, the this-is-what-we-make, this-is-what-we-sell mentality can impact negatively on a SMP. First, it defies the intent of the strategic marketing definition presented earlier. Second, it implies a lack of organizational sensitivity to properly serve markets and customers. (More on this point under the following topic, Managerial Participation.)

Primary Interest in Production Economies vs. Providing Need Satisfactions

How would you describe the power structure within the organization? If the criterion for deciding on new products is anchored to the production department, whose primary interest is production economies, there could be a narrow, inside-out orientation that dominates the decision-making process. Such an orientation reduces the strategic alternatives open to you within the SMP.

Conversely, the outside-in approach of providing need satisfactions presents the opposite and more desirable orientation of permitting the industry, customer, environmental, and competitive factors to dominate the planning process. Therefore, it is in your best interest to determine where the organizational power is located within your organization.

Managerial Participation

The third critical issue impacting the SMP consists of the amount and type of senior managerial participation. A delicate balance must be struck between too much or too little participation. The participation can be positive or negative, reflected in the degree of autonomy given to you as a manager and the amount of risk you will be permitted to take. All of these factors impact on your approach to planning.

In planning, you cannot underestimate the importance of the culture of your organization. Culture includes the behaviors, patterns, and rules of all employees interacting within your organization. It is the composite of all value systems identified by your company's orientation, levels of authority, the amount of risk tolerated, and the level of resources committed to a project, product, or market.

ORGANIZATIONAL CONDITIONS FOR DEVELOPING AN EFFECTIVE STRATEGIC MARKETING PLAN

Thus far, we have examined the evolution of planning and studied the critical issues related to the SMP. Now let's identify the organizational changes needed to develop an effective SMP. Here are examples to illustrate the point:

Senior management at Dow Chemical initiated dramatic organizational changes in 1981 when it moved from a primary role as manufacturer of basic chemicals to a more expansive mode of producer of specialty chemicals serving a collection of diverse markets.

The change led to new and exciting developments from agricultural products to new ventures in plastics for the automotive industry. Managers at all levels adopted a customer-oriented attitude they called an "outside-in approach." This attitude contrasted with their former inside-out, production orientation of maintaining a position as a low-cost producer of basic commodity chemicals.

Consider, too, Lee Iacocca's transformation of Chrysler Corporation in the 1980s from an unresponsive, production-driven organization on the edge of bankruptcy to a successful customer-driven company that has made remarkable strides through the 1990s to its current status as Daimler-Chrysler.

Iacocca began by trimming half its white-collar work force, wiping out layers of management to permit faster communications, and encouraging bold, entrepreneurial thinking to flourish. Planning once done exclusively at corporate headquarters was extended to the regional levels. Regional managers were trained and encouraged to plan strategically for growth in their own territory and to execute their plans with constant attention to customer needs, as measured by ongoing customer satisfaction studies.

Former CEO Bob Allen of AT&T shook up this once bureaucratic, highly regulated, super-conservative company. No longer could planning take place as in the days of a regulated monopoly with predictable price increases, complacency about competition, and uncritical of costs.

Allen pushed planning and decision making down — far down into the organization. Middle managers gained authority. They shed some of the old and tired conservatism — unacceptable now in a deregulated industry where ambitious domestic and global competitors fight aggressively for pieces of AT&T's market share.

Organizational Alternative

What if you are not in a high enough position to make such far-reaching organizational changes as those exhibited by Dow, Chrysler, and AT&T? What are your options? One organizational format that is exceedingly efficient for developing a SMP at the divisional, departmental, and product line levels is the team approach.

As a general rule, and where possible, your best approach to developing a SMP is to form a strategy team that represents every functional part of your organization, such as product development, finance, sales, marketing, and distribution (or any other function important to your operation.)

Using a team often overrides much of the resistance (sometimes adversarial) from other functional managers by merging their expertise, cooperation, and, most important, their support into your SMP.

Let's look at Dow Chemical for practical guidance. Over the past 20 years, the Midland, MI company has perfected the team approach as a way to integrate planning throughout all levels of the organization. It pushes decision making down through the layers of management to the lowest decision making level. And because of the multifunctional makeup of the team, it permits the implementation of the customer-driven, outside-in orientation among participating managers.

Dow uses such designations as Business Management Team, Product Management Team, Market Management Team, and Industry Management Team to identify different levels of team action.

Let's recap the reasons for using a team approach. Recall the definition of strategic marketing as a *total system of interacting business activities designed to plan, price, promote, and distribute want-satisfying products and services to end users in a competitive environment at a profit.*

To activate the definition calls for the interaction of individuals from different functions. It requires teamwork toward reaching such goals as protecting and growing existing markets and products to advancing into new and emerging markets with products that satisfy customers and solve their problems.

For those reasons the team approach acts as the most effective organizational format for developing the SMP. It is the easiest method for obtaining interaction and multifunctional participation when compared to the upheaval usually associated with initiating major organizational changes. You will find a list of duties and responsibilities in Chapter 5, Help Topics.

OUTCOMES OF THE STRATEGIC MARKETING PLAN

The whole purpose of the SMP — and the only practical reason for developing such a plan — is to develop strategies. Broadly defined, strategies are actions to achieve objectives that complement and support corporate policy.

To reinforce this assertion about planning, Dwight D. Eisenhower, the distinguished U.S. general of World War II fame and late U.S. president stated, *"The plan is nothing; planning is everything."*

Meaning: plans are useless unless implemented. Strategizing, thinking, conceptualizing, and implementing represent the action concepts associated with planning and thereby become the primary outcomes of the SMP.

Consequently, as you and a team begin developing a SMP, use the following guidelines to assess the value of your SMP:

■ Are there strategies to enlarge and penetrate existing markets? That means attracting new users, increasing sales to current users, and increasing customers' frequency of use as measured by such criteria as sales, profits, unit volume, and share of market.

■ Are there strategies for developing new markets? New markets are those that are emerging for your products and services because of changing buyer demands, neglected segments now available through new channels of distribution or because of a new technology, or poorly served markets surfacing due to a new capability to provide adequate service.

■ Are there clearly defined positioning strategies for your product or service? Positioning is defined in two ways: first, how your company or product is perceived by your prospects and customers. For example, what image does your product communicate in terms of quality, delivery, application, or reliability? Second, how is your product positioned against competitors? Is it firmly positioned against a dominant competitor through differentiation using superior quality, just-in-time delivery, or improved post-sales service? Or if you are the market share leader, is it positioned to actively deter a competitor as you match or exceed the competitor's innovation and thereby cancel out any product advantage?

■ Are there strategies to protect existing sales volume or share of market? This SMP guideline suggests that while looking for new markets and pursuing other enticing opportunities, it is important not to neglect existing customers.

■ Are there strategies to launch new products? Assuming that new products, line extensions, or modifications of existing products are included in your SMP, have you identified appropriate strategies to develop and launch or relaunch those products?

Finally, the dominant reasons why the SMP evolved as the preferred form of business planning is as follows:

Managers are able to develop a long-term strategic vision for a product, division, or company, depending on their level in the organization. Also, while the short-term marketing plan focused on immediate action, it lacked a strategic focus, whereas the SMP format ensures that action plans contribute to achieving strategic long-term goals.

Also, the SMP encourages the participation of various functional managers in the planning process through planning teams. Doing so permits an outward market-driven focus vs. continuing a narrow and inward production-driven orientation. And, most importantly, the SMP focuses on generating competitive marketing strategies in keeping with the growing intensity of global competition.

GETTING THE MOST OUT OF THIS BOOK

As you work through each chapter of the SMP, you will continually improve your knowledge of planning, regardless of what your company calls the process — strategic planning, business planning, or marketing planning. You will find application checks, real company examples, and case studies embedded throughout the book to help you link new skills back to your job.

Special Features

To assist you in making correct decisions and developing a customized SMP for your company, business unit, or product, the following special features are included in this book:

Help Topics

Chapter 5 is a convenient reference for you to access comprehensive information and in-depth guidelines as you go through the planning process. For best results, refer to Help Topics on an as-need basis as you develop each section of the SMP. For easy use, the topics are keyed to the applicable SMP section.

Also, beyond its specific use in the planning process, you will find Help Topics immensely practical as a general resource in designing business-building strategies and sharpening marketing management skills.

SMP Computer Disk

A computer disk for your office or home PC is enclosed with this book. It contains planning forms and guidelines that permit you to develop your own customized SMP. You can use the disk to see your plan evolve from its first draft through updates resulting from changing market and internal conditions to a final version that you submit to management (or a bank) for approval and funding.

Additionally, you can install SMP as a regular part of your management systems.

The book is divided into the following chapters:

Your Introduction to Strategic Marketing Planning: This chapter introduced you to the Strategic Marketing Plan (SMP) and presented an historical perspective on how planning evolved in the U.S.

Chapter 1: The Strategic Marketing Plan — Strategic Section: Using a real company to illustrate the planning techniques (only the name is disguised for confidentiality), you will begin the step-by-step process to see how the long-term strategic portion of the SMP is formed.

Chapter 2: The Strategic Marketing Plan — Tactical Section: Continuing with the case example, you will learn how to develop the 1-year tactical section of your SMP and how it links to the strategic section.

Chapter 3: Marketing Problem Solver: the Strategic Marketing Plan in Action: Actual case examples show how successful companies solved severe competitive problems — and won. Should your company face similar problems, you will find action strategies you can implement within your own organization. Again, references are made to the sections of the SMP that address those problems.

Chapter 4: Checklists for Developing Competitive Strategies: Where you need to evaluate the potential of a market or use a system to generate competitive strategies, several evaluation checklists are provided to add precision to your SMP.

Chapter 5: Help Topics: As indicated above under Special Features, Help Topics provide in-depth information and guidelines as handy references for developing Chapters 1 and 2, the specific chapters devoted to developing the SMP. This additional background information can assist you in adding meaningful content to your SMP.

Appendix: SMP Computer Disk

Also, as discussed under Special Features, you can use the disk in your own computer to customize your SMP. While maintaining the basic structure of the SMP, you are free to alter the forms to accommodate the special vocabulary and issues related to your industry and company. You can even add special forms or spreadsheets required by your organization and thereby make the SMP a permanent part of your operation.

Finally, there is one caution in using the SMP format: don't short-circuit the plan by skipping sections or altering the sequence in which the SMP is prepared. It is shown as a logical process leading you step-by-step from section to section, from the broad strategic focus to the narrow tactical implementation. The intent is to free up your mind to think broadly about your product or service, convert your thinking into a business perspective, and then follow through with action.

You are now ready to proceed to the next chapter and learn how to prepare your own SMP. As you go through the process, remember you are not alone. You have a good deal of assistance throughout this book to help you sharpen your planning skills. With planning as the mainstay requirement for every manager's job, honing those skills can serve you profitably over the course of your career.

Good luck and successful planning.

THE AUTHOR

Norton Paley has over 25 years of corporate experience in general management, marketing management, and product development at McGraw-Hill, Inc., John Wiley & Sons, and Alexander-Norton, Inc. He has authored seven books:

- *The Strategic Marketing Planner*
- *Action Guide to Marketing Planning and Strategy*
- *The Manager's Guide to Marketing Planning and Strategy*
- *Marketing for the Non-Marketing Executive*
- *Pricing Strategies and Practices*
- *Marketing: Principles and Tactics Everyone Must Know*
- *The Manager's Guide to Competitive Marketing Strategies, Second Edition*

In addition to advising management on competitive strategies and strategic planning, Paley also has extensive experience lecturing to managers, engineers, scientists, and marketing/sales personnel at such firms as American Express, Co., Babcock & Wilcox, Cargill, Inc. (worldwide), Chevron Chemical, Dow Chemical (worldwide), GTE, McDonnell-Douglas, Ohio Bell, Prentice-Hall, and W.R. Grace & Co. He has participated, as well, in lecture tours sponsored by the Republic of China and the U.S. Embassy for the Republic of Mexico.

Currently he writes a column on the Website of National Alliance of Sales and Marketing Executives and has been a featured columnist in *The*

Management Review and Sales & Marketing Management. Paley also publishes *The Successful Strategist* newsletter which covers case histories detailing the effective application of business-building strategies and tactics.

I

STRATEGIC
SECTION

1

THE STRATEGIC MARKETING PLAN

CHAPTER OBJECTIVES

Given the information in this chapter, you will be able to:

1. Outline the strategic section of the Strategic Marketing Plan (SMP).
2. Interpret the SMP guidelines by examining the plan of an actual company.
3. Apply the guidelines to developing your own SMP.

OVERVIEW

Now that you understand the history of planning and the evolution of the SMP as outlined in the previous chapter, you are ready to develop your own plan.

You can obtain optimum results for a SMP by following a process, which is diagrammed in Figure 1.1. (Each section of the SMP diagram will be highlighted as the material is discussed in the text.) As you examine the flowchart, notice that the top row of boxes represents the *strategic* portion of the plan and covers a 3- to 5-year time frame.

The bottom row of boxes displays the *tactical* 1-year marketing plan. Although these sections — strategic and tactical — are discussed in separate chapters for ease of explanation, in actual form it is the merging of the strategic plan and the marketing plan into one unified SMP that makes it a complete format. (The previous introduction explained the justification for merging the two formerly separate plans.)

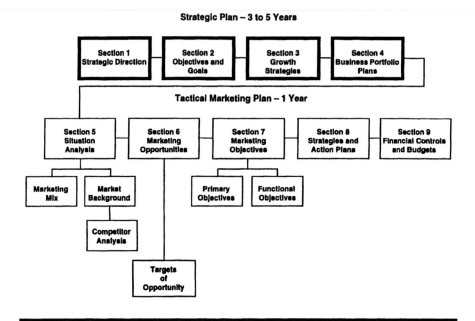

Figure 1.1 Strategic Marketing Plan

You will find that following the SMP process will add an organized and disciplined approach to your thinking, yet the process in no way confines your thinking or creativity. Instead, it enhances your inventiveness and extends a strategy vision that elevates the creative process. In turn, that strategy vision can pay off in abundant opportunities expressed through markets, products, and services.

This chapter and Chapter 2 address each section shown in Figure 1.1. To make the most comfortable learning experience for you, the following format is used for each section:

- *Planning Guidelines:* each section of the SMP is defined with point-by-point directions to help you master the process.
- *Application:* a sample plan of an actual company illustrates each part of the plan. Where appropriate, additional commentary is added to more fully explain the usage.
- *Working Draft:* as you go through each section, you can make notes and develop your own draft. When completed, you can transfer the draft and any subsequent updates to the SMP computer disk provided with the book.
- *Help Topics:* Chapter 5 provides you with comprehensive information on the more complex topics covered in this chapter and

Chapter 2. Referring to it often will ease your decision making and enhance your planning expertise.

THE STRATEGIC PLAN: LOOKING FORWARD 3 TO 5 YEARS

The top row in Figure 1.1, consisting of four boxes, represents the *strategic plan* portion of the SMP. The strategic plan is defined as the managerial process for developing and maintaining a strategic fit *between* the organization and changing market opportunities. It relies on developing the following sections: (1) a strategic direction or mission statement, (2) objectives and goals, (3) a growth strategy, and (4) business portfolio plans.

SECTION 1: STRATEGIC DIRECTION

Let's begin with the first box, Section 1, *Strategic Direction*. This is where you create a strategic direction — also known as a mission or vision — for your company, division, product, or service.

```
Section 1
Strategic Direction
```

Planning Guidelines

You can use the following questions to provide an organized approach to developing a strategic direction. Answering the questions will help you shape the ideal vision of what your company, business unit, or product/service will look like over the next 3 to 5 years. More precisely, it should echo your and your team's long-range philosophy, as long as it is consistent with overall corporate objectives and policy.

As you think about your strategic direction, consider the following six questions:

1. What are your firm's distinctive areas of expertise?
2. What business should your firm be in over the next 3 to 5 years? How will it differ from what exists today?
3. What segments or categories of customers will you serve?

4. What additional functions are you likely to fulfill for customers as you see the market evolve?
5. What new technologies will you require to satisfy future customer/market needs?
6. What changes are taking place in markets, consumer behavior, competition, environment, culture, and the economy that will impact your company?

The point of this exercise is that first, the responsibility for defining a strategic direction no longer belongs exclusively to upper management; second, there are a host of internal and external issues that can affect your SMP.

For best results, managers from various departments — marketing, product development, manufacturing, finance, and sales — should contribute to defining the strategic direction of the business or individual product.

Let's examine each of the above questions:

1. What are your firm's distinctive areas of expertise?

This question refers to your organization's (or business unit's) competencies. You can answer by evaluating the following:

■ Relative competitive strengths of your product or service based on customer satisfaction, profitability, and market share
■ Relationships with distributors and/or end-use customers
■ Existing production capabilities
■ Size of your sales force
■ Financial strength
■ R&D expenditures
■ Amount of customer or technical service provided

Further, where time and resources permit, you can delve into the question by conducting a strength/weakness analysis that serves as a marketing audit. (You will find a practical format for conducting a marketing audit in Chapter 4.)

2. What business should your firm be in over the next 3 to 5 years? How will it differ from what exists today?

The major work in this area of strategic thinking is attributed to Theodore Levitt,[1] of the Harvard Business School, in his classic article, "Marketing

---

[1] T. Levitt, "Marketing Myopia," *Harvard Business Review* (Sept./Oct. 1975), p. 28.

Table 1.1 Company Identity as Reflected by Orientation Concepts	
Product-Driven Orientation	*Market-Driven Orientation*
Railroad company	Transportation company
Oil company	Energy company
Baby food manufacturer	Child care business
Cosmetics company	Beauty, fashion, health company
Computer manufacturing company	Information processing company
Electrical wire manufacturer	Energy transfer business
Vacuum cleaner manufacturer	Cleaner environment business
Valve company	Fluid control company

Myopia." Using the railroads as a prime example, Levitt shows how the railway system declined in use as technology advanced, because executives defined the business too narrowly. He explains that to continue growing, companies must determine customers' needs and wants and not rely simply on the longevity of their products.

According to Levitt, a myopic view is grounded on the following four beliefs that begin in a manager's mind and permeate an organization: (1) growth is guaranteed by an expanding and affluent population, (2) there is no competitive substitute for the industry's major product, (3) excessive belief in mass production and rapidly declining unit costs as output rises, and (4) preoccupation with a product that lends itself to experimentation and manufacturing cost improvement.

The key point: looking out the window toward inevitable change, not into a mirror that reflects existing patterns, characterizes the market-driven vs. a product-driven organization.

Table 1.1 illustrates how organizations in a variety of industries express their identity between those two orientations of product driven vs. market driven. Note, too, how the differing perceptions would change the character of an organization and, in turn, become the underpinnings of a company's (or business unit's) strategic direction.

Thus, to continue growing, managers must create a viable strategic direction that looks critically at marketable trends and connects them with customers' needs and wants. Doing so avoids relying on the longevity of existing products to sustain company growth.

The implications of how you strategically position your business for the future determines the breadth of existing and new product lines and the range of existing and new markets served. If you are too narrow (myopic in Levitt's terms) in defining your business, the resulting product and market mix will be generally narrow, and possibly too confining for growth.

Conversely, defining your business too broadly can result in spreading capital, people, and other resources beyond the capabilities of the organization. You can create a balance by defining the scope of your business on two dimensions:

First, examine the culture, skills, and resources of your organization. Second, consider such factors as customer needs, business functions to be enhanced or added, and types of new technologies you need to compete successfully. The answers will emerge through the question and answer process suggested in this section.

3. What segments or categories of customers will you serve?

Customers exist at various levels in the distribution channel and in different segments of the market. At the end of the channel are end-use consumers with whom you may or may not come within direct contact.

Other customers in the distribution chain serve as intermediaries and typically perform several functions. Intermediaries include distributors who take possession of the products and often serve as a warehousing facility. Still other intermediaries repackage products and maintain inventory control systems to serve the next level of distribution. And there are value-added resellers that provide customer service, technical advice, computer software, or educational programs to differentiate their products from those of competitors.

Examining the existing and future needs at each level of distribution helps you project the types of customers you want to target for the 3- to 5-year period covered by the strategic portion of your SMP. Similarly, you will want to review various segments and target those that will provide the best opportunities over the planning period.

4. What additional functions are you likely to fulfill for customers as you see the market evolve?

As competitive intensity increases worldwide, each intermediary customer from distributor to dealer is increasingly pressured to maintain a competitive advantage. This guideline question asks you to determine what functions or capabilities are needed to solve customers' problems.

More precisely, you are looking beyond your immediate customer and reaching out further into the distribution channel to identify those functions that would solve your customers' *customers'* problems. Such functions might include providing computerized inventory control, after-sales technical support, quality control programs, just-in-time delivery, or financial assistance. Overall, this question relates to the "myopia" issue of defining the business in terms of customer needs.

5. What new technologies will you require to satisfy future customer/market needs?

Within the framework of the previous question and the practices of your industry, examine the impact of technologies to satisfy your customers' needs. Look at where your company ranks with such technologies as computer-aided design, computer-aided manufacturing, computer-integrated manufacturing systems that maintain high levels of quality, and electronic data interchange for rapid order processing and just-in-time delivery.

Also appraise such emerging technologies as expert diagnostic systems that utilize artificial intelligence for problem solving. Look, too, at the rapidly changing communications systems to link home office to field sales and the customer.

6. What changes are taking place in markets, consumer behavior, competition, environment, culture, and the economy that will impact your company?

This form of external analysis permits you to sensitize yourself to those critical issues related to markets, customers, competition, and the industry. They can range from local economic conditions to broad governmental regulations. As you will see, all can impact your SMP.

Answering these six questions allows you to make a long-term visionary inquiry that becomes the underlying support of your strategic direction — as long as it complements the overall mission of the organization. As you will see in a later section of the SMP, the strategic direction, in turn, permits you to accurately define markets, products, and services.

What follows is an *application* of a strategic direction for a single product line within a diversified healthcare organization in the U.S. It comes directly from its actual SMP. To maintain the company's anonymity, we will call it Tri-Tek.

The company manufactures hypodermic products for the healthcare field. Tri-Tek will be used to illustrate applications throughout the SMP. Only enough of the actual plan is provided to illustrate the guidelines. For security reasons, minor changes were made in the plan to disguise the actual identity of the company. Also, commentary is added where needed to further clarify the application.

APPLICATION

Strategic Direction

Our strategic direction is to meet the needs of consumers and healthcare providers for drug-delivery devices by offering a full line of hypodermic products and product systems. Our leadership position will be maintained through internal research and development, licensing of technology, and/or acquisition options to provide alternative administration and monitoring systems.

Commentary

Tri-Tek's primary product is the hypodermic needle. The strategic direction could have stated simply that the company is a manufacturer of hypodermic needles. That would have been too "myopic" and restrictive for growing and maintaining a dominant competitive position.

The broader interpretations of "drug-delivery devices" and "product systems" certainly incorporate Tri-Tek's core business of hypodermic needles. The important issue, however, is that it excites the mind to create fresh opportunities for product designers to develop new products and services.

For example, devices exist and are under development that eliminate the necessity for needles. Instead, delivering drugs to the body can be accomplished through new forms of pills and internally implanted pumps with sensors to control the release of the drug within the body.

Other devices that look like writing pens with drug-filled cartridges are alternatives to the syringe and needle. And still other product systems incorporate monitoring devices to measure medical effectiveness of the drug and automatically calculate the amount of dosages required for an individual patient.

With a measure of creativity even broader considerations of the strategic direction could impact on markets, products, technologies, and services. These include: disposal of the needles and syringes linked to increasing environmental concerns; product configurations by types of diseases, geographic location, culture, and demographics within a target population segment; and the severity of an illness and its contagious impact on unprotected groups.

Therefore, by conceiving a broader interpretation of a business — from railroad to transportation — helps avoid the negative impact of a shrinking market position due to older technologies. Taking time to develop a well-thought-out strategic direction provides an organized framework to extend your thinking to what your company or product line can or should become within an achievable time frame of 3 to 5 years.

Although the example used here represents a mid-size company, the same thought process could also be used for a product line within a larger organization or within a small, single-product company.

Look again at Tri-Tek's strategic direction. In addition to product systems and services, the statement refers to a "leadership position." Tri-Tek's existing position certainly could be maintained through internal R&D. However, the broader thinking also opens a pathway to new products, devices, systems, and services through licensing of technology, acquisition, joint ventures, and a variety of other forms of strategic alliances.

Working Draft

You are now ready to write your own first draft of a strategic direction. Initially, avoid the myopic, narrow approach and think as broadly as you can using the six guideline questions and the Help Topics in Chapter 5. Then, adjust your position within the range of narrow to broad direction, and write a statement that provides a realistic strategic direction for your product, business unit, or company.

As you reflect on the above questions and examples, also consider the culture of your organization. Is it passive, conservative, or aggressive? What value systems and patterns of behavior tend to govern the long-term and day-to-day management decisions? And look at available resources. Are there adequate funds available? Are the human resource skills adequate?

Serious deficiencies in your organization may prevent you from realizing your strategic direction. As you will see later in the planning process, you can address some deficiencies by developing SMP objectives that address organizational and human resource factors to help you perfect your vision.

Note, too, that while the strategic direction example is written in one paragraph, it can be stated in one sentence or two paragraphs. Write it in a format and in whatever length to communicate to your management a clear statement to cover 3 to 5 years.

Now begin to write your own working draft of a strategic direction. First, answer the following questions and then compress the output into a single statement.

1. What are your firm's distinctive areas of expertise?
2. What business should your firm be in over the next 3 to 5 years? How will it differ from what exists today?

3. What segments or categories of customers will you serve?
4. What additional functions are you likely to fulfill for customers as you see the market evolve?
5. What new technologies will you require to satisfy future customer/market needs?
6. What changes are taking place in markets, consumer behavior, competition, the environment, culture, and the economy that will impact your company?

SECTION 2: OBJECTIVES AND GOALS

```
Section 2
Objectives and
Goals
```

Planning Guidelines

State your objectives and goals both quantitatively and nonquantitatively. When developing objectives and goals (the second top box in Figure 1.1), your primary guideline is that they have a strategic focus. That is, they broadly impact your business in keeping with how you defined your strategic direction, and that the objectives cover a time frame of from 3 to 5 years.

This time period is reasonable for most businesses: short enough to be realistic and achievable in an increasingly volatile marketplace; long enough to be visionary about the impact of new technologies, changing behavioral patterns, the global marketplace, emerging competitors, and changing demographics.

Quantitative Objectives

Indicate in precise statements major performance expectations such as sales growth (dollars per unit), market share, return on investment, profit, and any other quantitative objectives required by your management. In this section of the SMP the objectives are generally broad and relate to the total business or to a few major segments. (In the tactical phase these will be more specific by products and markets.)

Nonquantitative Objectives

In addition, consider nonquantitative objectives as setting a foundation from which to build on to your organization's existing strengths and eliminate its internal weaknesses. In turn, your objectives help you realize your strategic direction. Your objectives could span diverse areas from organizational structure, distribution networks, and strategy teams to new product development.

Use the following examples to trigger additional objectives for your business. Above all, keep your objectives specific, actionable, realistic, and focused on achieving a sustainable competitive advantage.

Upgrading Distribution Channels

This objective relates to any intermediary between your organization and the end user (including distributors, dealers, and brokers). Upgrading could include management and sales training, technical support, installing inventory control systems, or even providing financial assistance.

Expanding Secondary Distribution

As an extension of the above objective, you may need to expand into new geographic segments, such as geographic areas that lack adequate distribution or sales representation. This objective is especially important when you cannot release the sales force from existing responsibilities and your only viable alternative is to expand through independent distributors.

Also, your organization may need additional linkages in the distribution channel. For example, although direct contact from manufacturer to distributor exists, there could be an opportunity to expand further into the distribution channel by contacting resellers at the next level of distribution.

Consolidating an Industry or Segment Position

As a protective measure to consolidate a leadership position, objectives could include: securing long-term sales contracts with key accounts, penetrating strategically important geographic territories by adding more sales and service personnel, or gaining maximum commitment from major distributors through technology transfer and financial assistance. Such objectives would help consolidate your market position and bar the entry of aggressive competitors.

Building "Specialty Product" Penetration

This objective considers both offensive and defensive moves. First, an offensive objective means developing a specialty product dedicated to penetrating a new market segment not held — or lightly defended — by a competitor.

Second, a defensive objective means protecting a dominant position. For instance, developing a specialty product that duplicates or imitates the competitive product, thereby eliminating the uniqueness of the competitor's innovation. Still another defensive objective is to introduce an interim specialty product to "buy time" until the next major product innovation is introduced.

Establishing or Improving Marketing Intelligence Systems

While this objective emphasizes organizing the inflow of information to identify noteworthy changes in the environment, industry, and customers, the primary focus remains on competitors. Specifically, the intent is to assess the future impact of the following factors:

1. Competitors' size — categorized by market share, growth rate, and profitability.
2. Competitors' objectives — both quantitative (sales, profits, return on investment [ROI]) and nonquantitative (product innovation; market leadership; and international, national, and regional distribution).
3. Competitors' strategies — analyzed by internal strategies (manufacturing capabilities, delivery, marketing expertise) and external strategies (distribution network, field support, market coverage, and ability to defend or build market share).
4. Competitors' organization — examined by organizational structure, culture, management systems, and people skills.
5. Competitors' cost structure — examined by pricing flexibility, ease or difficulty of exiting a market, and attitudes toward short-term vs. long-term profitability.
6. Competitors' overall strengths and weaknesses — identified by their internal systems and those market positions vulnerable to attack.

The total assessment serves as a window through which to develop a clear image of the actions you need to sustain a competitive advantage.

Focusing Training Actions

This objective considers internal and external training. Internal training reaches various levels of functional managers who need to interact with specific markets, customers, and product applications. Such functions include product management, customer service, technical support, and the sales force.

External training serves distributors' sales forces, service organizations, and customers. In this context, the primary aim of training is to maintain a competitive advantage through programs that assist customers in such areas as customizing services for their customers and finding creative approaches that add value to otherwise basic, undifferentiated products or services.

Launching New and Repositioning Old Products

Products are "new" when they are perceived as new by the marketplace. Therefore, it is appropriate for this objective to consider not only launching totally new products, but also reintroducing older products that have been differentiated through new applications, new packaging, or value-added services.

Upgrading Field Services

The range of field services includes checking levels of inventory, providing sophisticated technical service, or placing a customer-service individual at a customer's location for an indefinite period.

Improving Marketing Mix Management

The marketing mix consists of product or service, price, promotion, and distribution. There is generally a dominant component within the mix that acts as the driving force in achieving competitive advantage. Determining the optimum mix means you involve functional managers from such diverse functions as finance, sales, manufacturing, R&D, and distribution to shape the marketing mix objectives. (A checklist for evaluating your marketing mix against that of your competitor is included in Chapter 4.)

APPLICATION

Tri-Tek's Objectives and Goals

Quantitative Objectives

	200x (Year 1)	200x (Year 2)	200x (Year 3)
Gross sales	$8260	$8720	$8833
Returns	339	375	363
Cost of sales	2545	2632	2387
Gross profit	5376	5713	6083
Expenses			
Shipping	273	333	329
Selling	532	857	704
General and admin.	392	299	251
Total expenses	1197	1489	1284
Operating income	4179	4224	4799

Commentary

The quantitative objectives illustrated above comprise Tri-Tek's actual format. Additional quantitative objectives would include share of market, ROI, cash flow, or return on sales. Some organizations require extensive amounts of financial information in the SMP; others require only a minimal amount, such as sales, units, and profit margins. Your SMP should complement the financial format suggested by the financial manager or your next management level.

The following sample objectives are nonquantitative (or qualitative). You must distinguish between the quantitative objectives of the plan (illustrated above) and the nonquantitative objectives suggested in the guidelines of this section. In some instances quantification can be included with an objective for clarification, as noted in one of the following objectives:

NONQUANTITATIVE OBJECTIVES

1. Maintain Tri-Tek's low-cost producer status while introducing new improvements to existing products.

2. Aggressively maintain our dominant market share position in all market segments.
3. Maintain sufficient manufacturing capacity to absorb our competitors' market share in existing segments as well as serve new and emerging segments.
4. Launch new products to strengthen our leadership position in drug-delivery devices.
5. Maintain a level of 78% retail distribution and 53% retail market share for hypodermic products.
6. Increase trade distribution and block entry of competitors into the home-care segment of the market.

Commentary

Notice the strong parallel of Tri-Tek's objectives with its strategic direction. Phrases that describe the strategic direction include "full line of hypodermic needles" and "leadership position." And the objectives address those phrases. Again, the strategic direction provides a "vision" to project what the future can look like; objectives provide the precise outcomes.

Note, too, how these objectives have long-term strategic implications. Where possible, you can add quantitative information for each objective. However, it is not always necessary in this strategic section of the SMP.

The key point is that this planning format permits flexibility to accommodate the practices of individual organizations. Quantitative details can be added later in the plan, usually in the growth strategy section and certainly at the tactical 1-year portion of the SMP.

Working Draft

Now write a draft of your quantitative and nonquantitative objectives for a 3- to 5-year period.

SECTION 3: GROWTH STRATEGIES

> **Section 3**
> **Growth**
> **Strategies**

Planning Guidelines

This section outlines the process you can use to secure your objectives and goals. Think of *strategies* as actions to achieve your longer-term objectives; *tactics* as actions to achieve shorter-term objectives. Since the time frame of this section covers 3 to 5 years, strategies are indicated here. The 1-year portion, illustrated later in the plan, identifies tactics.

For best results in developing realistic growth strategies, you should base your decisions after analyzing your organization's internal capabilities. Such capabilities include performance, strategy, strategic priorities, costs, product portfolio, financial resources, and strength/weaknesses. (For a comprehensive discussion on each topic go to Chapter 5, Help Topic — *Looking at Your Company.)*

Overall, however, your thinking about strategies boils down to actions among the following:

- Growth and mature markets
- Long-term brand or product positioning
- Product quality
- Market share growth potential
- Distribution channel options
- Product, price, and promotion mix
- Spending strategies
- Specific marketing, sales, R&D, and manufacturing strengths to be exploited

In practice, where you have broad-based, long-term objectives you would need to develop multiple strategies for each objective. With other objectives where you find it difficult to be specific, it is appropriate to use general strategy statements. For example, you can form a committee to investigate an emerging market segment in the Pacific Rim; hire an outside consultant to conduct a feasibility study about a new laser technology; or locate a new distribution center to expand market coverage in the southwest. The specific actions for each would be detailed in the tactical portion of the SMP.

Formats can vary according to your individual or team's style. For instance, if you find it convenient, you have the option of merging the objectives and strategies sections by restating each objective from Section 2 and listing its corresponding strategies, as shown in the *Application.* Still another option is to write a general strategy statement followed by a detailed listing of subordinate objectives and strategies.

What follows is a general strategy statement derived from Tri-Tek's actual SMP, along with a selection of three of the six objectives from the previous section together with related strategies.

APPLICATION

General Strategy Statement

Tri-Tek will maintain industry leadership by addressing the full range of consumer and healthcare provider needs related to drug-delivery devices.

These needs include not only the marketing of delivery devices which are virtually painless, easy to read, and conveniently used, but also programs and educational services to aid in the achievement of normal bodily functions to maintain overall good health. These additional services will meet user needs both at the time of diagnosis and in the continuing treatment of the problem.

A dominant position in the drug-delivery device market will be maintained by developing market segmentation opportunities through continued product differentiation and innovation.

Objective 1:
Maintain Tri-Tek's low-cost producer status while introducing new improvements to existing products.
Strategies:
Reduce costs by 32.5% before 2002. Maintaining low-cost producer status gives our company the widest strategic flexibility in dealing with competitive assaults on our franchise. Potential areas of cost reduction:

Overhead reductions	4.5%
Waste reductions	7.0%
High-speed needle line	6.5%
Sales territory redesign	8.0%
Quality improvement and reduction in repair service	4.0%
Packaging improvements	2.5%
Total	32.5%

Improve existing products through improved dosage control and improved packaging to maintain a competitive advantage.

Objective 2:

Aggressively maintain our dominant market share position in all market segments.

Strategies:

■ Develop the Supra-Fine III needle to maintain superior product quality and performance vs. competition as it relates to injection comfort.

■ Increase spending levels on consumer/trade support programs to provide added value to product offerings, thereby decreasing attractiveness of lower-priced alternatives while maintaining brand loyalty.

■ Maintain broadest retail distribution and highest service levels to gain retailer support in promoting our brands and carrying adequate inventory levels.

■ Continue healthcare educational programs to gain professional recommendations at time of diagnosis and thereby maintain brand loyalty among users.

Objective 3:

Launch new products to strengthen our leadership position in drug-delivery devices.

Strategies:

■ Introduce a 40-unit syringe to address the needs of users on multiple-dose therapy. Converting users to a 40-unit syringe will insulate this group against competitive initiatives.

■ Develop and introduce a disposable pen–cartridge injection system to further segment the market and thereby reduce the competitive points of entry.

■ Become a full-line supplier of drug-delivery devices by broadening product offerings through internal R&D, joint venture, licensing, and acquisitions.

Commentary

Recall the overall planning guideline: the primary output of the SMP includes strategies to achieve competitive advantage. As noted in the above examples, Tri-Tek's strategies cover a wide range of activities and incorporate a variety of functions within the organization.

Accordingly, you can see the practicality of involving as many functional managers as possible in developing your SMP. Not only will their ideas prove helpful, but also they will internalize the strategies and be more motivated to implement them.

In turn, implementation is accomplished through each manager's functional plan that evolves from the SMP. The result: managers' participation from manufacturing, product development, finance, sales, and distribution makes the SMP come alive.

Working Draft

Now you are ready to develop a rough draft of strategies for each of your objectives.

SECTION 4: BUSINESS PORTFOLIO PLANS

```
┌─────────────────────┐
│                     │
│     Section 4       │
│ Business Portfolio  │
│       Plans         │
│                     │
└─────────────────────┘
```

Planning Guidelines

The business portfolio includes listings of *existing* products and markets and *new* products and markets. Following a logical progression, it is based on the strategic direction, objectives and goals, and growth strategies outlined in previous sections.

Key point: your strategic direction mirrors the content of your portfolio. That is, the broader the dimension of your strategic direction, the more expansive the range of products and markets in the portfolio. Conversely, the narrower the dimension of your strategic direction, the more limited the content of products and markets.

Use the following format and guidelines to develop your own business portfolio:

Existing Products/Existing Markets (Market Penetration)

Simply list those products you currently offer to existing customer groups or market segments. In an appendix of the SMP, you can document sales, profits, and market share data. From such information you can determine if your level of penetration is adequate and if possibilities exist for further growth.

For example, even minor changes in market and customer behavioral patterns may create fresh opportunities to increase market penetration by focusing in such areas as improving product quality, instituting just-in-time delivery, increasing technical support, improving customer service, or installing computerized inventory control systems.

After identifying new opportunities, it may be necessary for you to revisit Section 3 (Growth Strategies) and list actions you would take to implement the opportunities.

New Products/Existing Markets (Product Development)

Use this section to extend your thinking about new products to existing markets, in keeping with the strategic direction you created for your business. Again, recall the guideline that the broader the dimension of your strategic direction the broader the possibilities for the content of your portfolio.

If the definition of your business is too narrow, you may be limited in what you can list in this part of your portfolio. You still have the opportunity to go back to the strategic direction and recast it. You thereby open the possibilities for product expansion, if that is consistent with the overall aims of senior management.

In this section you are looking for new products that you can sell to current customer segments. These may include the specialty products discussed earlier or all new products.

What is a new product? Recall the definition that a new product is *new* when it is *perceived* as new by the customer. Therefore, product development could include added features, improved quality, new packaging, extended warranties, and other value-added items wrapped around existing core products. And, of course, product development includes totally new products.

Existing Products/New Markets (Market Development)

Another growth direction is to take your current products into new markets. Therefore, explore possibilities for market development by identifying emerging, neglected, or poorly served segments in which existing products can be utilized.

A classic case is 3M's Scotch Brand tape which has been market extended for use in offices, schools, homes, packaging, and scores of industrial applications. Another classic product, nylon, illustrates market development with applications of the product over the past 50 years in such diverse products as parachutes, clothes, tires, and carpets.

The possibilities are exciting. Yet caution is advised. Where, then, is the balance? How far afield should you go from your basic markets?

Again, go back to your strategic direction as a guiding beacon to direct your thinking. Think about those questions you answered to derive your strategic direction. What business should your firm be in over the next 3 to 5 years? What customer segments will you serve? What additional functions are you likely to fulfill for customers? What changes are taking place in markets and the environment? How will your organization participate in that future?

Here, too, it is extremely valuable to involve the next level of management in assessing risks and providing guidance on expansion. The risk in this instance is not with products. The products already exist. The risk is in the redeployment — and possible dispersion — of the sales force from its primary markets. Or it is the possible distraction of other functions of the organization from their focus on core products and markets. A further consideration is the added investment required to develop new markets.

It is also valuable to use a strategy team to help make assessments. Since the team members represent diverse functions of the business, they would take responsibility for implementing the strategies through their respective functions. (Go to Chapter 5, Help Topic — *Strategy Teams.*)

New Products/New Markets (Diversification)

This portion of the business portfolio is visionary, since it involves developing new products to meet the needs of new and yet untapped markets. New technologies, global markets, and new strategic alliances provide the framework from which this section evolves. These factors will assist you in participating in new markets, rather than riding existing businesses into maturity and then to decline.

Once again, interpret your strategic direction in its broadest context. Do not seek diversification for its own sake. Rather, the whole purpose of the exercise is for you to develop an organized framework for meaningful expansion.

Also, you will find that the other parts of the portfolio feed this portion. In practice, the number of new products into new markets will be the smallest part of the portfolio, because they carry the greatest risk. Yet organizations such as 3M, Intel, Motorola, AT&T, and General Electric will fill this portion of the portfolio extensively.

Known for their high levels of R&D, those visionary companies commit themselves entirely to future growth and leadership in their respective markets. This pattern exists more so than in those organizations making

	Existing Products	*New Products*
Existing Markets	1. Market Penetration	3. Product Development
New Markets	2. Market Development	4. Diversification

Figure 1.2 Business Portfolio Plan

commodity products, and with firms that lack the strategic vision to find their place in the future.

The grid in Figure 1.2 is a useful format to create your business portfolio of products and markets, both existing and new.

APPLICATION

	Tri-Tek's Existing Products	*Tri-Tek's New Products*
Existing Markets	• 24-gauge hypodermic needle • Diabetes • Allergy • Hospital • Clinics • Homecare	• 32-gauge hypodermic needle • SuperFine III needles • 40-gauge syringe/multiple-dose therapy system

New Markets	• AIDS
	  – Urban markets
	  – Ethnic populations
	  – Demographic segments
	• Pacific rim countries
		• Disposable pen
		  – Cartridge injection system
		• Implanted injection pumps with sensors

Figure 1.3 Tri-Tek's Business Portfolio Plan

Commentary

To illustrate the makeup of this section, Tri-Tek's business portfolio (Figure 1.3) is only a partial representation of products and markets from its actual plan. Supporting information on sales, units, profits, market share, and other quantitative information would be included in an appendix of the SMP.

Also, Tri-Tek's actual portfolio lists additional diseases for which hypodermic systems are needed and these would be placed in the appropriate quadrant. The information on population, ethnic, geographic, and demographic factors also breaks down into subsegments, which would drive new packaging, methods of treatment, educational programs, and types of distribution.

In practice, you will find that all four sections of the SMP are interconnected. For instance: (1) the strategic direction gives scope to your thinking by providing a company or product with a vision; (2) objectives permit you to list in quantitative and nonquantitative terms what you want to achieve; (3) growth strategies indicate how you will reach your objectives; (4) the business portfolio shows the effect of all the preceding work in the form of products and markets.

The interconnection also occurs as you add a new market or product to the portfolio. In that case you may need to return to the strategy section and identify how to develop the product and launch it into the market. Consequently, you are constantly creating opportunities and fine-tuning your SMP.

Working Draft

Now develop your rough draft of a business portfolio plan, using the grid in Figure 1.2 to categorize existing products/existing markets, new products/existing markets, existing products/new markets, and new products/new markets. Then, when ready, you can input the final version on the computer disk.

The business portfolio completes the strategic portion of the SMP. Now you are ready to proceed to the tactical 1-year marketing plan.

II

TACTICAL
SECTION

2

THE STRATEGIC MARKETING PLAN

CHAPTER OBJECTIVES

Given the information in this chapter, you will be able to:

1. Describe the components of the tactical part of the SMP.
2. Interpret the guidelines by applying them to an actual company's SMP.
3. Develop your own SMP.

OVERVIEW

The tactical marketing plan, shown in the highlighted area of the Strategic Marketing Plan (SMP; Figure 2.1) is not a stand-alone plan. It is but a portion of the total SMP consisting of the top row of boxes and the lower row of boxes.

Where commonalities exist among products and markets, one marketing plan can work as long as you make the appropriate changes in such areas as the sales force and the communications mix (advertising, sales promotion, and publicity). Where you face substantial differences in the character of your product and markets, then develop separate tactical plans.

As a precautionary measure, however, avoid the temptation indulged in by some managers who attempt to develop a plan for a business, division, or product line by jumping in at the middle of the SMP and beginning the process with the tactical 1-year marketing plan.

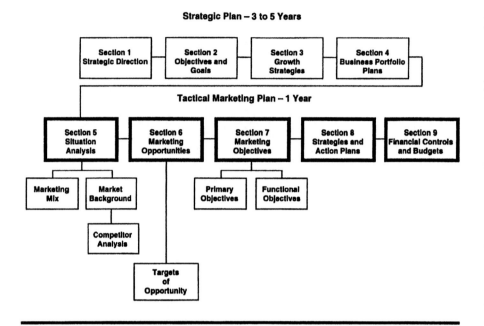

Figure 2.1 Strategic Marketing Plan

There are no short cuts. Reason: input to the tactical marketing plan flows from two directions: (1) from the strategic portion of the SMP (top row) containing the strategic direction, objectives, strategies, and business portfolio; (2) from the situation analysis (bottom row), which progresses to opportunities, annual objectives, tactics, and budgets. Also, the thought process that went into the strategic portion of the plan now flows down to feed the shorter-term, action-oriented marketing plan.

The tactical 1-year marketing plan — Sections 5 through 9 — is presented in the same format as used in the strategic part of the SMP in Chapter 1. That is, *planning guidelines* are provided to explain the thought process. And *applications* will continue with the Tri-Tek case. For ease of explanation, however, only one product from that company's business portfolio, the hypodermic needle, will be used to illustrate the planning process.

As with the strategic section, use *Help Topics* in Chapter 5 to provide worthwhile content to make your plan comprehensive and accurate. Also, you can use Chapter 3, *Marketing Problem Solver: the Strategic Marketing Plan in Action* for an extensive review of how actual companies apply the SMP to deal with real-world market difficulties.

Let's begin with Section 5, Situation Analysis.

SECTION 5: SITUATION ANALYSIS

```
Section 5
Situation
Analysis
```

The following three-part situation analysis describes in detail the past and current situation of your business:

Part I: Marketing Mix (product, price, distribution, promotion)
Part III: Competitor Analysis
Part III: Market Background

Each part is a subsection of the total situation analysis and defines the business in a detailed, factual, and objective manner. Approach your situation analysis by answering a fundamental question: "What are the key events in the development of my business?" Then compile historical data for a period of at least 3 years. Doing so provides an excellent perspective as you compare any significant events with the future trends you indicated for your market, industry, product line, or market segment as you defined them in your Strategic Direction (Section 1).

MARKETING MIX

Product

Planning Guidelines

Objectively describe the performance of your product or service by:

- Sales history, profitability, share of market, and other required financial data; where appropriate, you can graphically chart sales history with computer-generated forms
- Current position in the industry related to market share, reputation, product life cycle (introduction, growth, maturity, or decline), and competition
- Future trends related to environment, industry, customer, and competitive factors that may affect the position of your product

- Intended purpose of your product in terms of its applications or uniqueness
- Features and benefits of your product as related to quality, performance, safety, convenience, or other factors important to customers
- Other pertinent product information such as expected product improvements and additional product characteristics (size, model, price, packaging); recent features that enhance the position of your product; competitive trends in features, benefits, or technological changes; and changes that would add superior value to the product and provide a competitive advantage

APPLICATION

Product — Hypodermic Needles (24 Gauge)

Sales History

Year	200×	200×	200×
Net sales ($)	202,315	204,195	206,153
Units	754,405	769,614	768,397
Percent change from previous year	+6.8%	+1.8%	+1.9%
Market potential ($)	212,000	216,000	220,000
Market share (%)	88.6%	87.9%	87.6%

Position in the Industry

The 24-gauge needle, in the mature stage of its product life cycle, is categorized as a market leader according to the above share of market figures. Market research positions Tri-Tek as a technological innovator.

Future Trends

- Our dominant position will continue to be challenged by low-priced brands from the Far East
- Alternate injection systems such as the pen cartridge will compete with standard hypodermic needles
- Growth of new distribution channels (medical insurance plans) will alter buying behavior, removing end-use customers from the purchase decision

Intended Purpose of Our Product

Provide a reliable, safe, economical, and convenient delivery system of drugs to the body to maintain normal bodily functions, as well as provide systematic preemptive protection against disease.

Features and Benefits of Our Product

Needles and syringes satisfy design specifications of the medical establishment. Our syringes include permanently attached needles, storage capability for 25 needles, single-scale markings with large numbers, and special protective caps to ensure sterility. Our needles offer unmatched injection comfort.

Other

Our product rates as a high-quality, reliable drug-delivery device. Our packaging is convenient for use within all segments of the market, accompanied by easy-to-use instructions. A recognizable package displays Tri-Tek's corporate graphic logo, conveying the image of high-quality health products.

Working Draft

Using the following outline, begin gathering data that covers the following categories. You can then transfer this information to the SMP computer disk at a later date.

- Sales history:
- Position in the industry:
- Future trends:
- Intended purpose of product(s) or service(s):
- Features and benefits of product(s) or service(s):

Pricing

Planning Guidelines

History of Pricing

Examine the history of pricing policies for each market segment and/or distribution channel and consider their impact on the market position of your product.

Future Pricing Trends

Predict pricing trends as they pertain to product specification changes (including formulation and design), financial constraints, and expected market changes (trade/consumer attitudes, and competitive responses to price changes).

APPLICATION

History of Pricing Policies

Within the largest distribution channel (hospitals and clinics), Tri-Tek's price leadership position is maintained. One competitor, Majestic, has traditionally followed our prices with aggressive promotional discounts. A second competitor, Apollo, has established the lower-priced branded segment with a list price 27% below ours. (The names of competitors are disguised.)

Future Pricing Trends

For the next 12 months wholesale and retail prices are expected to remain at current levels. No major product innovations are anticipated during the planning period, and no new competitive entries are predicted to significantly alter the pricing trend.

Working Draft

Examine your company's history of pricing policies and future pricing trends.

Distribution Channels and Methods

Planning Guidelines

Current Channels

Describe your current distribution channels. Identify the functions performed for each stage in the distribution system (distributor, dealer, direct) and indicate levels of performance (sales volume, profitability, and percentage of business increases).

Where appropriate, analyze your physical distribution system, such as warehouse locations, inventory systems, or just-in-time delivery procedures.

Effectiveness of Coverage

Characterize the effectiveness of coverage of current channels by the programs and services provided.

Comment on effectiveness of distribution systems (distributors, dealers, direct). Specify the key activities performed at each point and indicate any areas that require corrective action. Also comment on the impact of future trends in distribution channels and methods.

Special Functions

Indicate special functions performed by your company's sales force for a particular distribution channel and the effect they had on the targeted market segments. Also include your distributors' sales forces, if applicable. Comment, too, on such approaches as "push" strategy (through distributors) or "pull" strategy (through consumers).

Finally, describe how effectively your sales force cover its assigned market area.

Target Accounts

List target accounts and their level of performance related to quantity and dollars. Add comments related to special needs of any account.

Future Trends

Indicate future trends in distribution methods and channels. Project what growth is expected in each major market segment. Also identify how this growth will affect your need for different distribution channels or methods of physical distribution.

APPLICATION

Current Channels

The largest distribution channel for our hypodermic needle products are hospitals and clinics, with 64.7% of unit sales volume distributed through these outlets. Drug stores and mass merchandisers account for the remaining category sales. Within the hospital segment, hospitals with 500 beds or more represent 60.2% of our unit sales volume followed by 30.8% of units in hospitals with 300 to 499 beds.

Effectiveness of Coverage

Our product has the broadest distribution penetration in the Northcentral and Southern divisions, as follows:

	Division	Market Penetration
Northeast	Boston	63%
	New York	58%
	Baltimore	52%
Northcentral	Detroit	92%
	Chicago	89%
	St. Paul	91%
Southern	Miami	88%
	Atlanta	93%
	Houston	92%
West Coast	Tacoma	73%
	San Francisco	69%
	San Diego	63%

Special Functions

Special sales functions include meeting with hospital administrators, holding workshops for nurses, conducting technical seminars for physicians, and checking for out-of-stock situations. In addition, maintaining in-hospital distribution of educational literature establishes brand recognition where continuation of hypodermic needle usage is required at home.

Target Accounts

Target account coverage requires making joint sales calls with our dealers' sales forces to maximize sales potential from each sales territory. Focusing on signing up hospitals to new 3-year, price-protected sales contracts ensures continuity of supplier–customer relationships.

Future Trends in Distribution Methods

Product volume within hospitals and clinics will continue to grow. Smaller dealers will leave the market or be absorbed by the larger ones that provide just-in-time delivery through computerized inventory control systems. Where dealers in emerging market segments are not available, our company must distribute directly to serve the dealer function.

Commentary

The above sampling of applications illustrate the type of information that goes into describing distribution. In your plan, you can add additional detail about the types of products, services, and specific sales activities. For example, you can make comparisons with your key competitors, provide insights on corrective actions to counter a threat, indicate how to displace a competitor, or identify how the Internet fits your market and product.

Target accounts have not been shown in this example, since it would simply contain a listing of accounts and is self-explanatory. For your working draft, as with other sections in this book, you may need to alter the format to fit your special requirements and specific terminology.

Working Draft

Analyze your distribution channels and methods by:

- Current channel
- Effectiveness of coverage
- Special functions performed by the sales force
- Target accounts by account, district, quantity, and revenue
- Future trends in distribution methods

Advertising and Sales Promotion

Planning Guidelines

Analysis

Analyze your advertising and sales promotion directed at each segment of the market or distribution channel based on the following elements: advertising dollar expenditures, creative strategy, media, trade promotions (dollars and type), consumer promotions (dollars and type), and other forms of promotion unique to your industry.

Competitive Trends

Identify and evaluate competitive trends in the same categories as above. Your advertising agency (or advertising department) and the sales force may prove helpful in providing this information.

Strategies

Identify your company's past and current advertising and sales promotion strategies by product and market segment and describe trends in these areas.

Other Support Strategies

Identify other support programs (publicity, educational, professional, trade shows, literature, films/videos, the Internet) that you have used and evaluate their effectiveness. Describe what programs you should employ.

APPLICATION

Analysis

- Copy strategy: Tri-Tek's primary advertising is aimed at hospital and clinic segments for 24-gauge hypodermic needles/syringes. Secondary levels of advertising focus on 32-gauge needles, SupraFine III, and the 40-unit syringe/multiple-dose therapy system. Such advertising reminds customers of our full line of high-quality products and product systems. Copy themes include clinical proof related to our unequaled injection comfort and superior quality to justify premium pricing.
- Media: magazines are used to target consumers who use hypodermic injection for ongoing therapy (pull strategy); professional journals reach the medical profession and the dealer (pull and push strategy). Current consumer magazines that target consumers are limited in their ability to reach more than 15 to 20% of the potential market. Alternative media options such as the Internet, direct mail, and broadcast are being explored.
- Other: direct mail, posters, and in-pack circulars deliver continuity programs to our buyers and buying influences.

The following describe competitive trends for two major competitors: Apollo and Majestic.

Copy Strategy

Apollo's plans in this area:

- Objective: encourage trial among purchasing agents

- Strategy: offer financial incentives on entire product line while reinforcing a high-quality image
- Tactics: feature bonus packs on syringes; offer free syringes and rebates with proof-of-purchase of competitive products

Majestic's plans in this area:

- Objective: encourage trial among physicians
- Strategy: attack all major competitors head on with claims that Majestic needles/syringes are made to hurt less and that the product choice should be made only by the patient
- Tactics: feature an active, healthy-looking individual that ties into advertising theme

Media

Both competitors utilize print media and on-pack offers exclusively. Print media is limited to health-related publications to achieve high efficiency at the expense of limited reach.

Other

Rebates and targeted direct mail are the primary promotional strategies. However, Majestic is more aggressive than Apollo in the frequency of its rebate and discount program. Overall, both Apollo and Majestic have become more aggressive in promoting their product lines to both hospitals and dealers. This aggressiveness is evidenced in increased advertising expenditures over the past 24 months.

Strategies

Tri-Tek's past and current advertising and sales promotion strategies have focused on maintaining a national leadership position. Where regional market share is threatened or where market intelligence calls for aggressive competitive action, fast promotional response is initiated against the target segment.

Other Support Strategies

- Professional programs: continue to generate professional recommendations for our company's products in health-related market segments where treatment depends on hypodermic drug-delivery products.

■ Conventions and trade shows: maintain a presence at key national and regional trade shows. Utilize new forms of video presentation to enhance the overall promotional strategy and support Tri-Tek's market leadership position in quality and technological advancement.

Commentary

The above sampling of applications shows how to write this portion of the situation analysis. Not all the information from the actual plan has been included, just enough to illustrate the planning guidelines. Your job is to add all pertinent information that provides a clear picture of your company's situation.

For instance, if you know actual advertising expenditures for your company and those of your competitors, display that comparative information. And, if your advertising agency has usable advertising research, include relevant portions.

Also, you will find it beneficial to highlight any critical issues that emerge from your situation analysis. You can then deal with them in the opportunities and strategy/tactic sections of your SMP.

This concludes part one of the Situation Analysis. After you prepare your working draft, begin Part II, Competitor Analysis.

Working Draft

Analyze the advertising and sales promotion directed at each segment of the market by:

- Copy strategy:
- Media:
- Other:

Identify and evaluate competitive trends in the same categories as you did for your analysis:

- Copy strategy:
- Media:
- Other:

COMPETITOR ANALYSIS

Planning Guidelines

Market Share

List all your competitors in descending-size order along with their sales and market shares. Include your company's ranking within the listing. Show at least three competitors (more if the information is meaningful).

Competitors' Strengths and Weaknesses

Identify each competitor's strengths and weaknesses related to such factors as product quality, distribution, pricing, promotion, management leadership, and financial condition. Also indicate any significant trends that would signal unsettling market situations, such as aggressiveness in growing market share or excessive discounting to maintain market position.

Attempt to make your competitive analysis as comprehensive as possible. The more competitive intelligence you gather, the more strategy options you have open to you. (To assist you in developing a quality analysis, go to the Developing Competitive Strategies Checklists in Chapter 4.)

Product Competitiveness

Identify competitive pricing strategies, price lines, and price discounts, if any. Identify competitors firmly entrenched in low-price segments of the market, those at the high end of the market, or competitors that are low-cost producers.

Product Features and Benefits

Compare the specific product features and benefits with those of competitive products. In particular, focus on product quality, design factors, and performance. Evaluate price/value relationships for each, discuss customer preferences (if available), and identify unique product innovations.

Advertising Effectiveness

Identify competitive spending levels and their effectiveness, as measured by awareness levels, competitive copy test scores, and reach/frequency levels (if available). Such measurements are conducted through formal advertising research conducted by your advertising agency, independent marketing research firms, or publications. Where no reliable quantitative research exists, use informal observation or rough measurements of advertising frequency and type.

Effectiveness of Distribution Methods

Compare competitive distribution strengths and weaknesses. Address differences in market penetration, market coverage, delivery time, and physical movement of the product by regions or territories. Where appropriate, identify major accounts where competitors' sales are weak or strong.

Packaging

Compare competitive products' package performance, innovation, and preference. Also review size, shape, function, convenience of handling, ease of storage, and shipping.

Trade/Consumer Attitudes

Review both trade (distributor or dealer) and consumer attitudes toward product quality, customer/technical service, company image, and company performance.

Competitive Share of Market (SOM) Trends

While SOM was previously included as a way of determining overall performance, the intent here is to specify trends in market share gains by individual products, as well as by market segments. Further, you must identify where each competitor is making a major commitment and where it may be relinquishing control by product and segment.

Sales Force Effectiveness and Market Coverage

Review effectiveness as it relates to sales, service, frequency of contact, and problem-solving capabilities by competitor and by market segment. Look to all sales-force performance within the distribution channel. For example, if you are a manufacturer, look at distributor coverage. Then examine distributors' coverage of their customers, which could be dealers, and finally end users.

APPLICATION

Competitors' Strengths and Weaknesses

Name	Share of market (SOM)	Strengths	Weaknesses	SOM trends
Tri-Tek	65%	Strong commitment to product improvements and product quality; broad distribution; low-cost producer	Weaker retail share compared to hospital share	Flat growth
Apollo	19%	Strong consumer promotion activities; higher retailer support relative to market share	Limited resources devoted to key buying influences; higher cost of goods. No commitment to product improvement	Declining share
Majestic	16%	Low selling price; overall high-quality product; highly automated production capabilities	Limited resources devoted to key buying influences; limited sales force; no professional education program	Slow build of share

Pricing

Brand	Distributor price	Direct price
Tri-Tek	$12.86	$17.98
Apollo	$12.50	$16.75
Majestic	$9.75	$13.60

Product Features and Benefits

Brand	Features	Benefits
Tri-Tek	Self-contained design Clear, bold scale Thin-line plunger tip	Convenient, no package Easy to see for greater accuracy Lines up precisely with scale markings for accurate reading — no waste

Brand	Features	Benefits
Apollo	Sterile soft packs No dead space Permanently attached needle	Easy-to-open package More accurate dosage; less waste Eliminates risk of needle separation
Majestic	Smooth plunger action Easy to read scale Individual safety seal packaging	Precise control of dosage Greater accuracy Ensures sterility until time of use

Commentary

This application contains only a sampling of the contents of this section. A full analysis would cover all the points specified in the planning guidelines. The comprehensiveness and quality of competitive information cannot be stressed enough. Your competitive strategy — the primary output of your SMP — and the desire to achieve competitive advantage rely heavily on this portion of the situation analysis. (Be sure to refer to Chapter 4 for the checklists supplementing this section.)

Now begin developing your working draft of a competitive analysis.

Working Draft

Analyze competitors' strengths and weaknesses by:

- Product competitiveness
- Pricing
- Product features and benefits
- Advertising effectiveness
- Effectiveness of distribution methods
- Packaging
- Trade/consumer attitudes
- Competitive share of market trends
- Sales force effectiveness

MARKET BACKGROUND

Planning Guidelines

This last part of the situation analysis focuses on the demographic and behavioral factors that determine market size and customer preferences (both trade and consumer) in a changing competitive environment.

You can derive data from primary market research (market segmentation studies, awareness, and usage studies) or data from secondary sources (trade and governmental reports). See extensive information provided on this subject in Chapter 5, *Help Topics*.

The information provided here is important because it serves as foundation material for developing Section 6 Opportunities, Section 7 Objectives, and Section 8 Strategies/Tactics. This information also highlights any gaps in knowledge about markets and customers and helps you determine the types of marketing research needed to make more effective decisions.

The following categories are considered as part of the market background:

Customer Profile

Define the profile of present and potential end-use customers that you (or your distributors) serve. Your intent is to look farther down the distribution channel and view the end-use consumer. Examine the following factors:

- *The Market Segments Distributors/Dealers Serve:* Make sure you address this question from your distributors' point of view.
- *Distributors' Overall Sales:* Concentrate on classifying the key customers that represent the majority of sales.
- *Other Classifications:* Profile your customers by such additional factors as type of products used, level of sophistication, price sensitivity, and service. Also indicate any target accounts that you can reach directly, thereby by-passing the distributor.
- *Frequency and Magnitude of Products Used:* Define customer purchases by frequency, volume, and seasonality of purchase. Additional information might include customer inventory levels, retail stocking policies, volume discounts, or consumer buying behavior related to price, point-of-purchase influences, or coupons.
- *Geographic Aspects of Products Used:* Define customer purchases regionally or territorially (both trade and consumer). Segment buyers by specific geographic area (e.g., rural, urban) or by other factors relevant to your industry.
- *Market Characteristics:* Assess the demographic, psychographic (lifestyle), and other descriptive aspects of the customers, including age, income level, and education. Examine level of product technology; purchase patterns and any distinctive individual or group behavioral styles; attitudes toward the company's products, services, quality, and image.

- *Decision Maker:* Define who makes the buying decisions and when and where they are made. Note the various individuals or departments that may influence the decision.
- *Customer Motivations:* Identify the key motivations that drive your customers to buy the product. Why do they select one manufacturer (or service provider) over another? Customers may buy your product because of quality, performance, image, technical/customer service, convenience, location, delivery, access to upper-level management, friendship, or peer pressure.
- *Customer Awareness:* Define the level of consumer awareness of your products. To what extent do they:
  - Recognize a need for your type of product?
  - Identify your product, brand, or company as a possible supplier?
  - Associate your product, brand, or company with desirable features?
- *Segment Trends:* Define the trends in the size and character of the various segments or niches. (A segment is a portion of an entire market; a niche is part of a segment.) A segment should be considered if it is accessible, measurable, potentially profitable, and has long-term growth potential. Segmenting a market also serves as an offensive strategy to identify emerging, neglected, or poorly served markets that can catapult you to further sales growth. You can also consider segments as a defensive strategy to prevent inroads of a potential competitor through an unattended market segment.
- *Other Comments/Critical Issues:* Add general comments that expand your knowledge of the market and customer base. Also identify any critical issues that have surfaced as a result of conducting the situation analysis — ones that should be singled out for special attention.

APPLICATION

Customer Profile

There are an estimated 15.7 million hypodermic needles used daily in the U.S. The breakdown is as follows:

Classification	Distribution Units
Hospitals	Distributor and direct, 5.6 million
Clinics	Distributor, 3.7 million
Home	Distributor and retailer, 3.6 million
Other	Distributor, 2.8 million

Hospitals classified as 500 beds and over are increasingly looking for the newer systems of injection that eliminate the standard needle and syringe. Smaller hospitals and clinics are price sensitive and remain committed to the standard method of drug delivery. Home usage, primarily by diabetics, is increasing at the annual rate of 2.4% annually.

Frequency and Magnitude of Products Used

Single-use needles and syringes comprise 89.5% of usage. Of the remaining 10.5%, usage consists of automatic infusion pumps, needleless jet injectors, and reusable glass syringes.

Daily injection frequency in all markets remains a key factor in the consumption of single-use syringes. Presently the market is characterized as follows:

Number of injections per day	Percent of users
1	54%
2	44%
3 or more	2%

Geographic Aspects of Products Used

See competitive analysis for geographic breakdown.

Customer Characteristics

Base	Usage of single-use needles and syringes in home market	
Sex	Male	44%
	Female	56%
	Median age at usage	42
	Median family income	$16.7K
Employment	Employed	37%
	Unemployed	63%
Race	White	80%
	Afro-American	15%
	Other	5%
Region	Northeast	19%
	Midwest	29%
	South	37%
	West	15%
Education	Median years of education	10.2

Decision Maker

At 65% of the hospitals, physicians make the brand selection in 58% of the purchasing decisions; 32% of the selections are made by purchasing agents; 10% by others, including nurses and administrators. Where drug-delivery systems increase in complexity, it is anticipated that physicians will account for 75% of purchase decisions.

Customer Motivation

Level of satisfaction (results of Tri-Tek's most recent independent survey of 2700 physicians).

	Tri-Tek	Apollo	Majestic
Complete satisfaction	85%	84%	76%
Moderate satisfaction	14%	13%	9%
Not very satisfied	1%	2%	15%
Not at all satisfied	—	—	—

Reasons for Purchase

	Tri-Tek	Apollo	Majestic
Price: cheaper/lower price	36%	11%	43%
Availability: bought what was available	12%	7%	21%
Product features: Likes brand	9%	20%	5%
Easier to use Comfort	14% 34%	4% 18%	4% 17%
Recommendation: By physician	62%	13%	25%

Customer Awareness

A marketing research firm conducted an awareness study to measure need recognition for disposable needles/syringes, brand identification, and seven feature/benefit categories. We used this study in conjunction with our advertising campaign to determine before and after awareness levels. We summarize the results below to show awareness at 6-month intervals.

Level of Awareness

	July 200x	Jan. 200x	July 200x
Tri-Tek	69%	71%	83%
Apollo	58%	59%	58%
Majestic	42%	45%	44%

Segmentation Trends

With the trend toward smaller (1/2-cc) syringes, but more frequent doses for most applications, the 1/2-cc syringe will grow at the expense of the 1-cc size. Introducing the 5/10-cc syringe and the pen–cartridge system will further segment the market, resulting in a further reduction in the importance of the 1-cc syringe.

Other General Comments/Critical Issues

- Can brand loyalty be maintained by improving our product, segmenting the market, and providing greater consumer value?
- How successful will pharmaceutical manufacturers be in expanding into the (drug-delivery) device business?
- Will the entry of low-priced competitors encourage the emergence of private-label brands?

Commentary

The above presentation is a digest of Tri-Tek's actual plan (only names and numbers have been disguised). The statistics used in the plan originate from informal general observation to formal statistical data uncovered by primary research.

The key issue behind developing a market background is sensitizing yourself about markets, people, and their behavior. Accept the notion that those buyers you dealt with 3 years ago had different needs from those you deal with today and will be different in wants, needs, and behavior 3 years from now.

Therefore, emphasize the use of meaningful marketing research in a way that fills any gaps in information about changing patterns of behavior among your customers. If you use distributors, then learn about your distributors' customers — those end users who actually consume your product.

Now complete the situation analysis by working on your rough draft of the market background.

Working Draft

Develop a customer profile by:

- The markets distributors/dealers serve
- Distributors' overall sales
- Other classifications
- Frequency and magnitude of products used
- Geographic aspects of products used
- Customer characteristics
- Decision makers
- Customer motivation
- Customer awareness
- Need recognition
- Brand identification
- Feature awareness
- Segmentation trends
- Other general comments/critical issues

SECTION 6: MARKETING OPPORTUNITIES

```
┌─────────────────────────┐
│      Section 6          │
│      Marketing         │
│    Opportunities       │
└─────────────────────────┘
```

Planning Guidelines

In this section you examine marketing strengths, weaknesses, and options. Opportunities will begin to emerge as you consider the variety of alternatives.

Try to avoid restricted thinking. Take your time and brainstorm. Dig for opportunities with other members of your planning team. If one doesn't exist, then put together a team representing different functional areas of the business (or persuade senior management to approve its formation).

Consider all possibilities for expanding existing market coverage and laying the groundwork for entering new markets. Also consider opportunities related to your competition. For instance, offensively, which of your competitors can be displaced from which market segments? Defensively, which competitors can be denied entry into your market?

As you go through this section, revisit your strategic portion of the SMP (the top row of boxes in Figure 2.1). While that portion represents a 3- to 5-year period, work must begin at some point to activate the strategic direction, objectives, growth strategies, and in particular the products and markets identified in the business portfolio section. Further, you should refer to the situation analysis in the last section, specifically the competitive analysis, for voids or weaknesses, which could represent opportunities.

Note the two-directional flow used to create opportunities: the future thinking that you composed for the strategic portion of the SMP now flows down to focus on 1-year opportunities. Then the situation analysis of the bottom row, the tactical marketing plan, exposes the voids and weaknesses representing opportunities.

Now review the following screening process to identify your major opportunities and challenges. Once you identify and prioritize the opportunities, convert them into objectives and strategies, which are the topics of the next two sections of the SMP.

Present Markets

Identify the best opportunities for expanding present markets through:

- Cultivating new business and new users
- Displacing competition
- Increasing product usage or programs by present customers
- Redefining market segments
- Reformulating or repackaging the product
- Identifying new uses (applications) of the product
- Repositioning the product to create a more favorable perception by consumers and to develop a competitive advantage over rival products
- Expanding into new or unserved market niches

Customers/Buyers

Identify the best opportunities for expanding your customer base through:

- Improving or expanding distribution channels

- Product pricing including discounts, rebates, volume purchases, allowances
- Product promotion covering advertising, sales promotion, publicity — including the promotional activities of the sales force
- Enhancing customer service, including technical support
- Trade buying practices, identifying where the buying power is focused or has shifted (from manufacturer to distributor or to end-user)

Growth Markets

Identify the major product growth markets in key areas (by geographic location) and specify which markets represent the greatest long-term potential.

Product and Service Development and Innovation

Identify the immediate and long-range opportunities for product development and innovation through:

- Adding new products to the line
- Diversifying into new or related products, product lines, and/or new items or features
- Modifying and altering products
- Improving packaging
- Establishing new value-added or customer services

Targets of Opportunity

List any areas outside your current market segment or product line not included in the above categories that you would like to explore. Be innovative and entrepreneurial in your thinking. These areas are opportunistic. Therefore, due to their innovative and risky characteristics, they are isolated from the other opportunities. Those you select for special attention are placed in a separate part of the objectives section of the SMP.

APPLICATION

Present Markets

Intensify promotion of drug therapy management systems and educational programs among consumers, physicians, and nurses. These systems and programs would displace Apollo and Majestic because of their poor performance in such programs. This action — technologically improving the market position of our product — will create new opportunities for increased usage.

Customers/Buyers

The mass merchandisers' importance within the consumer retail market will continue to grow at the expense of retail drugs. We will develop a new, dedicated sales team, hitting mass merchandisers during this planning period in order to attack Apollo and Majestic before they can mount a similar effort.

Growth in third-party payer plans may change buying behavior by removing consumers from the purchase decision. Price, therefore, may become a key purchasing variable for specific user groups. The pricing flexibility resulting from cost-cutting programs will position us to increase our customer base.

Growth Markets

As the overall market for drug-delivery systems grows, specific geographic areas will be a function of population shifts. Disease control within target groups in urban areas, such as those segments related to AIDS control, represents a growing market. (See Section 4, Business Portfolio for a comprehensive listing of existing products/new markets and new products/new markets.)

Product and Service Development and Innovation

Line extensions, modifications, and new package designs will strengthen our dominant share position within the needle/syringe segment. Introducing the cartridge injection system will address specific groups needing multiple daily injections.

Targets of Opportunity

Diversifying into drug-monitoring systems represents a major opportunity. Expansion into these systems will provide synergies through marketing an entire line of products. Such an approach provides market leverage to enter European and Pacific Rim countries as a single-source supplier.

Using the planning guidelines and the applications as reference, now prepare your working draft of opportunities.

Working Draft

List opportunities by:

- Present markets
- Customers/buyers
- Growth markets
- Product and service development/innovation
- Targets of opportunity

SECTION 7: MARKETING OBJECTIVES

```
Section 7
Marketing
Objectives
```

At this point, you have reported relevant factual data in Section 5 Situation Analysis and interpreted their meaning and consequences to your product line in Section 6 Marketing Opportunities. You must now set the objectives you want to achieve during the current planning period — generally defined as a 12-month period.

Once again, you will find it useful to review Sections 5 and 6. Also, it will help to review the strategic portion of the plan (the top row of boxes in Figure 2.1). It is in your best interest to be certain that actions related to your long-range strategic direction, objectives, and strategies are incorporated into your tactical 1-year objectives.

This section consists of three parts:

- Assumptions: projections about future conditions and trends
- Primary Objectives: quantitative areas related to your responsibility, including targets of opportunity
- Functional Objectives: operational parts of the business

ASSUMPTIONS

Planning Guidelines

For objectives to be realistic and achievable, you must first generate assumptions and projections about future conditions and trends. List only those major assumptions that will affect your business for the planning year as it relates to the following:

- *Economic assumptions:* discuss Gross Domestic Product (GDP), local economics, industrial production, plant and equipment expenditures, consumer expenditures, and changes in customer needs. Also document market size, growth rate, costs, and trends in major market segments.
- *Technological assumptions:* include depth of research and development efforts, the likelihood of technological breakthroughs, the availability of raw materials, and plant capacity.
- *Sociopolitical assumptions:* indicate prospective legislation, political tensions, tax outlook, population patterns, educational factors, and changes in customer habits.
- *Competitive assumptions:* identify the activities of existing competitors, inroads of new competitors, and changes in trade practices.

Commentary

List assumptions that relate to your business. It is not necessary to identify broad issues that fail to impact your business directly. For example, if the increase or decrease in GDP has no effect, don't list it. If population shifts and geographic considerations are major factors influencing your business, list them.

Consider, too, other potential factors about your company or industry, such as labor strife or belt-tightening budgetary restraints that may affect your plans. Make your assumptions realistic, focused, and practical.

APPLICATION

Economic Assumptions

- Those needing injections is projected to grow by 2.7% in the next 12 months
- The entry of low-priced competitors will not encourage the emergence of private label brands
- Third-party payers will not significantly change current buying patterns by taking the purchase decision away from the consumer

Technological Assumptions

- Cartridge devices will compete primarily with single-use syringes

■ No significant cannibalization of sales from our product line resulting from internal pumps and oral agents is anticipated

Sociopolitical Assumptions

■ Twice-daily injection regimens will increase to 57% of the target population from 49%
■ Greater government intervention is expected in drug and drug-delivery systems related to such diseases as AIDS

Competitive Assumptions

■ The basis of competition will continue to be product performance and differentiation
■ Competitive advantage will be achieved through extensive market segmentation by focusing goods and services on specific user groups

Working Draft

As you think about assumptions, it is appropriate to ask senior executives about how they view the above categories. Also confer with technical and financial individuals in your firm. They should provide clues about significant internal and external assumptions that would impact your SMP.

Categorize your assumptions by:

– Economic assumptions
– Technological assumptions
– Sociopolitical assumptions
– Competitive assumptions

PRIMARY OBJECTIVES

Planning Guidelines

Focus on the primary financial objectives your organization requires. Also include targets of opportunity you initially identified as innovative and entrepreneurial in Section 6.

Where there are multiple objectives you may find it helpful to rank them in priority order. Be sure to quantify expected results where possible. You can separate your objectives into the following categories:

Table 2.1 Primary Objectives								
	Current				Projected			
Product Group Breakdown	Sales ($)	Units	Margins	Share of Market	Sales ($)	Units	Margins	Share of Market
Product A								
Product B								
Product C								
Product D								
Other financial measures								

- *Primary objectives.* Current and projected sales, profits, market share, and return on investment (see Table 2.1 or use a form provided by your organization)
- *Targets of opportunity objectives.* Innovations in such areas as markets, product, price, promotion, and distribution
- *Functional objectives.* Product and nonproduct objectives

APPLICATION

Primary Objectives

(Since the Situation Analysis provided financial information, additional numbers are unnecessary here. Instead, this section includes a suggested form, Table 2.1, to define financial information that is usually reported in this portion of the SMP. Specific financial requirements usually originate from the ongoing reporting systems within the organization.)

Targets of Opportunity Objectives

Defend our needle/syringe leadership position by challenging the pen–cartridge system introduction, which looms as a competitive displacement threat. Introduce new computerized customer tracking systems within the mass merchandiser class of trade.

Working Draft

Develop primary objectives (use the form in Table 2.1 or the format required by your organization).

List targets of opportunity objectives.

FUNCTIONAL OBJECTIVES

Planning Guidelines

State the functional objectives relating to both product and nonproduct issues in the following categories:

Product Objectives

- *Quality.* Achieving competitive advantage by exceeding industry standards in some or all segments of your market
- *Development.* Dealing with new technology through internal R&D, licensing, or joint ventures
- *Modification.* Delivering major or minor product changes through reformulation or engineering
- *Differentiation.* Enhancing competitive position through function, design, or any other changes that can differentiate a product or service
- *Diversification.* Transferring technology or using the actual product in new applications, or diversifying into new geographic areas, such as developing countries
- *Deletion.* Removing a product from the line due to unsatisfactory performance, or keeping it in the line if the product serves some strategic purpose, such as presenting your company to the market as a full-line supplier
- *Segmentation.* Creating line extensions (adding product varieties) to reach a new market niche or defending against an incoming competitor in an existing market segment
- *Pricing.* Including list prices, volume discounts, and promotional rebates
- *Promotion.* Developing sales, sales promotion, advertising, and publicity to the trade and consumers
- *Distribution channel.* Adding new distributors to increase geographic coverage, developing programs or services to solidify relationships with the trade, removing distributors or dealers from the channel, or maintaining direct contact with the end user
- *Physical distribution.* Utilizing logistical factors from order entry to the physical movement of a product through the channel and eventual delivery to the end user
- *Packaging.* Using functional design and/or decorative considerations for brand identification

- *Service.* Broadening the range of services, from providing customers access to key executives in your firm to providing on-site technical assistance
- *Other.* Developing other categories as suggested in Targets of Opportunity

APPLICATION

Product Objectives (Sample Listing)

- *Differentiation.* Continue to generate added value for Tri-Tek's health-care products by communicating product improvements to the target audience
- *Segmentation.* Strengthen Tri-Tek's leadership position within the needle/syringe segment by addressing the trend in therapy toward smaller and more frequent injections
- *Pricing.* Maintain the premium price position across all healthcare product lines
- *Promotion.* Encourage continuity of purchase among current users, attract new and infrequent users, provide merchandising opportunities in support of trade programs
- *Packaging.* Achieve a consistent look across the entire line to enhance brand name recognition

Working Draft

Now prepare your rough draft. Keep in mind as you review the categories that competitive advantage, which incorporates long-term customer satisfaction, is the object of your efforts. Be selective, and make value judgments about each objective in relation to the advantages you will gain.

As in most of the listings of this SMP, you may wish to edit the following list to incorporate your own trade terminology.

- Quality
- Modification
- Differentiation
- Diversification
- Deletion
- Segmentation
- Pricing
- Promotion

- Distribution channel
- Physical distribution
- Packaging
- Service
- Other

NONPRODUCT OBJECTIVES

Planning Guidelines

Although most of the following activities eventually relate to the product or service, some are support functions which you may or may not influence. How much clout you can exert depends on the functions represented on your planning team.

- *Targeted accounts.* Indicate those customers with whom you can develop special relationships through customized products, distribution or warehousing, value-added services, or participation in quality improvement programs
- *Manufacturing.* Identify special activities that would provide a competitive advantage, such as offering small production runs to accommodate the changing needs of customers and to reduce inventory levels
- *Marketing research.* Cite customer-tracking studies that identify key buying factors and include competitive intelligence
- *Credit.* Include any programs that use credit and finance as a value-added component for a product offering, such as rendering financial advice or providing financial assistance to customers in certain situations
- *Technical sales activities.* Include any support activities, such as 24-hour hot-line telephone assistance that offers on-site consultation to solve customers' problems
- *R&D.* Indicate internal research and development projects as well as joint ventures that would complement the Strategic Direction identified in Section 1 of the SMP
- *Training.* List internal training as well as external distributor and end-user programs
- *Human resource development.* Identify types of skills and levels of performance among individuals who would make the SMP operational
- *Other.* Include those specialized activities that may be unique to your organization

APPLICATION

This segment contains only a sampling of Tri-Tek's actual SMP nonproduct objectives.

- *Manufacturing.* Maintain low-cost producer status as product improvements are implemented
- *Technical sales activities.* Maintain sales focus of the brand by providing consumers with information and technical assistance to demonstrate the unequaled injection comfort of our product; project Tri-Tek's dedication to meeting the needs of people dependent on drug-delivery systems
- *Training.* Maintain full marketing support for professional educators

Working Draft

Use the following categories to develop your nonproduct objectives.

- – Targeted accounts:
- – Manufacturing:
- – Marketing research:
- – Credit:
- – Technical sales activities:
- – R&D:
- – Training:
- – Human resource development:
- – Other:

SECTION 8: STRATEGIES AND ACTION PLANS (TACTICS)

```
Section 8
Strategies and
Action Plans
```

Strategy is the art of coordinating the means (money, human resources, materials) to achieve the ends (profits, customer satisfaction, growth) as defined by company policy, strategic direction, and objectives.

In this section, strategies have to be identified and put into action. You must assign responsibilities, set schedules, establish budgets, and determine checkpoints. Make sure that the planning team actively participates in this section. They are the ones who have to implement the strategies.

This section is the focal point of the SMP. All the previous work was done for one reason, and one reason only: to develop strategies and tactics. To refine the definition further: strategies and tactics are actions to achieve objectives. Strategies to achieve longer-term objectives; tactics to reach shorter-term objectives.

Planning Guidelines

Restate the functional product and nonproduct objectives from Section 7 and link them with a brief description of the course of action — strategies and tactics — you will use to reach each objective. Then put all actions together into a summary strategy.

One of the reasons for restating the objectives is to clarify the frequent misunderstanding between objectives and strategies. Objectives are *what* you want to accomplish; strategies are *how* (actions) to achieve objectives. If you state an objective and don't have a related strategy, you may not have an objective. The statement may be an action for some other objective.

APPLICATION

This segment contains only a sampling from Tri-Tek's SMP.

Product Strategies/Tactics

Differentiation Objective

- Continue to generate added value for Tri-Tek's healthcare products by communicating product improvements to the target audience

Strategy/Tactics

- Introduce SupraFine III needle to maintain superior product quality and performance vs. competition as it relates to injection comfort
- Develop marketing plans for third-quarter introduction

Responsibility: Marketing and Technical Sales.

Segmentation Objective

- Strengthen our leadership position within the needle/syringe segment by addressing the trend towards smaller and more frequent injections

Strategy/Tactics

- Introduce a 40-unit syringe to address the needs of target groups for multiple-dose therapy
- Integrate promotional activities on the entire product line to coincide with the new product introduction
- Develop marketing plans for introduction during the second quarter

Responsibility: Marketing.

Pricing Objective

- Maintain price leadership across all healthcare product lines

Strategy/Tactics

- Hold manufacturers' list price at 200× levels.

Responsibility: Marketing and Finance.

Promotion Objective

- Encourage continuity of purchase among current users; attract new and infrequent users
- Provide merchandising opportunities in support of trade programs

Strategy/Tactics

- Maximize effectiveness of consumer promotion events by coordinating them with trade programs and presenting them to the trade with sufficient lead time to gain their support
- Coordinate trade promotions with distribution allowances and extended dating programs
- Utilize combinations of counter-card rebate offers and in-pack programs to reach category and brand users
- Submit promotion plans in the first quarter

Responsibility: Marketing.

Packaging Objective

- Achieve a consistent look across the entire line to enhance brand name recognition

Strategy/Tactics

- Revise packaging to include new SupraFine III and product improvements
- Determine key consumer benefits and revise packaging graphics to provide consistent look across all sizes
- Designs to be submitted during the second quarter

Responsibility: Marketing and outside agencies.

Nonproduct Strategies/Tactics

Manufacturing Objectives

- Maintain low-cost producer status as product improvements are implemented

Strategy/Tactics

- Continue to implement quality control (QC) program
- Install new cost-reduction program
- Develop a prototype for a disposable pen–cartridge system with the assistance of product designers and marketing
- Submit status and recommendation reports by second quarter

Responsibility: Manufacturing/Engineering.

Technical Sales Activities Objectives

- Maintain sales focus of the brand by providing consumers with information and technical assistance to demonstrate the unequaled injection comfort of our products and project Tri-Tek's dedication in meeting the needs of people dependent on drug-delivery systems

Strategy/Tactics

- Achieve a level of 90% distribution of "Getting Started" take-home kits

■ Develop video presentation with key medical professionals for use in hospitals and clinics

Responsibility: Marketing.

Training Objective

■ Maintain marketing support behind professional educators

Strategy/Tactics

■ Continue technical education program for internal sales staff and distributors' sales staff to gain professional recommendations at time of diagnosis and maintain brand loyalty
■ Submit training plan by the third quarter

Responsibility: Human Re᠐ources.

Summary Strategy

Planning Guidelines

Summarize the basic strategies for achieving your primary objectives. Include a discussion of alternative and contingency plans available if situations arise to prevent reaching your objectives. Relate these alternatives to the overall SMP.

Consider the following additional strategic issues:

■ Changes needed to the product or package
■ Changes needed to prices, discounts, or long-term contracts
■ Changes needed to advertising strategy, related to the selection of features and benefits, or copy themes to special groups
■ Changes needed in media plan
■ Promotional strategies for private label, dealer and/or distributor, consumers, and sales force incentives

APPLICATION

Tri-Tek's industry leadership will be maintained by addressing our full range of drug-delivery systems for healthcare. These include not only the marketing of delivery devices that are virtually painless, easy to read, and convenient to use, but also programs and educational services to aid in the achievement of improved healthcare. The dominant strategies include the following:

- Segment the market through product differentiation and innovation
- Maintain low-cost producer status by achieving cost reductions of 32.5% by 200x
- Develop a nonreusable syringe
- Initiate anti-reuse campaign
- Introduce the Supra-Fine III needle
- Introduce a 40-unit syringe for multiple-dose therapy. Superior quality and low-cost producer status continue to be critical element strategies for success; if internal R&D and cost-reduction programs do not meet projections, joint ventures will be pursued

Working Draft

Now write a draft using the format shown above.

SECTION 9: FINANCIAL CONTROLS AND BUDGETS

> **Section 9**
> **Financial Controls**
> **and Budgets**

Planning Guidelines

Having completed the strategy phase of your SMP, you must decide how you will monitor its execution. Therefore, before implementing it, you have to develop procedures for both control (comparing actual and planned figures) and review (deciding whether planned figures should be adjusted or other corrective measures taken).

This final section incorporates your operating budget. If your organization has reporting procedures, you should incorporate them within this section.

Included below are examples of additional reports or data sheets designed to monitor progress at key checkpoints of the plan and permit either major shifts in strategies or simple midcourse corrections:

- Forecast models
- Sales by channel of distribution
  - Inventory or out-of-stock reports
  - Average selling price (including discounts, rebates, or allowances) by distribution channel and customer outlet
- Profit and loss statements by product
- Direct product budgets
- R&D expenses
- Administrative budget
- Spending by quarter

As an overall guideline — regardless of the forms you use — make certain that the system serves as a reliable feedback mechanism. Your interest is in maintaining explicit and timely control so you can react swiftly to impending problems. Further, it should serve as a procedure for reviewing schedules and strategies. Finally, the system could provide an upward flow of fresh market information which, in turn, could impact on broad policy revisions at the highest levels of the organization.

APPLICATION

Examples of Tri-Tek's financial data were provided in other sections of the SMP.

Working Draft

Insert your company's forms or use the forms provided in the various sections of the SMP.

Summary

You now have the formal structure of the SMP. Once again a caution: don't short-circuit the plan by skipping sections or altering the sequence in which the SMP is prepared. It is shown as a logical process leading you step-by-step from section to section, from the broad to the narrow, and from the strategic focus to the tactical implementation.

The intent is to free up your mind to think broadly about your product or service and convert your thinking into a business perspective, followed by implementation. Further, the systematic process permits your next level of management — the level that approves and funds your plan — to observe the thought processes that went into the SMP.

The only other part left in your SMP is an optional appendix. Your appendix should include the following items: copies of advertising campaigns for your product as well as those of your competitors, market data from market research, additional data on competitors' market strategies and pricing schedules, and details about product features and benefits.

Functional Managers' Plans

Finally, the SMP serves as a core plan from which other functional managers create subplans. For example:

The *sales manager* develops a sales plan by territory, indicating how sales people are deployed, trained, and compensated. It specifies types of promotional support as well as target customers that require special attention.

The *advertising manager* prepares copy strategy and media plans as well as designs sales promotion activities such as trade shows, direct mail campaigns, Internet campaigns, video presentations, and educational workshops.

The *financial manager* develops financial measures related to operating performance such as cash flow, return on investment, and return-on-sales. Those measures monitor the financial health of the operating unit and aid in projecting financial needs to the organization.

The *human resource manager* determines skills training, compensation programs, and new hiring needs to support the SMP.

The *R&D and manufacturing managers* set in motion plans to support the strategies of the SMP as they relate to product innovations, packaging, and manufacturing cost efficiencies.

The above functional managers, and others, are part of the Business Management Team (BMT) referred to in Chapter 1. Thus, the imperative is to initiate a team approach to develop the SMP, thereby coordinating the usually diverse functions into a cohesive, market-driven organizational force.

How do you seize the opportunity to convert the SMP into action? Go to Chapter 3 and see real company examples of how marketing-related problems are solved through the effective application of business-building strategies.

You will observe how some problems parallel those you may be facing. Then refer to the section of the SMP where that type of difficulty is handled. You then have the opportunity to alter your working draft and begin inputting the refined plan into the SMP computer disk.

Schedule for Strategic Marketing Planning

The purpose of a planning schedule is to demonstrate that effective planning is a participative process requiring input from all levels of management. While Figure 2.2, a calendarized schedule, displays an optimum situation, the activities and units of responsibility may vary within each organization.

In practice, many organizations with formalized planning systems will take a 6-month period to develop an operating plan. If a company is working on a calendar year, the process begins in July and is usually submitted to top management by November or early December.

Planning Activity	Unit Responsible	Week(s) No.										
1. Marketing research conducts situation analysis and generates background data.	Marketing research	▮										
2. Marketing research develops assumptions about future environment and identifies current position.	Marketing research		▮									
3. Top management sets corporate objectives.	Top management			▮								
4. Marketing vice-president interprets corporate objectives and derives marketing objectives with input of strategy team or product manager.	Vice-president marketing				▮							
5. Sales and expense forecasts are established.	Marketing research controller					▮						
6. Product managers develop optimum strategies for their assigned lines and review with marketing vice-president.	Product managers, vice-president marketing					▮						
7. Product managers design detailed action programs and review with general sales manager.	Product managers, general sales manager							▮				
8. Product managers write up their proposals and submit them to marketing vice-president.	Product manager							▮				
9. Marketing reviews and coordinates individual product plans.	Vice-president marketing								▮			
10. General sales manager assigns district volume objectives.	General sales manager								▮			
11. District managers develop district sales plans in consultation with sales people.	District sales managers											
12. General sales manager reviews and integrates district sales plans.	General sales manager											
13. Product managers prepare financial summaries.	Product managers											
14. Controller prepares operating budget.	Controller											
15. Top marketing reviews and approves marketing plan.	Top management											

Figure 2.2   Schedule for Strategic Marketing Planning

III

THE STRATEGIC MARKETING PLAN IN ACTION

3

MARKETING PROBLEM
SOLVER

Given the information in this chapter, you should be able to:

■ Use SMP techniques to solve competitive marketing problems
■ Strengthen your planning skills by applying the lessons of actual case histories to solving your marketing problems
■ Link sections of the SMP to specific marketing problems

OVERVIEW

As indicated in previous chapters, the primary outputs of strategic marketing planning are competitive marketing strategies. Using actual case examples, this chapter illustrates how the planning process helps solve competitive marketing problems — perhaps ones you currently face.

To strengthen your planning skills and enhance your ability to use the SMP process in practical applications, the following format is used:

1. A competitive problem is identified.
2. An actual case example is used to illustrate each problem.
3. Action strategies explain how the company solved the problem.
4. References indicate the SMP section where you would address such a problem.

The following case examples are included in this chapter:

1. How do you sustain growth in a mature market? (Campbell Soup Co.)
2. With large multinational organizations tending to dominate a market, what strategies are possible? (National Semiconductor Corp./Xerox Corp.)

3. How can you use SMPs to identify long-term opportunities and manage day-to-day operations? (Emerson Electric Co.)

4. When developing a SMP, how can you use competitor analysis to justify the time and expense of gathering the information? (Texas Instruments Inc.)

5. How do you deal with off-shore competitors selling into your market with prices 30 to 40% below yours? (Cummins Engines)

6. How do you cope with the possibility of your product becoming a dinosaur? (Moore Corp.)

7. How can you implement relationship marketing to block the actions of enterprising competitors? (Baldor Electric Co.)

8. What defensive strategies are effective to protect market share? (Haworth Inc.)

9. How can you maneuver into a niche already occupied by market leaders? (Nu-Kote Holding Inc.)

10. How can you justify the high up-front expenditures for new product development with the inevitable drop in prices as products move rapidly into the mature stage in their life cycles? (Microsoft, Intel, IBM, Eastman Kodak)

11. What strategies can help reverse a steep decline in a company's sales? (Emery Worldwide)

12. How can a small company apply customer-driven marketing techniques to grow against dominant competitors? (QAD Inc.)

13. Is there a way to create a competitive advantage in a basic industry heavily dominated by low-cost competitors? (Russell Corp.)

14. How do you transform a commodity product into a brand name? (Thor-Lo Inc.)

15. How do you position your products effectively against market leaders? (A. Schulman Inc.)

16. What strategies can outdistance competitors when entering a new market? (Safeskin Corp.)

17. What strategies can you use to regain lost market share? (Quaker State Corp.)

CASE EXAMPLES

Case Example #1: Campbell Soup Co.

Problem: *How do you sustain growth in a mature market?*

Managers at Campbell Soup Co. introduced a radical change in strategy to deal with a mature market for its soup products. They shifted from mass marketing to regionalization. For Campbell, regionalization is demonstrated by the following example.

In Texas and parts of Southern California where consumers like food with a zesty taste, Campbell makes its nacho cheese soup spicier. In Northern California the same soup is produced in a milder form.

In a parallel example of regionalization, a local sales manager used part of her ad budget to sponsor a radio promotion at a major sports event. In still another example, a local Campbell manager arranged for hot samples of selected soups to be distributed to thankful skiers at a mountain resort.

To move toward regionalization, Campbell shifted its focus by pushing decision making down to levels that are closer to the consumer. That move required more market-by-market planning. For instance, managers tailored their products, advertising, promotion, and sales efforts to fit different regions of the country — and even individual neighborhoods within a city.

In turn, the regionalization strategy required more skilled managers to develop comprehensive marketing plans, determine competitive strategies and tactics, and then be able to identify the financial implications of those strategies. As a result, such calculations as return on investment (ROI), return on sales, market share, break-even analysis, and marketing expense-to-sales ratios took on even greater meaning with regionalization.

Now, compare this strategy with the traditional centralized Campbell approach of developing a single set of products and marketing programs for a mass market which was formerly viewed with little or no differentiation.

With the changes in strategy, not only are middle managers required to act as business managers, but local sales staffs are transformed into autonomous marketers as the company divided the U.S. into 22 regions. Now every regional staff develops its own marketing strategies and takes responsibility for implementing plans to deal with mature markets.

Action Strategy

For Campbell, the approach to mature markets is regionalization. Other labels given to the approach are segmentation, target marketing, and niche marketing. And there is *mass customization* which serves the mass market through computer-integrated manufacturing and other forms of technology that can customize a product for various customer groupings.

For your purpose, begin by recognizing that segments are not static. You will find it necessary to resegment or regionalize your markets for other opportunities. For Campbell, success is based on satisfying market segments by differentiating the product.

In short, segmenting markets is a creative process. Go beyond the standard approaches of demographic, geographic, and behavioral segmentation. Examine your markets and determine if additional approaches permit you to resegment for fresh opportunities.

To trigger your thinking look at some of the following factors:

- Segment by common buying factors
  - Performance
  - Delivery
  - Price
  - Quality
  - Service (customer and/or technical)
- Segment by measurable characteristics
  - Customer size
  - Customer growth rate
  - Customer location(s)
- Segment by type of competitors and their respective strategies and strengths/weaknesses
- Segment by common sales and distribution channels
- Segment by business opportunities created through a technology breakthrough, new legislation, a competitor exiting the market, or blocking inroads of a new competitor, and similar situations.

Also, be aware of over-segmenting as well as under-segmenting your market. As a guideline, use the following criteria to determine the viability of your segment:

- Is the segment of sufficient size and purchasing power to be profitable?
- Does the segment have growth potential?
- Is the segment of negligible interest to major competitors, especially if there is an aggressive leader in the total market?
- Does your organization (division, business unit) have the necessary skills and resources to serve the segment effectively?
- Do you have the ability to defend against an attacking major competitor?
- Can your group develop strategies to maintain a competitive advantage?

Additional in-depth coverage of segmentation is in Chapter 5, Help Topics.

SMP Reference

Section 4 (Business Portfolio) and Section 6 (Marketing Opportunities).

Case Example #2: National Semiconductor Corp./Xerox Corp.

Problem: *With large multinational organizations tending to dominate a market, what strategies are possible?*

National Semiconductor Corp. and Xerox Corp. forged a unique supplier–customer alliance. They reflect the leading edge of a new-wave strategy on how to deal with aggressive multinational and other offshore competitors.

The alliance relies on mutual trust. Here is how it works: Xerox accesses National's secret techniques for designing integrated circuits. National, in turn, sees Xerox's closely guarded sales projections and new product strategies and serves as Xerox's primary supplier.

The advantages of the supplier–customer alliance are the following:

- Xerox uses National's technology to create custom chips. The competitive advantage for Xerox is in achieving product uniqueness and differentiation, which cannot be easily duplicated. National gets primary supplier status, which seals up the business, assures accurate production schedules, and maintains reliable deliveries. The alliance also serves as a formidable defense against incoming competitors.
- The product differentiation avoids a frontal attack against cutthroat competitors in the commodity end of the market.
- The alliance blends the unique talents of both companies into a common purpose. The purpose is to sustain a competitive advantage at the end of the distribution chain: the ultimate customer. Also, the customized products tend to be tougher to duplicate by competitors.
- The alliance forces a market-driven, customer-first attitude from all participating managers. Such an attitude contrasts with the commodity, production-driven mentality that creates havoc in most industries.

Action Strategy

Forming joint alliances to create product differentiation and provide for customer satisfaction is but one part of the equation; the other is determining how competitors might behave toward the alliance. Consider the following types of competitor behavior:

- *Passive competitor.* Characterized as slow to react, this competitor believes it holds a solid position in the market and has customer loyalty. Or it may lack resources, have disorganized (or complacent) management, and display an overall laid-back mentality. This type of competitor presents major opportunities for aggressive strategies. However, first find out the reasons for the passive behavior.

- *Discerning competitor.* Selective actions, such as attacking competitors' key accounts, might provoke an aggressive competitive response from this type of competitor. Yet a price reduction or adding value to your product might not produce a counter move. Determine those selective actions that would produce a threatening competitive response. Detecting such behavior is vital to developing competitive strategies.

- *Aggressive competitor.* This type of competitor charges forward with quick and vigorous actions. In some instances the competitor sends out strong challenging signals simply on the news of your new product or service. The telltale signals indicate that any action you take will be hotly contested. In such a case, your response is to avoid a direct confrontation at all costs. Instead, focus on detecting weaknesses in your competitor's market coverage. Do so by examining the marketing mix (product, price, promotion, and distribution) for opportunities to use your strengths against the competitor's weaknesses.

- *Unpredictable competitor.* This type of competitor is elusive without predictable behavior. The company's actions appear highly flexible, and it shapes itself rapidly to market situations. This competitor might have a lean organization with few layers of management which permits hands-on managers to exercise authority and responsibility right down to the field level. Careful monitoring through competitor intelligence by field sales and product managers is essential to prevent a surprise counterattack to your strategies.

SMP Reference

Section 3 (Growth Strategies) and Section 5 (Situation Analysis).

Case Example #3: Emerson Electric Co.

Problem: *How can you use SMPs to identify long-term opportunities and manage day-to-day operations?*

Emerson makes basic products essential to a variety of industries, such as refrigerator compressors, pressure gauges, and garbage disposals. What distinguishes this St. Louis, MO company from the herd is its dazzling record of 36 uninterrupted years of increased earnings, without significant price increases since the mid-1980s. During the highly competitive 1980s, Emerson staunchly endured the challenges of low-cost Brazilian, Korean, and Japanese competitors.

Several factors contributed to Emerson's success:

1. Management recognized early on that low-cost, aggressive competitors would remain a permanent part of the global scene and would intensify into the next decade.
2. It exerted the discipline to secure cost-efficient operations at every level of the organization.
3. Management demonstrated the flexibility to focus on growth markets and exit those segments with little chance of turning a profit, such as defense and construction, and niche businesses such as gardening tools.
4. It realized that cost cutting was only one part of the success equation to sustain growth. The other, that strategic marketing planning should function as the primary operating system for managing both long-term objectives and day-to-day operations.

A single example sums up Emerson's accomplishments. Ten years ago a Japanese plant could offer temperature sensors for washing machines for 20% below Emerson's prices. Today, Emerson's costs are below those of the Japanese, and the company has regained market share. Rigorous planning, then, is at the heart of Emerson's system for managing growth.

To make the planning system work, Emerson:

■ Surveys all employees periodically to assure input and participation from every functional area of the business; such input permits additional strategy options to surface that can be evaluated, refined, and implemented

■ Identifies customers' problems early, while they are still manageable, enabling marketing and sales to take immediate action

■ Keeps vigilant watch on troublesome competitors so that managers lose no time in redirecting their efforts where needed

■ Tracks sales growth, new product development, and market expansion as benchmarks to monitor the plan

Action Strategy

Like Emerson, you can utilize strategic marketing planning to grow present markets, spot growth markets, recognize new product innovations, and stay alert to current opportunities. The following screening process will help you zero in on clear pathways for growth. Once identified and prioritized, you can then convert them into long- and short-term marketing objectives, strategies, and tactics.

1. Present Markets

To identify the best opportunities for expanding present markets, you should:

- Investigate emerging businesses or acquire new users for your product
- Determine how to displace competition — a particularly significant move in no-growth markets
- Increase product usage by your current customers and redefine market segments where there are changes in customers' buying patterns
- Work jointly with customers on innovative ideas to reformulate or repackage the product according to their specific needs
- Identify new uses (applications) for your product
- Reposition the product to create a more favorable perception over rival products
- Investigate where to expand into new or unserved market niches

2. Customers

To identify the best opportunities for expanding your customer base, you should:

- Improve or expand distribution channels
- Refine your product pricing policies to match market share objectives
- Enrich your communications, including advertising, sales promotion, and publicity
- Deploy the sales force to target new customers with high potential
- Enhance customer service, including technical service and complaint handling
- Identify changes in trade buying practices, where the buying power may have shifted from manufacturer to distributor or to end user

3. Growth Markets

To identify the major growth markets, you should:

- Target key geographic locations, specifying which markets or user groups represent the greatest long-term potential

4. New Product Development

To give priority to "hot" candidates for new product and service development that will impact on immediate and long-range opportunities, you should:

- Focus on new products that can be differentiated and that have the potential for an extended life cycle
- Search for ways to diversify into new or related products, product lines, and/or new items or features
- Examine techniques to modify products by customer groups, distribution outlets, or individual customer applications
- Work on improving packaging to conform to customers' specifications and to distinguish your product from its rivals
- Establish new value-added services

5. Targets of Opportunity

To focus on areas outside your current market segment or product line not included in the other categories, you should:

- Be innovative and entrepreneurial in your thinking; however, refer to your strategic direction (SMP Section 1) as a guideline to how far your company can realistically diversify from its core business and still retain its vitality

SMP Reference

Section 6 (Marketing Opportunities) and Section 7 (Marketing Objectives).

Case Example #4: Texas Instruments Inc.

Problem: *When developing a SMP, how can you use competitor analysis to justify the time and expense of gathering the information?*

Texas Instruments Inc. made phenomenal progress in attracting customers to its custom-designed computer chips when it decided to battle the Japanese head-to-head in high-volume dynamic random access memory (RAM) markets. The competitive attitude infused the company with new vitality at a time when other U.S. competitors were retreating from the market. As a result, a number of aggressive strategies were implemented.

For example, Texas Instrument managers:

■ Guaranteed monthly shipping quotas to customers that wanted to institute just-in-time inventory programs
■ Innovated by working on a system that simulated a customer's proprietary chip design, tested it, and delivered the results overnight
■ Counted on a string of new product successes; researchers worked hard to develop a single-chip version of a powerful processor tailored for artificial intelligence applications; it also produced a memory chip capable of storing data four times the capacity of the most advanced Japanese counterpart at that time
■ Asserted its aggressive fighting-back attitude by filing a suit charging Japan's eight leading producers with infringing on its patents for computer memory chips

Action Strategy

Texas Instrument's ability to develop aggressive SMPs were based on satisfying customer needs and on a thorough competitive analysis that helped forge its strategy. While there are numerous approaches to understanding competitors, the following criteria should be your primary considerations:

■ Competitor's size — categorized by market share, growth rate, and profitability
■ Competitor's objectives — related to quantitative (sales, profits, ROI, market share) and nonquantitative (technology innovation, market leadership, international, national, or regional distribution, etc.) measures
■ Competitor's strategies — analyzed by internal strategies (speed of product development, manufacturing capabilities, marketing expertise) and external strategies (distribution network, joint R&D relationships, market coverage, and aggressiveness in defending or building share of market)
■ Competitor's organization — examined by structure, culture, systems, and people

- Competitor's cost structure — examined by how efficiently it can compete and the ease or difficulty of exiting a business
- Competitor's overall strengths and weaknesses — identified by areas of vulnerability as well as areas of strength that can be bypassed or neutralized

If there is any one area of the SMP that deserves your major attention, it is in the competitive analysis. By scrutinizing competitors' strengths, weaknesses, and intentions, you can develop effective competitive marketing strategies.

SMP Reference

Section 5 (Situation Analysis), Competitor Analysis section. Also see the supplemental work forms in Chapter 4 to conduct a more comprehensive competitor analysis.

Case Example #5: Cummins Engines

Problem: *How do you deal with off-shore competitors selling into your market with prices 30 to 40% below yours?*

Cummins Engines, the diesel engine manufacturer, fought aggressively against two formidable Japanese competitors: Komatsu and Nissan. The first indication of a problem came from Cummins' customers, Navistar and Freightliner. Both companies reported they were testing Japanese medium truck engines.

Knowing the Japanese strategy of using an indirect approach into a market, Cummins saw the medium engine entry as a strategic threat. The entry could lead to the next step of penetrating Cummins' dominant share of the U.S. market for heavy-duty diesel truck engines. Cummins managers saw the strategy pattern evolve:

1. The Japanese competitors entered the market with prices 40% below prevailing levels to quickly buy market share.
2. They found a poorly served and emerging market segment in medium-size engines.
3. They developed a quality product and were prepared to expand their product lines. ·

Faced with the problem, Cummins managers took the following actions:

- Cummins launched into the medium-size truck engine market with four new engine models. This timing, however, was coincidental. Cummins had been planning this market entry for 5 years through a joint venture with J.I. Case, a farm machinery producer that uses diesel engines.
- Cummins immediately cut prices of the new engines to the Japanese level. As the then CEO Henry Schacht observed, "If you don't give the Japanese a major price advantage, they can't get in."
- Cummins cut costs by one third. This action was the toughest job in what was perceived as a bare-bones, efficient manufacturing operation. Overhead was reduced by using more flexible machinery and cutting excess inventory from a 60-day supply to a 4-day supply.
- Cummins managers gained participation from suppliers on suggestions about cost cutting. The result: lowering of material costs by 18%. This impressive reduction was achieved by changing the traditional adversarial attitude toward suppliers to one of fostering cooperative relationships.

The strategy worked as an effective defense, particularly as it relates to Cummins' concern about its heavy-duty diesel business. Into the early 1990s, Cummins held more than a 50% market share in North America, and not a single Japanese engine powered a U.S.-built tractor-trailer.

Action Strategy

A number of strategy lessons come out of the Cummins case. First, there are options open to you against a price attack. You observed some of those actions above. But the action must begin with a mental attitude of "fighting back" and not giving up market share without a battle.

Second, blunting a competitor's price attack by lowering one's own price is conditional on a set of factors related to your organization vs. key competitors. It is necessary in your competitive analysis to compare cost structures based on the following considerations:

- Determine the number of employees needed on a project and then calculate a breakdown of direct labor and overhead costs
- Use relative costs of raw material and components to determine if components should be made or outsourced
- Calculate the investment in inventory, plant, and equipment
- Determine if there are any unique manufacturing or marketing innovations that could affect costs
- Look at sales costs as they relate to the number of plants, warehousing locations, and other distribution procedures

Although the above factors relate primarily to a manufacturing situation, the approach is applicable to nonmanufacturing and service organizations. It is applicable to any organization that expends resources to operate a business.

Examining such factors needs the active participation of financial, manufacturing (or the equivalent function of a service provider), sales, and all other functional managers. Therefore, it is extremely valuable to form a strategy team of managers from the various functions who can assist in the study of all necessary factors. The aim is to develop strategies to meet the threat; in this case, countering a price attack.

SMP Reference

Section 5 (Situation Analysis), with particular attention aimed at determining the delivery, manufacturing cost, and product availability of competition.

Case Example #6: Moore Corporation

Problem: *How do you cope with the possibility of your product becoming a dinosaur?*

Moore has been making business forms for over 100 years. In fact, Moore invented the ubiquitous multipart form. The Toronto-based firm prospered until 1990 when it suffered a precipitous fall in income and a sharp 16% decline in sales, which finally bottomed out by 1993. Market share also dropped from a respectable 30% 2 decades ago to a paltry 13%.

Two questions arise. What triggered the staggering decline? What strategies did Moore's management use to reverse the situation? Let's deal with each — with the intent of applying the lessons to your own operation.

The problem: as many of Moore's corporate customers embraced restructuring, reengineering, and other streamlining approaches to maintain a competitive edge, they also used sophisticated technology to capture, move, and store massive amounts of information electronically. The result: paper consumption took a nosedive and the dinosaur syndrome threatened Moore's business.

Moore's Strategies

Further investigation revealed that while Moore's sale of paper forms lessened, the business wasn't altogether dead. Hard-copy invoices, labels, and other documents needed to comply with government, legal, and various customer needs continued to limp along. However, actual projections indicated industry-wide sales of forms would continue its near-decade-old decline.

Facing the potential dinosaur problem, management responded with alternative objectives that focused on three types of actions:

1. *Positioning.* The initial objective was to reorient and reposition Moore from an old-line forms printer to a 21st century organization able to design the flow of office information, both digitally and on paper. The new position moved Moore into database management, selling such items as computer software that turn out electronic forms. Projections indicate this part of the business will grow by 25% a year.

2. *Product mix.* Recognizing that a balance is needed between paper forms and electronic media, management set in motion a series of acquisition and joint venture objectives to recast the product mix. Rapid movement led Moore to form the following relationships: acquired Jetform Corp., a leading supplier of electronic-forms software; forged an alliance with Electronic Data Systems Corp., a computer-consulting firm, to help Moore's customers manage the accelerating flow of information; created a joint venture with Xerox Corp. that permits Moore's customers to customize documents and instantly transmit their designs to the nearest Moore plant for printing.

3. *Relaunch Products.* Noting the increasing use of bar coding to track products in a variety of markets had the mushrooming effect of actually increasing paper usage and gave new life to Moore's direct mail and labels group. In labels alone, sales jumped 30%, due to additional innovations as backing-less labels that promise to save the U.S. Postal Service 60% on its changes of address.

Action Strategy

One striking lesson in Moore's turnaround is not to roll over and claim that a business is totally outdated. Forging alternative objectives, such as joining new product development with technology, can help a company regain lost market share.

Making a changeover is one thing, creating a new perception or a new position that will stick in customers' minds is quite another challenge. If you face a situation of transforming the image of your product into a new market position, follow these guidelines:

- Be certain your position is *distinctive* and doesn't create confusion or misinterpretation, so that a competitor is mistakenly identified with your position.
- Select a position that conforms to your firm's unique, core competencies, so that competitors cannot easily duplicate the differentiating factors for which you can claim *superiority.*
- Communicate your position in precise terms through product application, sales promotion, and advertising. For example, determine what constitutes your position. Do you position your product with a single benefit, such as lowest cost? Do you use a double-benefit position of lowest cost and best technical support? Or do you select a multibenefit position of lowest cost, best technical support, and state-of-the-art technology?

These benefit positions, in turn, lay the foundation for developing the tactical programs that you incorporate into a marketing mix, consisting of product, price, promotion, and distribution.

SMP Reference

Section 1 (Strategic Direction), Section 2 (Objectives), and Section 3 (Growth Strategies).

Case Example #7: Baldor Electric Co.

Problem: *How can you implement relationship marketing to block the actions of enterprising competitors?*

Baldor considers relationship marketing and the total orientation toward satisfying unfilled wants and needs as more than just a management buzzword. In the mid-1990s, with sales of $418 million, the Fort Smith, AR company was dwarfed by two stalwart rivals, Reliance Electric and General Electric, competitors in electric motors that power pumps, fans, conveyor belts, and the variety of automated components used in modern factories.

"If you have good relationships, you can weather the bad times," declared Baldor CEO Roland Boreham Jr. Relationships, according to Boreham, extend beyond customers and include workers at Baldor, where there has not been a single layoff since 1962. Even during the recession of 1991, workers were busy increasing inventory and expanding the product line in readiness for the eventual upswing in business. Since 1991, sales have skyrocketed by 46%.

Customer Relationships

Focusing on fulfilling customers' wants and needs at Baldor means providing customers with the motors they need, on time, and according to their specifications. The company accomplishes this by building up ready-to-go inventory early in the production cycle, permitting it to fill an order overnight for the numerous motors it stocks — ranging in size from 1/50 h.p. to 700 h.p. It assembles all other sizes on short order from a database that includes over 20,000 different specifications.

The core ingredients behind Baldor's ability to sustain sound customer relationships are: (1) a bulk of its inventory is stored in 31 warehouses strategically located around the country in proximity to customers' locations; (2) each warehousing facility is owned and operated by an independent Baldor sales representative who is in continuing contact with other reps around the country; and (3) each facility is linked by computer, so that constant availability is "online" to respond to a customer's urgent request for a motor to prevent a potential manufacturing interruption.

Result: unsurpassed customer relationships for reliability, responsiveness, and flexibility where almost any size motor ships on virtually an overnight schedule — and exceeds the capabilities of most of its formidable competitors.

Action Strategy

With the customer as the centerpiece behind Baldor's success, examine the following eight steps of a customer satisfaction program for your own operation:

1. *Define customer requirements and expectations.* Begin by establishing continuous dialogue with customers to define their current and future expectations. Gather information by personal customer contact — usually obtained by the sales force. Then match customer expectations against promises made in the sales presentation. The feedback often falls into such basic areas as orders being shipped complete and on time and complaints being handled rapidly and to the customer's satisfaction.

2. *Maintain a system of customer relationship management.* Ongoing customer contact is a key component of the program. It means

assigning permanent customer contact people, such as customer service, sales, and technical service to selected customers. Each contact person is then empowered to initiate actions to resolve customers' problems.

Other features of customer relations include toll-free telephone lines and online "expert systems" that connect customers to information on inventory, production, and technical problem-solving assistance. Overall goal: achieve a preferred supplier status with 100% conformance to expectations.

3. *Adhere to customer service standards.* All quality plans, product performance, and customer relationships are driven by customers' standards. Most often those standards are measured by the time it takes to handle complaints, the number of on-time shipments compared to previous time periods, and the amount of invoicing errors, freight claims, and product returns.

    Once indexed, the information is forwarded to a steering committee made up of various functional managers for evaluation and action.

4. *Make the commitment to customers a company ritual.* A commitment means guarantees that include: stock orders shipped the same day received, technical service teams sent to customers' locations when needed, specialized training provided to customers' employees, products that conform to data supplied by customers, and a 24-hour "hot line" for support services.

5. *Resolve complaints to achieve quality improvement results.* Empower customer-contact personnel to resolve customer problems on the spot. In particular, sales reps should follow up complaints and make a formal report to a Customer Satisfaction Committee.

6. *Determine what constitutes customer satisfaction.* Develop an index to measure customer satisfaction. With customer feedback as the input, assemble information from various sources, such as direct customer contact, customer audits, independent surveys, quality assurance cards with shipments, suggestions, inquiries, and complaints.

7. *Deliver customer satisfaction results.* Circulate the results so that functional managers can design customer satisfaction objectives for the following year.

8. *Compare customer satisfaction levels.* Contrast your results with those of competitors and with industry standards through formal and informal benchmarking. Then share the results with distributors to help them improve their customer satisfaction ratings.

SMP Reference

Section 2 (Objectives) and Section 6 (Marketing Opportunities).

Case Example #8: Haworth Inc.

Problem: *What defensive strategies are effective to protect market share?*

Haworth, a manufacturer of office furniture, meandered from its beginning in 1948 as a single-product company making wood and glass office partitions, and remained small until 1975. Then came the big break when Haworth management exploited a product opportunity pioneered by market leader, Herman Miller, Inc.

Following a business trend, Herman Miller introduced movable office panels that permitted dividing open spaces into offices. Haworth took that product into the next generation by adding factory-installed wiring inside the panels. For the customer, that innovation eliminated the time and cost of hiring union electricians to wire a new office. Instead, panels were simply snapped together.

Then the inevitable happened. Competitors entered the market with knock-off products. Haworth pounced with unrelenting speed to counter the threat. The Holland, MI firm took legal action charging those competitors with patent infringement as its primary weapon to block their entry. Haworth won multimillion-dollar settlements from Herman Miller and Steelcase (Herman Miller's settlement alone was $44 million).

With the hefty court settlements and the surge in revenues from its highly successful prewired panels, Haworth methodically began an expansion policy to protect the market share it had won:

■ Haworth acquired companies and moved out of the one-product category to become a full-line office furniture maker.

■ The company developed a line of inexpensive office furniture to parallel the needs of a growing distribution channel through low-end outlets, such as Office Depot. For example, Haworth's swivel chair sold for $30 in contrast to market leader Steelcase's $120.

■ Concurrent with manufacturing an inexpensive line, Haworth invested in efficient production systems. It streamlined manufacturing processes. For instance, raw materials such as metal, wood, and plastic move by robot from machine to machine, where they are formed into desks, chairs, and panels. And production systems accommodate to the growing trend toward mass customization, with computers that direct product modifications to match individual customer's needs. Thus, if a customer wants a table 3 in. shorter than the standard model, the assembly line can accommodate to the change.

■ New products and product systems continue to flourish as a defense against competitors' threats to market share. For example, borrowing from the computer industry's use of open architecture that integrates competing components into an operating system, Haworth worked on an open system where its products will work with products made by competitors.

For example, at one point each office product manufacturer used proprietary items such as hinges that won't allow noncompeting panels to be attached. Haworth solved that problem, thereby giving it an edge to establish a beachhead into customer locations without the big sell of asking the customer to make a massive switchover.

Results: By the mid-1990s, Haworth's effective application of strategy had pushed revenues to $1.2 billion and outpaced its competitors in the race for market share.

Action Strategy

Overall, it's often cheaper to protect existing market share in which you already have an investment and a stake in its growth than to gain new market share. Specifically, consider using these guidelines:

1. Where a competitor attempts to clone your product innovation to gain market entry or reduce your market penetration, blunt its efforts by rapidly matching the innovation. In doing so, you deprive the competitor of promotional impact and any product advantage.

   Remember the old cowboy movie shouts of, "Cut 'em off at the pass?" That's precisely what you should be doing: cut off competitors' entry into your market. Haworth pulled off that strategy by cutting off their competitors' knock-off products through legal offense.

2. Believe in the maxim, "The best defense is a good offense." In the context of competitive strategy, that means employing continuous innovation and continuous improvement. Your aim is to protect your market share by becoming as invincible as possible.

3. Search for possibilities within the marketing mix. For example, Haworth's active defense included a new low-end product line, cheap pricing, and mass-market distribution through Office Depot.

Further, Haworth continued its active defense by innovating with open systems.

Altogether, the greatest execution of opportunistic strategy is to create a situation that discourages a competitor from even entering your territory because of the formidable barriers you have established.

SMP Reference

Section 3 (Growth Strategies), Section 6 (Marketing Opportunities), and Section 7 (Marketing Objectives).

Case Example #9: Nu-Kote Holding Inc.

Problem: *How can you maneuver into a niche already occupied by market leaders?*

Nu-Kote sells refill cartridges for inkjet and laser printers. It's not the most glamorous of businesses. Nevertheless, such companies as Hewlett-Packard, Canon, and Epson have taken dominant market positions in actively selling replaceable cartridges. So it wasn't easy for a tiny company like Nu-Kote to find a viable niche, especially where those biggies wielded their promotional and branding strength.

What makes the case instructive is the marketing savvy Nu-Kote managers used to devise a maneuvering strategy. Also notable was the discipline and courage they displayed to remain in the fray and not be intimidated to pull out.

For starters, Nu-Kote management was quick to recognize how the giant printer makers applied the classic Gillette razor and razor blade strategy to computer printers and replacement cartridges. For example, one of Hewlett-Packard's color inkjet printers sells for under $300. The color and black disposable ink cartridges each sell for about $29. The gross margins on inkjet printer cartridges run as high as 60%, vs. 40% or less on printers. Thus, HP's strategy focuses on selling the printer at a lower profit and picking up the higher margins from the disposable cartridge replacements.

Given those governing factors, here's where Nu-Kote boldly entered the market and defined its niche. The Dallas-based company undercut HP's prices by selling reconditioned cartridges for inkjet and laser printers at around one third less than the cost of new cartridges from the leaders.

Here's how the system works: Nu-Kote buys new HP cartridges from distributors, detaches the print head and adapts it so that it simply reattaches to other ink reservoirs. The first Nu-Kote cartridge costs about the same as a HP replacement cartridge. After that, a customer can purchase Nu-Kote's snap-on ink reservoirs for $21 per complete refill. That compares with $29 from HP.

Nu-Kote also gathers old laser cartridges from office supply stores and repair services, replaces the photoelectric drum and adds a new supply of the toner powder needed to produce an image. The remanufactured laser printer cartridges retail for $50 vs. $85 for a new brand-name cartridge.

The result: Nu-Kote's sales skyrocketed to nearly $500 million by maneuvering into a niche-component business.

Action Strategy

Few marketing strategies are more difficult to execute than maneuver. First, it requires defining the most roundabout route to the customer, rather than suffer the consequences of a direct confrontation against a stronger market leader. Nu-Kote maneuvered by remanufacturing replacement cartridges.

Next, maneuvering requires that you assess your resources and evaluate market conditions before moving toward a niche. That means weighing both the advantages and dangers of maintaining a market presence for the long haul. For instance, Hewlett-Packard's possible retaliation against Nu-Kote's low-price strategy would entail eliminating the price differential and promoting the quality pledges associated with buying its brand-name cartridge.

Finally, before you undertake a maneuver strategy, be aware of these guidelines for success:

■ *Know your market.* Pinpoint the critical strategic points for market entry. Initially look at geographic location, availability of distributors, and buying motives of the targeted buyers. What entry point would give you the best possibility to maneuver?

■ *Assess competitors' intentions and strategies.* Evaluate how energetically competitors will challenge your intrusion into their market domain. Are they willing to forfeit a piece of the business to you as long as you don't become too aggressive?

■ *Determine the level of technology required.* While technology adeptness often wins many of today's markets, there are still numerous low-tech niche opportunities open to a smaller company — as exhibited by Nu-Kote. Where does your company fit on the technology issue?

- *Evaluate your internal capabilities and competencies.* One of the cornerstones to maneuvering in today's market is the ability to turn out a quality product equal to or better than competitors. In Nu-Kote's case, remanufacturing a refill ink cartridge and managing internal operations to achieve a pricing advantage were the underpinnings of its success. What are your company's outstanding competencies?
- *Maintain discipline and vision.* Attempting to maneuver among market leaders takes confidence, courage, and know-how in developing a winning strategy. Certainly, Nu-Kote's management displayed such qualities by imbuing a winning spirit among all levels of workers. How would you assess your company's willingness to challenge a market leader?
- *Secure financial resources.* Upper-level management support is necessary to obtain the finances to sustain an ongoing activity. If competitors detect any weakness, they can easily play the waiting game for the financially unsteady organization to cave in. What type of support can you count on?
- *Develop a launch plan to market the product.* Shape a marketing mix that incorporates a quality *product*, appropriate *distribution*, adequate *promotion*, and a market-oriented *price* to attract buyers. In Nu-Kote's case, keeping a one-third price differential was a dominant part of its marketing mix. Which part of the mix would represent your driving force?
- *Maintain a discerning awareness of how customers will respond to your product offering.* Use market research to gain insight about what motivates various groups to buy your product. For Nu-Kote, it is a remanufactured product, priced low to attract a sufficient number of buyers. What immediate action can you undertake to target a niche and avoid a head-on confrontation with a market leader?

SMP Reference

Section 3 (Growth Strategies), Section 6 (Marketing Opportunities), Section 7 (Marketing Objectives), and Section 8 (Strategies and Action Plans).

Case Example #10: Microsoft, Intel, IBM, Eastman Kodak

Problem: *How can you justify the high up-front expenditures for new product development with the inevitable drop in prices as products move rapidly into the mature stage in their life cycles?*

The above large companies as well as many smaller firms that rely on new products and technologies to stay ahead of competition face the problems of rapid price deterioration and shorter product life cycles.

Marketing wisdom developed during the harsh competitive years of the 1980s counseled that to avoid the intense price competition from offshore competitors, develop new and differentiated products and add value to existing ones. For the most part that strategy worked, particularly among high-tech firms.

Here's the paradox: new products often mean extensive R&D, retooling of equipment and processes, commitment to high quality, and long-term capital investment before payout. Yet, as the pace of technology increases and production costs decrease, competitors respond rapidly with cloned products, causing product life cycles to shorten and prices to tumble. The pattern then repeats itself for another round.

Faced with this dilemma, companies anchored to new product development are responding with creative strategies to replace some of the traditional, ironclad marketing techniques. For example, Computer Associates Inc. gave away a large quantity of a new software program as part of one of its product introductions. However, conventional pricing techniques to launch a new product generally followed one of two strategies: use either skim (high) price or penetration (low) price.

Teleport Communications Inc. offered to upgrade their customers' systems with enhanced fiber optics technology at no cost. For the most part, however, the traditional approach is to sell the new technology at a premium price, particularly if first-in to the market.

What's the thinking behind such actions?

First, some managers believe the value of favorable word-of-mouth publicity outweighs the cost of the initial give-aways and results in faster acceptance of product innovations to potentially large numbers of new customers.

Second, other managers reason that locking in a customer with new technology secures the customer for successive new technology cycles and keeps out competitors. They also figure on making money by selling additional services and peripherals. By accepting the principle that in this era of unprecedented innovations, as the power of technology goes up and prices go down with increasing frequency, the marginal cost of upgrading is offset by the benefits of long-term customer–supplier relationships.

Third, still other managers find that the traditional pattern of paced pricing for each stage of the product life cycle is becoming outdated. Reason: mass markets with standardized products are giving way to mass customization where specialized products are sold to solve specific customer problems. Thus, pricing strategy is aimed at redefining value and tying into the long-term relationships with customers — as illustrated above by the give-aways and free upgrades.

Action Strategy

In practice, the new strategies are still evolving to fit the myriad products and industries — from tools to services to autos. Here are some factors to consider as the new paradigms unfold:

1. Retain the strategies that still work for you. However, that doesn't mean sticking to the old saw, "If it ain't broke, don't fix it." Instead, recognize that strategies have life cycles. As with products, in time they will mature and decline. Therefore, watch the evolving patterns of other industries (as illustrated above) and look for creative adaptations to your own use.

   You may want to experiment with give-aways with some products or free services with other offerings — if, of course, you can clearly recognize a future payout. And don't overlook revisiting the classic strategies, such as Gillette's timeless give-away-the-razor-and-sell-the-blades approach.

2. The conventional wisdom about preventing products from reaching a mature or commodity stage in the life cycle bears rethinking. Take a fresh look at that notion, too. Evidence suggests that room exists in the market for standard, reliable, no-frills products. However, you may want to tweak the strategy by enhancing your products with a competitive advantage, such as technical backup, rapid delivery, or extra guarantees.

   The effort may reward you with an optimum position, somewhere between an enhanced commodity and a differentiated product. Above all, however, the big prize goes to managers who discover new applications for their products.

3. Finally, there is one organizational concept that began in the 1980s and is being embraced by an increasing number of firms, large and small: the cross-functional team that was discussed in previous chapters. Where utilized for product development, marketing planning, and strategy implementation, teamwork mobilizes internal thinking and generally produces exceptional results.

   And where a team deliberately extends itself to incorporate the thinking of customers, the collaboration has proven enormously effective in solving competitive problems.

SMP Reference

Section 4 (Business Portfolio) and Section 6 (Marketing Opportunities).

Case Example# 11: Emery Worldwide

Problem: *What strategies can help reverse a steep decline in a company's sales?*

Emery, an overnight-delivery service and cargo company, faced unrelenting losses at the rate of $97 million a year back in 1990. In 1994, Emery reported a striking turnaround with operating profits at $77 million — a $207-million swing in just 4 years. What's behind Emery's strategies that can apply to your business?

Initially, Emery managers viewed the competitive environment and made two meaningful observations: their chief rival, Federal Express, picked up more envelopes at a single New York City location in 1 day than Emery picked up in all of New York State. Next, whereas Emery charged an average of $6/lb to pick up and deliver an envelope, its costs were $16/lb.

For Emery, a piercing diagnosis emerged of a clear-cut competitive disadvantage. Diagnosis is one thing; forming meaningful conclusions and taking action is quite another matter.

Management devised the following prescription for its ailing operations:

- Exit the letter-mail and small-package segment of the overnight delivery business, the niche dominated by the formidable Federal Express and United Parcel Service.
- Concentrate resources on a market segment they defined as overnight delivery of mid- and heavy-weight freight and packages weighing over 70 lb, a segment in which Federal Express and United Parcel would have to play catch-up with Emery.
- Bring in new clients by motivating salespeople with big bonuses. In only 2 years, revenues attributed to the program jumped by 37%. In one situation, Emery signed an $880-million, 10-year contract with the U.S. Postal Service.
- Do the inevitable: cut expenses, trim staff, shrink terminal space, and whatever else would be necessary to reduce the per-package handling costs.

Marketing results: Emery seized 24% of the over-70-lb freight market. Its nearest competitor, Burlington Air Express, has a 13% share.

Action Strategy

Emery's astuteness in doing the basic analysis and defining a vacant market segment resulted in its outstanding performance. For instance, selecting segments depends on a group of variables, including knowledge of *customer needs and behavior* and *competitor capabilities*. Grasping the significance of each will add greater precision to selecting viable segments.

Customer Needs and Behavior

If you maintain an ongoing customer analysis that accurately defines the needs and wants of customer groups and individuals, you satisfy a primary ingredient of successful segmentation. Specifically, analyzing needs and behavior requires you to:

- *Categorize segments.* Begin by adding structure to your view of the market. Doing so allows you to properly allocate marketing and sales resources for the greatest impact. For example, categorize your segments by geographic location, demographics, product attributes, market size, common buying factors, shared distribution channels, and any other factors that are unique to your industry.
- *Determine purchase patterns.* Next, analyze purchasing variables so you can develop customized packages of benefits that will increase your chances of success by segment and key customers.

    For example, divide customer purchase patterns into two categories: *regular use* and *infrequent special application* of your product. Review how customers perceive your product benefits in terms of *price/value, convenience,* or *prestige* factors. Analyze and rank customer loyalty as *nonexistent, medium,* or *strong.* Examine customer awareness and readiness to buy your product as *unaware, informed, interested,* or *intending to buy.* And evaluate your buyers' existing (and evolving) needs related to *product quality, delivery, guarantees, technical services,* or *promotional support.*

Competitor Capabilities

While customer analysis lets you examine how to attract and satisfy customers, competitor analysis gives you a picture of your competitors' capabilities by segment. For example, view competitors from the following perspective:

1. How they segment their markets.
2. How customers select rival products.

3. What purchasing patterns their behavior exhibits.
4. How competitors develop their marketing strategies and how likely they are to dislodge you from a particular segment.

You can utilize this information in several ways: to position your product line in a market niche unattended by competitors; to identify competitors' weaknesses in their product, price, promotion, or distribution mix; and to create your own counterstrategies for immediate or future use.

Finally, observe with the utmost alertness what approaches you use to enter a segment against an existing competitor. As illustrated by Emery, understanding where the vacant segments are and taking into account the competitors' capabilities to deter your moves are the core ingredients for success.

SMP Reference

Section 2 (Objectives), Section 6 (Marketing Opportunities), and Section 7 (Marketing Objectives).

Case Example #12: QAD Inc.

Problem: *How can a small company apply customer-driven marketing techniques to grow against dominant competitors?*

QAD occupies a highly successful market position as a supplier of computer software to manufacturing companies. Its venerable position is secure (or as safe as any company can be in a volatile field) by clinging to two fundamental strategies.

First, QAD adheres to a product strategy tested against the toughest standard of all: *satisfying customer wants.* For instance, the Carpinteria, CA company makes every effort to understand the unique characteristics of a customer's business.

In one case, a customer initially required only a basic software program to track incoming orders. In time that requirement progressed with the addition of pieces of software to perform new tasks such as inventory control, materials planning, forecasting, and cash management. All those tasks, and more, were then integrated as modules into a seamless whole to run an entire factory.

Second, QAD mastered the techniques of taking large software programs and dividing them into subtasks, then combining and recombining them to produce new programs. Such technical mastery creates customized programs for each of its customers.

Key point: understanding a customer's business and maintaining a customer-driven orientation isn't just some mechanical gesture at QAD. Managers imbed themselves into a customer's business and know it inside and out. That means understanding the workings of all types of factories that manufacture everything from automotive parts, medical products, electronic components, to shoes.

Carrying the strategy still further means integrating such knowledge into software products that define each type of business, while keeping ever present in mind the profile of the user who will operate the program. For example, QAD programmers avoid esoteric and technical jargon in developing instructions. Instead, software is written so that users from various backgrounds and levels of training can easily follow instructions and perform their functions.

Results: in 1 year revenues jumped by 39% and more than a hundred-fold from a decade ago.

Action Strategy

First, instill a mindset in yourself and in those with whom you work that keeps your customers' needs in the forefront of product development and service. Sustaining such an attitude is one part of the success formula. The second, and more critical part, is to install a systematic approach that permits you to learn about your customers' business.

Here is one system that works. Explore customers' needs and problems in two broad categories that would appeal to their self interests: *revenue-expansion* and *cost-reduction* opportunities. This approach will chalk up positive results for your customers. In due course, it should also help you provide applicable products and services.

To conduct the analysis, ask the following questions:

Revenue-Expansion Opportunities:
- What approaches would reduce customer returns and complaints?
- What processes would speed up production and delivery to benefit your customer? (This is an area in which QAD focused.)
- How can you improve a customer's market position and image?
- How would adding a name brand impact your customers' revenues?
- What product or service benefits would enhance your customers' operation?
- How can you create differentiation that gives your customers a competitive advantage?
- How would improving reordering procedures impact revenues?

Cost-Reduction Opportunities:
■ What procedures would cut customers' purchase costs?
■ What processes would cut customers' production costs?
■ What systems would cut customers' production downtime?
■ What approaches would cut customers' delivery costs?
■ What methods would cut customers' administrative overhead?
■ What strategies would maximize customers' working capital?

Several of those areas reach beyond the traditional role of marketing. Therefore, involve product developers and other nonmarketing managers to interpret findings and translate them into product design solutions.

Finally, implementing the process is a sticky problem, especially so when it involves nonmarketing groups into actively thinking about such areas as customers' needs, market growth, and competitive advantage. There is no easy solution.

For starters, however, enlist the assistance of the senior executives in your group or company. Have them brief those nonmarketing personnel on the benefits of paying attention to market-driven issues for the welfare of the company as well as their personal career growth — and even survival. If that doesn't do the trick, you might recommend that an orientation seminar be used to help instill the appropriate attitudes.

SMP Reference

Section 6 (Marketing Opportunities), Section 7 (Marketing Objectives), and Section 8 (Strategies and Actions Plans).

Case Example #13: Russell Corporation

Problems: *Is there a way to create a competitive advantage in a basic industry heavily dominated by low-cost competitors?*

Russell Corp. is one of the largest producers of athletic uniforms in the U.S., with a grip on 35 to 40% of the U.S. market. The uniqueness of Russell is that this Alabama-based sportswear maker survives against its Asian competitors and still commands a leading share of the market.

The core strategy behind Russell's success is summed up by one of the company's executives: "It's pretty hard to make a football uniform on Monday in Japan or Korea and get it over here by Friday." Russell has outfitted the NBA and virtually every NFL team.

But uniforms account for only 35% of Russell's sales. Half of its billings come from simpler items: T-shirts, fleeced sweatshirts, warm-up suits sold through department stores, and discount chains such as Sears and Wal★Mart, as well as private-label arrangements with Nike and Levi Strauss.

The company's strategy also employs a cost-improvement approach. As a result, Russell's production lines are about the quietest, cleanest, and most automated in the industry.

Action Strategy

Russell created a clear-cut competitive advantage. Listed below are potential survival strategies to achieve your advantage.

- *Price advantage.* Through offshore sourcing, internal belt-tightening, or installing new equipment and systems, find a way to offer users a product comparable to that of your competitors at a lower price. Organizations in every sector of the economy are desperately searching for ways to lower costs.
- *No-frills product.* Provide a segment of the market with a product that has fewer features or minimal services. Such a product could use a different package or another name to eliminate confusion and minimize cannibalizing sales from a main-line product.
- *Upscale product.* Launch a higher-quality product that may include improved warranties, after-sales support, installation, or improved packaging. However, be sure that your company's image can support a move upscale and that you have selected the appropriate segment that is willing the pay the higher price.
- *Product expansion.* Introduce a large number of product versions, thereby offering buyers more choices. This strategy lends itself to applications, sizes, shapes, models, and features. It also blocks any open market niches through which a competitor can enter.
- *Product innovation.* Use product or service innovation as an offensive strategy with which to attack a competitor's position. Muster extensive competitor analysis to determine areas of strengths and weaknesses from which the innovation can be initiated.
- *Improved services.* Services can include customer service and technical service. Technical advice, hot-line service, repair service, or availability of spare parts are all examples of such service. This strategy also includes value-added approaches, such as providing financial packages for customers, establishing quality control systems, installing computerized inventory control systems, or providing computer-based expert diagnostic systems utilizing the new technology of artificial intelligence for problem resolution.

■ *Distribution innovation.* Examine creative new approaches to managing channels of distribution or improving existing ones. This strategy is especially appropriate when some competitors alter their distribution strategies, such as changing from pushing through distributors to pulling through end users. Also, there is an opportunity to strengthen relationships with distributors who may give you extra support because of disagreements with their former suppliers after being shunted aside and who need new sources of supply.

■ *Cost-improvement.* Initiate ways to achieve lower manufacturing costs. The technologies abound through computer-aided design, computer-aided manufacturing, and computer-integrated manufacturing systems that are increasingly becoming more affordable for even the smallest company. Many systems are now used on microcomputers as compared with its original applications with large mainframe computers.

■ *Market identification.* Continue to monitor changing customer behavior and unfilled needs and wants. Establish end-user and distributor councils to identify emerging, neglected, or poorly served niches that represent opportunities for new products and services.

SMP Reference

Section 3 (Growth Strategies), Section 6 (Marketing Opportunities), Section 7 (Marketing Objectives), and Section 8 (Strategies and Action Plans).

Case Example #14: Thor-Lo Inc.

Problem: *How do you transform a commodity product into a brand name?*

Thor-Lo, a manufacturer of athletic socks, turned an unglamorous commodity into a remarkably successful branded item. There's a good deal of marketing savvy to be gleaned from this success story.

First, Thor-Lo's product developers would not consciously acknowledge that their product was a commodity. Instead, they talked about producing "foot equipment" rather than athletic socks. (Here is another practical application of developing a functional strategic direction, as discussed in Chapter 1.) This strategic direction was not a play on words, but a mindset and a visionary statement that converted into innovations.

Second, managers translated their vision into a tangible product. They observed that the $500-million sport sock market was served by organizations that used either a low-cost manufacturing strategy or attached a designer label to distinguish their socks. For the most part, however, the items were look-alikes — usually cotton, white, and perhaps with a stripe or two.

Capitalizing on "foot equipment" as the idea generator for the new product strategy, Thor-Lo's designers first developed a specialty sport sock with a roll-top terry cloth ridge that prevented the sock from drooping. With that success Thor-Lo's president, James Throneburg, conceived a sock that could protect the foot against the pounding of hard athletics. He designed a sport sock with as much terry cloth as could be packed into the sole, without making it too thick in the arch. That item triggered the major breakthrough to vault the privately held company over its rivals.

Third, with the exceptional success of the padded sock, managers then shifted to segmentation as their expansion strategy. Sport-specific socks were soon developed for tennis, cycling, hiking, aerobics, and basketball. The dense padding was skillfully placed in areas where the foot takes the most bruising. (Sport-specific socks are about a $200-million-a-year business at retail, with Thor-Lo's share at about 50%.) Beyond sports, Thor-Lo managers further segmented the market on demographic and life-style criteria, providing specialty socks for senior citizens, and those needing preventive healthcare for their feet.

Fourth, managers launched their differentiated sport socks as a Thor-Lo brand. The features that made the brand unique also provided the conditions for premium pricing. Prices were set at about double that of the existing brands. Retailers, enticed by the generous increase in actual dollars, quickly carried the line.

Fifth, promotion complemented the overall product strategy. Using the unique benefits of the product as the dominant theme, promotions capitalized on endorsements from such prestigious personalities as tennis star Martina Navratilova praise from the American Podiatric Medical Association, and favorable reports published in medical journals. They also capitalized on the implied endorsement of the U.S. Postal Service, which approved Thor-Lo as an official sock supplier.

Finally, recognizing the inevitability of competitors introducing low-priced knock-offs, Thor-Lo invested almost 20% of its revenue in R&D and new knitting machines. The two-pronged strategy aimed at (1) extending the life of the product through new designs to maintain a competitive edge, and (2) fending off aggressive competitors by bolstering its cost-efficient manufacturing operation.

Action Strategy

To develop a successful competing brand, be certain you apply a differentiation strategy to distinguish your product from the standard offerings in the market. And do so in a manner whereby you don't cannibalize sales from one line to another. Follow these useful guidelines:

- *Features and benefits.* Focus on those characteristics that complement the basic function of the product. Start with your core product. Then envision adding unique features and services; ideally, ones based on users' expectations. (Thor-Lo visualized "foot equipment.")
- *Performance.* This factor relates to the level at which the product operates — including quality. (Thor-Lo achieved high performance by inserting padding adjusted to the sport.)
- *Acceptance.* This characteristic measures how close the product comes to established standards or specifications. (Conforming to endorsers' standards proved a valuable strategy to Thor-Lo's market acceptance.)
- *Endurance.* This factor relates to the expected operating life of the product. (Consumers perceived that in addition to comfort, thick socks would outlive ordinary ones and so were worth the higher price.)
- *Dependability.* This attribute measures the probability of the product breaking or malfunctioning within a specified period. (Dependability is a criterion most often applicable to engineered products.)
- *Appearance.* This factor covers numerous considerations ranging from image, function, look, or feel. Different from performance, appearance integrates the product with all its differentiating components, including packaging.
- *Design.* This factor unites the above differentiating components, as well. While design encompasses the appearance, endurance, and dependability of the product, there is particular emphasis placed on ease of use and appropriateness to the function for which it was designed.

SMP Reference

Section 6 (Marketing Opportunities), Section 7 (Marketing Objectives), and Section 8 (Strategies and Action Plans).

Case Example #15: A. Schulman Inc.

Problem: *How can you position your products effectively against market leaders?*

A. Schulman Inc. produces plastics that go into such diverse products as auto dashboards, moldings, and furniture. The company has produced extraordinary results during a 5-year period by doubling sales and tripling earnings.

Its performance triumphs in a competitive environment against such mighty companies as Dow, Monsanto, Quantum, BASF, and Hoechst.

Let's examine the key success strategies:

■ Schulman excels in filling rush orders for customers by making special weekend runs in its U.S. and European factories to satisfy customers' urgent requests.

■ Schulman talks quality and product differentiation, not price. While the industry giants focus heavily on commodity plastics, Schulman concentrates on higher-priced specialty products. Managers search for areas of differentiation with features that can't be easily duplicated by competitors.

■ In its early years of growth, Schulman established strong customer relationships with smaller organizations, with those that were generally neglected by the market leaders. Now, using superior technology to add value to product offerings and by continuing its customer-driven relationships, it is expanding to serve such names as General Motors, Ford, and 3M.

■ Commitment to a market-driven attitude is a hard and fast policy at Schulman. Its labs do not develop compounds and then search for markets. Rather, salespeople and engineers work closely with customers on ideas that solve problems. Those ideas are then converted into customized products to provide solutions.

■ About 65% of Schulman's sales are outside the U.S. Beyond its presence in Canada, U.K., and Europe, the Akron, OH company cultivates thriving relationships with Japanese companies, such as Mitsubishi. These alliances provide unique applications for auto moldings and dashboards for Toyota and Honda plants in the U.S.

Action Strategy

If you want to position your product effectively against market leaders, consider some of the following action strategies suggested by the Schulman example:

1. Select a competitive advantage that larger competitors cannot perform efficiently.

   Action: employ market research, such as customer tracking studies, to identify possibilities for differentiation.

2. Commit to quality and service as an organizational priority.

Action: initiate programs that encourage individuals at various functions to strive for quality. These are not one-time motivational talks, but continuous training.

3. Focus on specialty products that command premium prices; leave the commodity price segment to others.

   Action: practice segmenting your market for specific product applications. Get closer to your customers and their problems.

4. Establish long-term alliances with customers to grow with them and to build technology and product relationships.

   Action: encourage trust with customers or suppliers so that sensitive information can be shared for mutual interests.

5. Maintain a market-driven orientation throughout the organization — within all functions — to maintain a competitive advantage.

   Action: organize strategy teams made up of functional managers. Then, use the teams' SMPs as lines of communications to respond rapidly to market opportunities.

6. Seek global opportunities that complement long-term objectives.

   Action: through joint ventures, licensing, or exporting develop a global presence — if consistent with your corporate mission.

7. Partner salespeople with customers to provide product solutions to customers' problems.

   Action: go beyond traditional forms of sales training. Instead, teach salespeople how to think like strategists so they can help their customers achieve a competitive advantage.

8. Identify market niches that are emerging, neglected, or poorly served.

   Action: reassess how you segment your markets. Search for additional approaches beyond the usual criteria of customer size, frequency of purchase, geographic location. Look for potential niches related to just-in-time delivery, performance, application, quality, or technical assistance.

SMP Reference

Section 2 (Objectives), Section 3 (Growth Strategies), Section 4 (Business Portfolio), and Section 6 (Marketing Opportunities).

Case Example #16: Safeskin Corp.

Problem: *What strategies can outdistance competitors when entering a new market?*

Remember the familiar adage, "Build a better mousetrap and the world will beat a path to your door?" Well, an innovative small company, Safeskin Corp., offers a twist to that ending. Rather than expect others to beat a path to its door in a wildly competitive field, the company pursues an aggressive selling path, while relying on its enhanced product (the better mousetrap) to avoid becoming another look-alike commodity.

Safeskin's case provides valuable lessons for any manager facing an uphill price battle where there are similar products struggling for every sales dollar.

The case began in 1987, when the Centers for Disease Control alerted healthcare professionals to protect themselves from their patients' body fluids. With the rapid spread of the AIDS virus, the demand for disposable latex gloves soon skyrocketed.

In 1988, Safeskin entered the latex glove market when it was plagued with shortages. About that time such big companies as Johnson & Johnson, Baxter Healthcare, and Ansell had established strong market positions and were gearing up to meet the accelerating demand.

Not wishing to fall into the commodity trap against giant competitors, the San Diego-based company determined that it must differentiate its product. To execute the strategy, managers assessed user needs. They found that many doctors and nurses wearing latex gloves for long periods felt sick from allergic reactions and dermatitis.

Armed with that valuable information, Safeskin designed and manufactured a latex-type glove that prevented the allergic reactions about which numerous doctors complained. The hypoallergenic latex gloves rolled out in 1989.

With the product in hand, the second part of the strategy shifted to marketing and distribution. Safeskin managers recognized the folly of pursuing the traditional approaches of selling their higher-priced gloves through their standard distributors. They felt implementing such a strategy would bog them down against the increasing number of determined competitors.

Instead, Safeskin management circumvented the distribution network and hired top sales people from such companies as U.S. Surgical and Johnson & Johnson who had contacts among doctors and other healthcare workers using gloves. Safeskin then hired a well-respected doctor to educate his colleagues to the advantages of the new and improved glove over the less-expensive ones. Relying on this pull-through marketing approach, doctors began influencing hospital purchasing agents to order the premium Safeskin gloves.

Continuing to observe market behavior, Safeskin managers also noted that significant numbers of physicians and nurses were using cornstarch powder in their gloves to make it easier to take on and off. The problem was that powder proved unacceptable in sterile hospitals and laboratories. Thus, the next leap forward in product development for Safeskin occurred with the development of the first powder-free hypoallergenic gloves, introduced in 1991.

Result: Safeskin maintains over 50% of the powder-free exam glove market.

Action Strategy

Two primary lessons emerge from the mousetrap adage: first, make a superior product truly based on meeting customers' needs and solving their problems. Second, pinpoint a well-researched market that permits you to maximize the impact of your promotion and gain a competitive advantage.

Too often the product is the focus without adequate attention to those who will use your product or service. Thus, when ready to move into a market, use the following criteria to provide a comprehensive picture for a go, no-go decision:

1. *Suppliers.* If a few dominant suppliers maintain control over the flow of materials that result in the control of prices, then a powerful influence is exerted on all the other forces within the industry. Accordingly, review supplier practices for clues to future patterns of supplier behavior, which in turn will shape your strategies.
2. *Existing competitors.* Examine the intensity of competitive actions. For instance, decide which competitors seem likely to retaliate against movements in price. Review the amount of advertising and identify the themes of the competitors' advertisements. Determine if environmental, technological, or other issues are changing the character of the market.
3. *Emerging competitors.* In conducting a market analysis, there is a tendency to focus only on existing players. The wrenching lesson from organizations that blindly entered markets and failed is that they did not analyze emerging competitors with the same intensity they applied to existing ones. This issue is particularly pertinent with the proliferation of new and powerful competitors resulting from joint ventures, mergers, and acquisitions.
4. *Alternative product offerings.* As with analyzing emerging competitors, give similar emphasis to alternative products or services. In this type of analysis it is valuable to employ the skills and knowledge of R&D and manufacturing. Also tap the expertise of outside

industry experts who are more likely to be aware of substitute products.

Finally, keep the customer as the primary focal point around which you make your assessments and you'll reduce the risk of entering a new market.

SMP Reference

Section 5 (Situation Analysis) and Section 6 (Marketing Opportunities).

Case Example #17: Quaker State Corporation

Problem: *What strategies can you use to regain lost market share?*

Quaker State Corp., a producer of motor oil, is making a valiant effort to recover market share lost during the 1980s to such aggressive rivals as Pennzoil, Valvoline, Havoline, and Castrol.

Quaker's tumble from market share dominance had many causes. Among them, the company's policy of maintaining premium prices in a selling environment where motor oil was viewed by retailers as a commodity and a loss leader. Also, Quaker avoided discounts and rebates to retailers — unlike those competitors that bombarded customers with such offers.

Practices changed during the 1990s when new management took the helm. The Oil City, PA company began the difficult fight to recoup market share. Soon, the following winning marketing strategies emerged.

Quaker State's Strategies

1. *Market research.* Managers initiated consumer research, an activity that was virtually nonexistent during the headlong plunge in sales and market share. Analysis revealed that first, Quaker State lacked strong brand awareness among consumers. Second, basic product knowledge that Quaker assumed was known by consumers was at a low level. For example, when Quaker's engineers were invited to observe focus group sessions, they were startled to find that consumers could not define synthetic oil and were confused by traditional motor-oil labels containing such information as 10W-30.
2. *Brand development.* Armed with the market research, managers began the formidable job of building brand identity, including supplying ample product information to customers and consumers.

Beginning with a segmentation approach, they targeted the fast-growing markets for light trucks, sport-utility vehicles, and minivans. Their initial product entry was Quaker State 4×4 which was launched with a consumer-style ad campaign to establish brand recognition.

3. *Pricing.* Challenging the traditional industry practice of using motor oil as a loss leader and relying on rebates, Quaker positioned its new product at a premium price and offered retailers generous margins in return for more shelf space for Quaker's products.

4. *Market expansion.* Concurrent with the segmentation approach, Quaker implemented a forward integration strategy by acquiring its biggest distributor, Specialty Oils of Shreveport, LA. The maneuver nearly doubled Quaker's oil sales to $800 million. Future expansion plans also called for increasing Quaker's Q Lube and other fast-oil-change outlets.

Result: from Quaker's low point of 11% market share, the decline stopped and a sharp upward curve began to current levels of about a 16% share.

Action Strategy

The Quaker case clearly demonstrates that researching your markets, targeting emerging segments, and tailoring unique products to suit market needs are proactive strategies that pay off in regaining market share.

However, there is another effective strategy to rebuild market share: customer retention. Managers are just beginning to direct their efforts to retaining customers and savoring the economies associated with the strategy in times of restricted budgets.

Let's look at average costs for new customer acquisition in a business-to-business market:

- Cost of an average sales call (including salary, commission, benefits, and expenses) $290
- Average number of calls to convert a prospect into a customer   × 5
- Cost of acquiring a new customer (advertising/promotion expenditures are not included) $1450

Now, let's look at the projected lifetime value of a customer:

- Annual customer revenue $5000
- Average years as a customer   × 2

- Average profit margin   × .10
- Customer lifetime value $1000

Conclusion: it costs more to acquire a new customer than you'll get in lifetime value, that is, unless you can find a way to decrease selling expenditures, reduce the number of sales calls, or increase lifetime value.

On the other hand, retaining the loyalty of a customer is far more cost effective, since the acquisition costs are sharply reduced or eliminated altogether.

Let's examine how you can install a customer retention program:

- *Measure retention rate over a sustained period.* If you have a few large company clients, the calculation is simple. With a large customer base, the use of percentages or actual customer counts will give you a clear measurement.
- *Isolate the causes of customer defections.* Customers that discontinue business or move to an area not serviced by your firm is one thing. Those leaving because of poor product quality, excessive pricing, shabby customer service, or faulty order processing is quite another matter and cause for concern. Then, focus on specific corrective actions and incorporate them into your marketing plan.
- *Calculate how much profit you would forfeit from lost customers.* This is expressed as a customer's lifetime value, as illustrated above.
- *Determine what it would cost your company to reduce the defection rate.* As long as the cost is less than the lost profit, the expenditure is justified.

SMP Reference

Section 7 (Marketing Objectives), Section 8 (Strategies and Action Plans), and Section 9 (Financial Controls and Budgets).

SUMMARY

The intent of this chapter was to show you how real companies, of all sizes and in diverse industries, solved difficult business problems. Some of those problems flowed out of deteriorating internal organizational conditions; others arose from an uncompromising competitive environment.

It is conceivable that you, too, could be facing some or all of those tough situations. Therefore, the sole purpose of highlighting the assorted case problems is to demonstrate that developing and implementing *action strategies* is the dominant ingredient in overcoming numerous internal and external obstacles.

The overriding lesson: rely on your SMP to churn out action strategies and tactics to guide your actions through the maze of organizational and market conditions.

IV

CHECKLISTS FOR DEVELOPING COMPETITIVE STRATEGIES

4

CHECKLISTS FOR DEVELOPING COMPETITIVE STRATEGIES

Given the information in this chapter, you should be able to:

1. Develop a competitive advantage analysis.
2. Conduct a competitive strategy analysis to improve the performance of your Strategic Marketing Plan (SMP).
3. Assess the condition of your marketing capabilities by using a marketing audit.

OVERVIEW

"The plan is nothing; planning is everything."

Dwight D. Eisenhower

The insightful quote above indicates that masterminding, strategizing, and implementing are the driving forces behind the effectiveness of your SMP. A number of aids in the form of checklists and a marketing audit can assist you in those efforts.

DEVELOPING COMPETITIVE STRATEGIES

There are two parts to developing competitive strategies and thereby improve the credibility of your SMP:

Part I: Competitive Advantage Analysis

The first part consists of a comprehensive checklist to analyze the strengths and weaknesses of your company vs. those of your competitors in the key areas of the marketing mix (product, price, distribution, and promotion). While the factors for rating strengths and weaknesses are applicable to most companies and product lines, you may find it useful to edit the list and customize it with precise factors pertinent to your business and industry.

The intent of the analysis is to (1) determine where there are opportunities to attack the weaknesses of competitors, and (2) expose potential weaknesses through which competitors can devise strategies against you.

Part II: Competitive Strategies Analysis

The second part consists of a more expansive group of checklists to help you determine competitors' strategies. Accordingly, the analyses warrant more interpretation, judgment, and insight than Part I. Here, your intent is to dig behind the mere facts and determine the patterns of competitors' behavior. For instance, look at such patterns as when and how your competitors enter a market, their introductory pricing strategies, the type of promotional support they give to the sales force, their overall distribution strategies, or their after-sales support service.

You may never be able to predict with complete accuracy the behavior of competing managers. But there is a good chance of predicting general forms of competitor actions. You thereby can anticipate actions, avoid surprise, and develop contingency plans. It is still a time-honored truth that surprise is a major success factor in implementing strategies and tactics. You need to avoid being surprised by your competitor. Yet, you should create surprise when attacking competitors.

HOW TO CONDUCT THE ANALYSIS

As recommended throughout this book, the ideal approach to developing the SMP is to use the team effort. Continue working with your team in this part of the analysis.

For best results have each team member privately conduct the analysis by using the 1 to 10 rating scale for each item on the checklist. Then reconvene the team and review each individual's comparative ratings, along with the supporting information behind the ratings.

Where there are extreme differences in results, have the members go through a second round of ratings, this time armed with the information discussed at the first meeting. Once again reconvene the group and aim for consensus. Continue the procedure until a reliable result is produced.

Where possible, attempt to validate the results through formal marketing research. Above all, remember the purpose of the analysis is to:

- Add more precision to your SMP
- Devise competitive marketing strategies that will permit you to sustain a competitive advantage

Checklists for Developing Competitive Strategies

Part I: Competitive Advantage Analysis

1–10 rating, 10 = best

A. PRODUCT/SERVICE	Your Firm's Product/Service	Competitor A	Competitor B	Competitor C	List Advantage and Define Strategy
Quality					
Features					
Options					
Style					
Brand name					
Packaging					
Sizes					
Services					
Warranties					
Returns					
Versatility					
Uniqueness					
Utility					
Reliability					
Durability					
Patent protection					
Guarantees					

B. PRICE	Your Firm's Product/Service	Competitor A	Competitor B	Competitor C	List Advantage and Define Strategy
List price					
Discounts					
Allowances					
Payment period					
Credit terms					
Financing					

C. DISTRIBUTION	Your Firm's Product/Service	Competitor A	Competitor B	Competitor C	List Advantage and Define Stragtey
Distribution Channels:					
Direct sales force					
Manufacturers' reps					
Distributors					
Jobbers					
Dealers					
Market coverage					
Warehouse locations					
Inventory control systems					
Physical transport					

D. PROMOTION	Your Firm's Product/Service	Competitor A	Competitor B	Competitor C	List Advantage and Define Strategy
Advertising					
Consumer					
Trade					
Personal selling					
Incentives					
Sales aids					
Samples					
Training					
Sales promotions					
Demonstrations					
Contests					
Premiums					
Coupons					
Telemarketing					
Internet					
Publicity					
Other					
TOTAL SCORE					

Part II: Competitive Strategies Analysis

Market _____

1–10 rating by market or product. 10 = best

A. MARKET DIMENSION (List product/market segments)	Your Firm's Product/Service	Competitor A	Competitor B	Competitor C	Total Current Sales ($)	Total Potential Sales ($)
Segment 1						
Segment 2						
Segment 3						
TOTAL						

B. MARKET ENTRY	Your Firm's Product/Service	Competitor A	Competitor B	Competitor C
How do competitors usually enter a market? Is there a market leader among the competitors? Who are the followers? Identify by:				
First-in Strategy 　　Product: 　　Price: 　　Distribution: 　　Promotion:				
Follow-the-Leader Strategy 　　Product: 　　Price: 　　Distribution: 　　Promotion:				

B. MARKET ENTRY	Your Firm's Product/Service	Competitor A	Competitor B	Competitor C
Last-in Strategy				
Product:				
Price:				
Distribution:				
Promotion:				

C. MARKET COMMITMENT	Your Firm's Product/Service	Competitor A	Competitor B	Competitor C
How much commitment do competitors give to a specific market in terms of people, dollars, research, and products?				

D. MARKET DEMAND	Your Firm's Product/Service	Competitor A	Competitor B	Competitor C
How flexible are competitors in changing strategies for different market situations? Which competitors ...				
Prune markets when demand slackens?				
Concentrate on key markets when demand increases?				
Harvest profits when sales plateau?				

E. MARKET DIVERSIFICATION	Your Firm's Product/Service	Competitor A	Competitor B	Competitor C
How have competitors responded to diversification opportunities?				
Allocated additional resources to new segments?				
Added another stage of distribution?				

Product

1–10 rating by market or product. 10 = best

A. POSITIONING	Your Firm's Product/ Service	Competitor A	Competitor B	Competitor C
How efficient are competitors in monitoring customer perceptions and identifying customer niches? Related to:				
Positioning a single brand				
Positioning a multiple brand				
Repositioning older products				

B. PRODUCT LIFE CYCLE	Your Firm's Product/ Service	Competitor A	Competitor B	Competitor C
How efficient are competitors in extending the life cycle of their products? Related to:				
Promoting more frequent usage				
Finding new users				
Finding more uses for products				

C. PRODUCT COMPETITION	Your Firm's Product/Service	Competitor A	Competitor B	Competitor C
To what extent do competitors attempt to gain a larger share of a market? By introducing:				
New packaging				
Competing brand				
Private label				
Generic product				

D. PRODUCT MIX

Where do competitors stand in width and depth of product lines? Related to …	Your Firm's Product/Service	Competitor A	Competitor B	Competitor C
Single product				
Multiple products				
Product systems				

E. PRODUCT APPLICATION

How much manufacturing and application flexibility do competitors display as related to:	Your Firm's Product/Service	Competitor A	Competitor B	Competitor C
Standard products				
Private-label products				
Standard product, modified				

F. NEW PRODUCTS

What has been the pattern of competitors related to the following areas of new product development?	Your Firm's Product/Service	Competitor A	Competitor B	Competitor C
Innovation				
Modification				
Line extension				

F. NEW PRODUCTS (continued)	Your Firm's Product/Service	Competitor A	Competitor B	Competitor C
Diversification				
Remerchandising or reformulating existing products				
Market extending (existing products)				

G. PRODUCT AUDIT	Your Firm's Product/Service	Competitor A	Competitor B	Competitor C
How flexible have competitors been in managing their product lines as displayed by:				
Line reduction				
Line elimination				

Price

1–10 rating by market or product. 10 = best

A. NEW PRODUCTS	Your Firm's Product/Service	Competitor A	Competitor B	Competitor C
What has been the pattern of competitors in pricing new products? Do they tend to use:				
Skim (high) pricing				
Penetration (low) pricing				
Follow-the-leader pricing				
Cost-plus pricing				

B. ESTABLISHED PRODUCTS	Your Firm's Product/Service	Competitor A	Competitor B	Competitor C
What has been the pattern of competitors in pricing established products? Do they tend to use:				
Slide-down (gradual reduction) pricing				
Segment pricing				
Flexible pricing				
Preemptive (reacting to competitors') pricing				
Loss-leader pricing				

Promotion

1–10 rating by market or product. 10 = best

A. ADVERTISING	Your Firm's Product/Service	Competitor A	Competitor B	Competitor C
To what extent do competitors use advertising to do the following:				
Support personal selling				
Inform target audience about availability of product				
Persuade prospects to buy directly from advertising				
Integrate the Internet as part of the overall advertising effort				

B. SALES FORCE	Your Firm's Product/Service	Competitor A	Competitor B	Competitor C
What is the profile of competitors' sales forces related to:				
Sales force size				
Sales force territorial design				
Compensation systems				
Training				
Technical or service backup				

C. SALES PROMOTION	Your Firm's Product/Service	Competitor A	Competitor B	Competitor C
How well do competitors integrate sales promotion with their advertising and sales force strategies? Is sales promotion used to:				
Encourage more product usage				
Induce distributor and dealer involvement				
Stimulate greater sales force efforts.				

Distribution

1–10 rating by market or product. 10 = best

A. CHANNEL STRUCTURE	Your Firm's Product/Service	Competitor A	Competitor B	Competitor C
What has been the distribution strategy of competitors in reaching customer markets? Related to …				
Direct distribution to the end user				
Indirect distribution through intermediaries (distributors, dealers)				
Direct sale to end user				
Impact of E-commerce on distribution strategy				

THE MARKETING AUDIT

An immensely valuable evaluation tool, the Marketing Audit, is found on the following pages. Consisting of 100 questions, it is an accurate diagnostic tool to determine the condition of your marketing capabilities. Taking the time to conduct the audit takes some of the risk out of planning, strategizing, and implementing. For instance, you have the opportunity to anticipate the weaknesses and strengths from both your side and that of your competitors and make hard decisions based on analysis and fact, not speculation.

What also follows is that the boldness or timidity of your plans will be determined by your ability to execute balanced strategies within the internal capabilities of your organization matched to the market environment of customers and competitors.

As with a physical examination or a financial audit, the aim of the marketing audit is to highlight a set of symptoms for further evaluation. Then, with the detailed output, you can take corrective actions or modify plans to meet those circumstances. Thus, the marketing audit permits you to conduct a structured analysis of internal and external considerations divided into three areas:

1. Your firm's marketing environment.
2. Marketing management procedures and policies.
3. Tactical aspects of your marketing mix.

You can conduct the analysis by using the same team approach described in Developing Competitive Analysis. Where possible, however, it is more beneficial to gain an objective outside opinion from an individual or group that can add a broader perspective to evaluating the competencies of your organization.

Part I: Reviewing the Firm's Marketing Environment

Consumers (End Users)

1. Who are our ultimate buyers?
2. Who or what influences them in their buying decisions?
3. What are our consumers' demographic and psychographic profiles?
4. When, where, and how do they shop for and consume our product?
5. What need(s) can our product or service satisfy?
6. How well does it satisfy?
7. How can we segment our target market?
8. How do prospective buyers perceive our product in their minds?

9. What are the economic conditions and expectations of our target market?
10. Are our consumers' attitudes, values, or habits changing?

Customers

11. Who are our customers — that is, are they intermediate buyers (wholesalers and/or retailers)?
12. Who or what influences them in their buying decisions?
13. Where are our customers located?
14. What other products do they carry?
15. What is their size and what percentage of our total revenue does each group represent?
16. How well do they serve our target market?
17. How well do we serve their needs?
18. How much support do they give our product?
19. What factors made us select them and them select us?
20. How can we motivate them to work harder for us?
21. Do we need them?
22. Do they need us?
23. Do we use multiple channels, including E-commerce?
24. Would we be better off setting up our own distribution system?
25. Should we go direct?

Competitors

26. Who are our competitors?
27. Where are they located?
28. How big are they overall and, specifically, in this product area?
29. What is their product mix?
30. Is their participation in this field growing or declining?
31. Which competitors may be leaving the field?
32. What new domestic competitors may be on the horizon?
33. What new international competitors may be on the horizon?
34. Which competitive strategies and tactics appear particularly successful or unsuccessful?
35. What new direction is the competition pursuing?

Other Relevant Environmental Components

36. What are the legal constraints affecting our marketing effort?
37. To what extent do government regulations restrict our flexibility in making marketing decisions?

38. What requirements do we have to meet?
39. What political or legal developments are looming that will improve or worsen our situation?
40. What threats or opportunities do advances in technology hold for our company?
41. How well do we keep up with technology in the lab and in the plant?
42. What broad cultural shifts are occurring in segments of our market that may impact our business?
43. What consequences will demographic and geographic shifts have for our business?
44. Are any changes in resource availability foreseeable?
45. How do we propose to cope with ecological constraints?

Part II: Reviewing Marketing Management Procedures and Policies

Analysis

46. Do we have an established marketing research function or use outside resources?
47. Do we conduct regular, systematic market analyses?
48. Do we subscribe to any regular market data service?
49. Do we test and retest carefully before we introduce a new product?
50. Are all our major marketing decisions based on solidly researched facts?

Planning

51. How carefully do we examine and how aggressively do we cope with problems, difficulties, challenges, and threats to our business?
52. How do we identify and capitalize on opportunities in our marketplace?
53. What procedure do we use to determine gaps in customers' needs?
54. Do we develop clearly stated and prioritized short-term and long-term marketing objectives?
55. What are our marketing objectives and do they complement our strategic direction?
56. Are our marketing objectives achievable and measurable?
57. Do we have a formalized procedure to develop a Strategic Marketing Plan?
58. Do we use management by objectives (MBO)?
59. What are our core strategies and tactics for achieving our marketing objectives?

60. Are we employing a push–pull strategy in dealing with our customers and consumers?
61. How aggressively are we considering diversification?
62. How effectively are we segmenting our target market?
63. Are we allocating sufficient marketing resources to accomplish our marketing tasks?
64. Are our marketing resources optimally allocated to the major elements of our marketing mix?
65. How well do we tie in our SMP with the other functional plans of our organization?

Implementation and Control

66. Is our SMP (or any business plan) realistically followed or just filed away?
67. Do we continuously monitor our environment to determine the adequacy of our plan?
68. Do we use control mechanisms to monitor achievement of our objectives?
69. Do we compare planned and actual figures periodically and take appropriate measures if they differ significantly?
70. Do we systematically study the contribution and effectiveness of various marketing activities?

Organization

71. Does our firm have a high-level marketing function to analyze, plan, and oversee the implementation of our marketing effort?
72. How capable and dedicated are our marketing personnel?
73. Is there a need for more internal training, incentives, supervision, or evaluation?
74. Are our marketing responsibilities structured to best serve the needs of different marketing activities, products, target markets, and sales territories?
75. Does our entire organization embrace and practice the marketing concept?

Part III: Reviewing Strategy Aspects of the Marketing Mix

Product Policy

76. What is the makeup of our product mix and how well are its components selling?

77. Does it have optimal breadth and depth?
78. Should any of our products be phased out?
79. Do we carefully evaluate any negative ripple effects on the remaining product mix before we make a decision to phase out a product?
80. Have we considered modification, repositioning, and/or extension of sagging products?
81. What additions, if any, should be made to our product mix?
82. Which products are we best equipped to make ourselves and which items should we buy and resell under our own name?
83. Do we routinely check product safety and product liability?
84. Do we have a formalized and tested product recall procedure?
85. Is any recall imminent?

Pricing

86. To what degree are our prices based on cost, demand, and/or competitive considerations?
87. How would our customers react to higher or lower prices?
88. Do we use temporary price promotions and, if so, how effective are they?
89. Do we suggest resale prices?
90. How do our wholesale or retail margins and discounts compare with those of the competition?

Promotion

91. Do we state our advertising objectives clearly?
92. Do we spend enough, too much, or too little on advertising'?
93. Are our ad themes and copy effective?
94. Is our media mix optimal?
95. Do we make aggressive use of sales promotion techniques?

Personal Selling and Distribution

96. Is our sales force large enough to accomplish our marketing objectives?
97. Is it optimally organized according to geographic, market, or product criteria?
98. Is it adequately trained and motivated, and characterized by high morale, ability, and effectiveness?

99. Have we optimized our distribution setup, or are there opportunities for further streamlining?
100. Does our customer service meet customer requirements?

As a final note: conditions within your company are likely to change and that is unquestionably true of the volatile markets of today. Therefore, to make precise decisions (or recommend changes to the next level of management), it is indispensable to skillful management to give your operation a once-a-year checkup. You will find the marketing audit as well as the other checklists in this chapter useful tools to assist in clarifying your thinking and permitting you to grasp the sum and substance of your firm in its operating environment.

V

HELP TOPICS

5

HELP TOPICS

As you develop your Strategic Marketing Plan (SMP), use the ample resources of Help Topics to add greater precision to your thinking. The wide range of topics covered in this chapter provide valuable in-depth information that you can apply to various sections of the SMP. Making liberal use of the information will add to the quality of the plan you submit to management for approval, or to a lender for funding.

Help Topics is divided into 12 parts. Each part begins with a table of contents with references to each section of the SMP.

PART 1:
COMPETITIVE STRATEGY

Contents	
HELP TOPICS	*Applies to SMP in*

1.1 Competitive Strategy
1.2 Strategy Defined for Your SMP
1.3 Implementing Strategy
        Impact of Human Will
        Distracting Competition
1.4 Strategy Principles
        Speed
        Indirect Approach
        Concentration
        Alternative Objectives
        Unbalacing Competition
	Sections 3 and 8

1.1 COMPETITIVE STRATEGY

Why should you be concerned with competitive strategy?

First, strategy has been the key planning challenge since the 1980s, and it will continue to dominate the thinking and actions of executives into the 21st century. Second, it remains the primary focus of your SMP. Third, competitive strategies are the measurable output of your SMP through which actions are taken to achieve your objectives.

Competitive strategy encompasses such diverse issues as the

- Competitive capabilities of both your company and your competitors
- Changing demographics
- Shifting customers' buying patterns
- Globalization of companies, markets, and products
- Saturated markets
- Price wars initiated by hostile competitors
- Rapid technological change
- Shortened product life cycles

Your ability to develop competitive strategies and implement them through a well-developed plan is, and will remain, the hallmark of a good manager and critical to the survival and growth of a company. To acquire that unique skill, you need to understand what strategy is and how to incorporate it into your SMP.

Put into practical terms, the following strategy applications are directed within a two-pronged effort: first, to sustain an advantage over competitors; second, to satisfy customers' needs and establish a strong relationship for a prolonged period.

Strategy applications include:

- Seeking competitive advantage
- Establishing long-term customer relationships
- Incorporating market intelligence into decision making
- Determining optimum product positioning to satisfy customer needs and deter competitive threats
- Identifying areas for market expansion and penetration
- Developing an ongoing stream of products and services

1.2 STRATEGY DEFINED FOR YOUR SMP

As you develop your SMP, keep in mind the broader definition of strategy: strategy is the art of coordinating the means (money, human resources, and materials) to achieve the ends (profit, customer satisfaction, and company growth) as defined by company policy and objectives.

Strategy is further defined at three levels:

1. *Higher-level corporate strategy* directs your company's capabilities toward fulfilling your firm's strategic direction without exhausting its material and human resources. Specifically, that means shaping strategies with the long-term view of sustaining your company's potential for ongoing market development with profitable growth.
2. *Mid-level strategy* operates at the division, business unit, department, or product-line level. While contributing to the company's

overall mission, it is more precise than corporate strategy. It covers a period of 3 to 5 years (SMP Sections 1 through 4) and focuses on quantitative and nonquantitative objectives.

Here, the intent is to provide for continued growth by (a) penetrating existing markets with existing products, (b) expanding into new markets with existing products, (c) developing new products for existing markets, and (d) developing new products for new markets. (These items form the structure of SMP Section 4.)

3. *Lower-level strategy or tactics* requires a shorter time frame (usually 1 year) and correlates most often with the annual marketing plan (SMP Sections 5 through 9). Tactics are actions designed to achieve short-term objectives and link up to longer-term objectives and strategies.

   These precise actions cover such definable issues as pricing and discounts, advertising media and copy approaches, sales force deployment and selling aids, distributor selection and training, product packaging and service, and selection of target segments for a product launch.

1.3 IMPLEMENTING STRATEGY

Ultimately, the effectiveness of your SMP boils down to the skill, motivation, and boldness of your actions opposed to those of your competing manager. Yet, with the immense quantities of computerized reports available, many managers rely exclusively on quantified data to implement marketing plans and strategies.

Mistakenly, they often consider the market as a set of impartial factors that can be predicted, analyzed, and managed through a variety of logic-based techniques. While correct calculations and well-coordinated objectives are indispensable for devising marketing strategies, they are not sufficient for handling unpredictable business conditions and erratic buying behavior.

Thus, the practice of marketing emerges as a battle of mind against mind, manager against competing manager, marketing strategy against competitor's strategy. It is essentially a conflict of human wills. Therefore, strategies must meet and counter unpredictable human responses.

Impact of Human Will

To understand how strategy correlates with the human will, consider what happens when a firm enters a new market. At once the newcomer is likely to encounter resistance from existing companies already dominating the market.

Therefore, the prime purpose of strategy is to *lessen resistance.* Meaning: the goal of strategy is not head-to-head conflict with competitors, the effect of which would drain a company's resources and increase resistance. Rather, the aim of strategy is to initially *surprise, upset,* and *confuse* the competition of your intentions. In turn, those actions are followed by a rapid concentration of your resources at points of opportunity, such as markets that are emerging, neglected, or poorly served.

Surprise takes place at two levels — physical and psychological:

1. At the *physical* level, it entails a series of moves to upset and confuse the competitor's plans through a sudden attack on a market segment. For instance, a move might impair a company's ability to supply outlets or make deliveries on time by dislocating its distribution and organization. That move depends on calculations of market conditions, competitors' resistance, timing, geography, distribution, and transportation. Thus, you can see the importance of inputting such calculations into your SMP.

2. At the *psychological* level, surprise and confusion are the effects any disruptive physical move has on the mind of the competing manager. It relies on surprise to distract and upset the competing manager into making sudden and faulty decisions. When the competing manager feels trapped and unable to counter your moves quickly enough, he or she may hastily form mistakes in judgment, and thus play the market into your hands. Therefore, surprise depends on a calculation of the conditions that are likely to affect the will and mindset of the competition.

To create surprise and confusion, the physical and psychological elements must join together for strategy to work. The intent is to (1) distract the competing manager from interfering with your own efforts, (2) disperse his attention among many unprofitable avenues, and (3) dislocate him from his grip on the market. Overextended and limited in his options, the opposing manager will be less able to oppose your moves.

Distracting Competition

To distract your competition, you may have to deploy your marketing efforts temporarily in order to appear being spread out. Once you have weakened your competition, however, you must *concentrate* your strength at the point of greatest market potential. The familiar marketing terms given to such concentration are *segmentation, niches,* or *target markets.*

The best way to achieve this concentration is to develop *alternative market objectives* (SMP Sections 2 and 7). If the competing manager is certain of your aim, he has the best chance of blunting your efforts. By taking a line that threatens him with alternative objectives, you distract his attention, divide his efforts, and place him on the "horns of a dilemma." By leaving yourself a number of options, you ensure the achievement of at least one objective, perhaps more. Therefore, your SMP must be flexible enough to respond to changing circumstances.

In sum, your aim is not to battle the competition directly, but rather to use strategy to surprise, unbalance, and weaken the competitor, while concentrating your company's strength at market opportunities. And it all boils down to manager vs. manager, one person competing against another.

As you consider your strategy, be aware of the following guidelines for success, most of which apply to SMP Sections 1 through 4.

- *Know your market.* Pinpoint the critical strategic points for market entry. Initially look at geographic location, availability of distributors, and buying motives of the targeted buyers. Which point of entry would give you the best possibility to maneuver?
- *Assess competitors' intentions and strategies.* Evaluate how energetically competitors will challenge your intrusion into their market domain. Are they willing to forfeit a piece of the business to you as long as you don't become too aggressive?
- *Determine the level of technology required.* While technology adeptness often wins many of today's markets, there are still numerous low-tech niche opportunities open to a smaller company. Where does your company fit on the technology issue?
- *Evaluate your internal capabilities and competencies.* One of the cornerstones to maneuvering in today's market is the ability to turn out a quality product equal to or better than those of competitors. What are your company's outstanding competencies?
- *Maintain discipline and vision.* Attempting to maneuver among market leaders takes confidence, courage, and know-how to develop a winning strategy. How would you assess your company's willingness to challenge a market leader?
- *Secure financial resources.* Upper-level management support is necessary to obtain the finances to sustain an ongoing activity. If competitors detect any weakness, they can easily play the waiting game

for the financially unsteady organization to cave in. What type of support can you count on?

■ *Develop a launch plan within your SMP to market the product.* Shape a marketing mix in the tactical section of the SMP (Sections 7 and 8) that incorporates a quality *product*, appropriate *distribution*, adequate *promotion*, and a market-oriented *price* to attract buyers. Which part of the mix would represent your driving force?

■ *Maintain a sensitive awareness of how customers will respond to your product offering.* Use market research to gain insight about what motivates various groups to buy your product. What immediate action can you undertake to target a niche and avoid a head-on confrontation with a market leader?

1.4 STRATEGY PRINCIPLES

As you immerse yourself into the practices of developing winning strategies, five principles emerge as the underpinnings for developing competitive strategies, and apply to SMP Sections 3 and 8.

The principles include *speed, indirect approach, concentration, alternative objectives,* and *unbalancing competition.* A thorough understanding of these pragmatic standards is critical for you to implement business-building strategies.

Speed

Speed is essential to marketing. There are few cases of overlong, dragged-out campaigns that have been successful. The draining of resources without achieving planning objectives has killed more companies than almost any other factor.

Extended deliberation, procrastination, cumbersome committees, and unwieldy organizational hierarchies from home office to field sales are all detriments to success. Drawn-out efforts divert interest, diminish enthusiasm, and depress morale. Individuals become bored and their skills lose sharpness. The gaps of time created through lack of action give competitors a greater chance to react and blunt your efforts.

In today's hotly contested markets, a manager must evaluate, maneuver, and concentrate marketing forces quickly to gain the most profit at least cost and in the shortest span of time. The proverb "opportunities are fleeting" or "the window of opportunity is open" has an intensified truth in today's markets. Speed is essential to overtake the lead and exploit any advantages gained.

Organizing for Speed and Quick Reaction

Two factors make it possible for you to react with speed. First, new technologies in product development, communications, and computerization afford you the opportunity to react quickly and decisively, in a ratio of a short span of time to a large amount of space. The second factor for maximum speed — the essential ingredient — is an *efficient organization*.

In a small organization the founder or president is at the helm. He or she is in a unique position to control both policy making and execution. Because decisions do not have to be channeled through others, they are unlikely to be misinterpreted, delayed, or contested. For the most part, they can be implemented with consistency and speed.

While there exists a preponderance of small businesses, the composition of many have swung to the multiproduct firms with an array of services. In turn, this movement is creating the new breed of diversified firms created by leveraged buyouts, consolidations, joint ventures, and special purpose alliances. With these developments are problems of organization. New people, new products, new positions, and new levels of authority blending into one organization may well result in a cumbersome, inflexible operation.

Individuals in the field often feel that there are obstructions in the decision-making process that prevent moving into new markets. Missed opportunities are common, and "go" decisions get stuck for reasons other than the competition. Even first-line managers think that there are too many people at the staff level or in service departments and not enough on the job with revenue-producing responsibilities.

The large office staffs and the shortage of efficient managers are sources of constant complaint. As a result, an increasing number of companies have followed the trend of downsizing and reengineering to reduce their staffs to efficient "lean and mean" levels.

Your own experience may well support the obvious conclusion that an organization with many levels in its decision-making process cannot operate with speed. This situation exists because each link in a chain of command carries four drawbacks:

1. Loss of time in getting information back.
2. Loss of time in sending orders forward.
3. Reduction of the top executive's full knowledge of the situation.
4. Reduction of the top executive's personal influence on managers.

Therefore, to make your marketing effort effective and if in your power to influence, reduce the chain of command. The fewer the intermediate levels, the more dynamic the operations tend to become. The result is improved effectiveness of the total marketing effort and increased flexibility.

A more flexible organization can achieve greater market penetration because it has the capacity to adjust to varying circumstances, follow alternative objectives, and concentrate at the decisive point. You can enhance organizational flexibility by using a cross-functional strategy team made up of junior and middle managers representing different functional areas of the organization.

Application

To increase the speed of your operations and improve your flexibility, do the following:

1. Reduce the chain of command in your company and increase the pace of communications from the field to the home office.
2. Utilize junior managers for ideas, flexibility, and initiatives for identifying and taking advantage of new opportunities.
3. Use cross-functional strategy teams that tap any cultural diversity that exists in your firm, thereby benefiting from multiple perspectives.

Indirect Approach

The object of the indirect approach is to circumvent the strong points of resistance and concentrate in the markets of opportunity with a *competitive advantage* built around product, price, promotion, and distribution. Historical examples abound: Xerox (copy machines), Black & Decker (professional power tools), and the Japanese and German firms (small automobiles) illustrate an indirect attack centered on product innovation, market segmentation, and product positioning.

Using the indirect approach to position a product or service consists of a two-pronged effort: *customer relationships* and *competitive position*. Attempt to include them in your objectives and strategies at both the strategic and tactical levels of the SMP.

Customer Relationships

As basic as it sounds, bonding with customers remains the controlling factor in positioning. Managers must infuse all company personnel, from salespeople to packers and shippers, with an attitude that strengthens · customer relationships.

In particular, where face-to-face contact permits interaction with customers, delve into the processes customers use to conduct business. What are their priority needs? What special problems do they face to remain competitive? Ultimately, the point is to resolve customers' problems with innovative products and services. When you do so, include the resulting products and services in the Business Portfolio (SMP Section 4).

Therefore, as part of the bonding process, get out in the field and talk directly to customers on a regular basis. Such visits include marketing and sales personnel, as well as to senior management and technical individuals.

For instance, companies such as Deere & Co. routinely send out manufacturing and technical personnel to call on customers and track down information about product performance and technical problems. Customers often view such contact by nonmarketing individuals whose interests center on resolving operational problems as helpful, unobtrusive, and nonthreatening.

To properly interpret and quantify the intelligence you have gathered from these face-to-face visits, it is wise to verify the findings through formal market research. This process benefits you with benchmarks to measure product performance, customer service, distribution efficiency, pricing strategy, and promotion effectiveness, all of which help to monitor the progress of your SMP.

Competitive Position

Once you activate the customer bonding and the market intelligence procedures, you can use the new benchmarks to determine how your market position compares with that of competitors. The key issues here are the *perceptions* embedded in the customers' minds about your company and its products and how they stack up against those of your competitors.

Application

To use an indirect approach, do the following:

1. Search for emerging, neglected, or poorly served market segments through competitive analysis and then fill those gaps with products. (SMP Section 4.)
2. Identify a competitive advantage centered on price, product, promotion, or distribution (the marketing mix). (SMP Sections 3 and 8.)
3. Use movement, surprise, speed, and alternative objectives to surprise, confuse, and upset your competitor. (SMP Section 2.)

4. Once you have gained a point of entry, move toward market expansion. (SMP Sections 2, 3, and 4.)

Concentration

Concentration has two uses in business terms.

First, it means directing your resources toward a market or group and fulfilling its specific needs and wants. In modern marketing practices concentration is used in target marketing, segmentation, and niche marketing.

Second, as applied to strategy, concentration means focusing your strengths against the weaknesses of your competitor.

How do you determine the weaknesses of the competitor? You use *competitive analysis* in your strategy development to detect the strength–weakness relationship. Internal analysis — used at both the strategic and tactical level of your SMP — allows you to identify your unique competencies or natural strengths. External analysis allows you to identify your competitor's weaknesses.

Application

To concentrate in a market, do the following:

1. Use competitive analysis to identify your competitors' weaknesses and your company's strengths.
2. Concentrate on an unserved, poorly served, or emerging segment of the market that you have determined represents growth and, in turn, could help launch you into additional market segments.
3. Introduce a product (or product modification) not already developed by existing competitors in the overall product category.
4. Develop multilevel distribution by private labeling your product for existing suppliers, concurrent with establishing your own brand. Therefore, if one strategy falters the alternative strategy wins.
5. Follow up by expanding into additional market segments with the appropriate products so you can envelop the entire market category.

Alternate Objectives

There are four central reasons for developing alternative, or multiple objectives, in SMP Sections 2 and 7:

1. On a corporate scale, most businesses have to fulfill a variety of long- and short-term objectives and require various approaches for

their attainment. Therefore, a wide range of objectives are needed with a variety of timeframes.

2. As already discussed, the strategy principle of concentration is implemented successfully only by applying alternative objectives.

3. Alternative objectives permit enough flexibility to exploit opportunities as they arise. By designing a number of objectives, you hold options for achieving one objective should others fail.

4. Most important, alternative objectives keep your competitors from detecting your real intentions. By displaying a number of possible threats, you force a competing manager to spread his resources and attention to match your action.

While you have dispersed intentionally in order to gain control, you cause him to disperse erratically, inconveniently, and without full knowledge of the situation. Thus, you cause the opposing manager to lose control. You can then concentrate rapidly on the objective that offers the best potential for success.

As noted earlier, since the major incalculable is the human will (the mind of one manager against the mind of a competing manager), the intent of alternative objectives is to unbalance the opposing manager into making mistakes through inaction, distraction, wrong decisions, false moves, or misinterpretation of your real intent. You thereby expose a weakness that you can exploit through concentration of effort. This unbalancing or distraction is achieved through movement and surprise.

Application

To use alternative objectives, do the following:

1. Consider such areas as customer service, improved delivery time, extended warranties, sales terms, after-sales support, packaging, and management training as sources of alternative objectives.

2. Identify alternative niches in the initial stages of attack to cause distraction among your competitors.

3. Exploit your competitors' confusion by concentrating your efforts on the weak spots that represent opportunities.

Unbalancing Competition

While the overriding output of your SMP are strategies, its indisputable bottom-line goals translate to outperforming competition, satisfying evolving customers' needs and wants, and sustaining the profitable long-term growth of markets. In that demanding context, how do you unbalance and thereby outperform competition?

First, victory in many competitive situations is not necessarily due to the brilliance of the attacker, but to the mistakes of the opposing manager. If brilliance plays a roll at all, it is in the manager's deliberate efforts to develop situations that confuse and unbalance the competition. Moreover, unbalancing fulfills the ultimate purpose of the strategy: the reduction of resistance.

One major approach to outperforming competition is to try an unbalancing action. For example, announce a new product that could make the competing manager's product line obsolete. Even a press release about a yet-to-be released product line can "make 'em sweat" and create panic — and mistakes.

Most often, this unbalancing is developed in the tactical sections of your SMP and through the day-to-day activities that range from the threat of legal action to the effects of mergers and acquisitions.

Application

To unbalance competition, do the following:

- Identify the areas in which the competition is not able (or willing) to respond to your actions. (Use the competitor analysis checklists in Chapter 4 for this purpose.)
- Make a conscious effort to create an unbalancing effect through surprise announcements. For example, tout your new computerized ordering procedures, just-in-time delivery, or technical on-site assistance. The unbalancing effect will have the greatest impact to the extent that you are able to maintain secrecy until the last possible moment.
- Utilize new technology to unbalance competitors and make them scramble to catch up. Investigate the various technologies applied to marketing, such as electronic data interchange (EDI) to speed delivery from manufacturer to customer, interactive video systems, and the Internet to enhance your promotion and distribution strategies.

Strategy Lessons

From these principles and strategies of competitive marketing strategy, five major lessons stand out:

1. While the tools of marketing (advertising, sales promotion, field selling, marketing research, distribution, and pricing) are physical

acts, they are directed by a mental process. The better thought-out your strategy, the more easily you will gain the upper hand, and the less it will cost.

2. The tougher you make your marketing practices, the more your competitors will consolidate against you. Result: you will harden the resistance you are trying to overcome. Even if you succeed in winning the market, you will have fewer resources with which to profit from the victory.

3. The more intent you are in securing a market entirely of your own choosing and terms, the stiffer the obstacles you will raise in your path and the more cause competitors will have to reverse what you have achieved.

4. When you are trying to dislodge your competitor from a strong market position that will be costly to abandon, leave that competitor a quick way to retreat from the market.

5. If you face a situation of transforming the image of your product into a new market position, follow these guidelines:

    – Be certain your position is *distinctive* and doesn't create confusion or misinterpretation, so that a competitor is mistakenly identified with your position.

    – Select a position that conforms to your firm's unique, core competencies, so that competitors cannot easily duplicate the differentiating factors for which you can claim *superiority*.

    – Communicate your position in precise terms through product application, sales promotion, and advertising. For example, determine what constitutes your position. Do you position your product with a single benefit, such as lowest cost; do you use a double-benefit position of lowest cost and best technical support; or do you select a multibenefit position of lowest cost, best technical support, and state-of-the-art technology?

    These benefit positions lay the foundation for developing the tactical sections of your SMP that incorporates the marketing mix, consisting of product, price, promotion, and distribution. (SMP Sections 7 and 8.)

PART 2:
LOOKING AT YOUR MARKET

Contents	
HELP TOPICS	*Applies to SMP in*

2.1 LOOKING AT YOUR MARKET

The purpose of looking at your market is to uncover opportunities and threats that result in alternative strategies and, ultimately, to competitive advantage. The most comprehensive approach to looking at your market is to concentrate on four market spheres: *analyzing customer groups, identifying competitor behavior, viewing the industry,* and *scanning the environment.*

2.2 ANALYZING CUSTOMER GROUPS

Strategic marketing is a total system of interacting business activities designed to plan, price, promote, and distribute want-satisfying products and services to organizational and household users at a profit.

From this functional definition you can see that the customer is the center of marketing's attention — and your entire SMP. To produce want-satisfying products and services, you must know what your customers want, where they can find what they want, and how to communicate to them that you are able to meet their needs and solve their problems.

In both the strategic and tactical sections of the SMP, use the following guidelines as you look at your market:

- *Define your customers by demographic and psychographic (behavioral) characteristics.* Observe changes in the character of your markets. For instance, look for any unmet customer needs that would enable you to respond rapidly in the form of products, services, methods of delivery, credit terms, or technical assistance. Talk with customers to detect their most troublesome problems and frustrations. Meet with sales people and draw them out on ways in which to innovate.
- *Examine customer usage patterns or frequency of purchase.* Watch for alternative and substitute products that could represent an opportunity to replace competitive products. Also observe deviations in regional and seasonal purchase patterns. Check for changes from past purchasing and usage practices that could translate into opportunities.
- *Survey selling practices.* Innovations often occur in selling. Stay tuned-in to current trends in promotional allowances, selling tactics, trade discounts, rebates, point-of-purchase opportunities, or seasonal/holiday requirements. Here, again, stay close to sales people for such information. Encourage them to input all behavioral information about perceptions dealing with your product, delivery, company image, complaint handling, and any other factors that influence a sale and contribute to a long-term relationship.
- *Survey channels of distribution.* Examine your distribution methods and look for opportunities to customize services consistent with the

characteristics of the segment. Pay attention to warehousing (if applicable) and what could be fertile possibilities to innovate, such as electronic ordering and computerized inventory control systems. Look, too, at the direct marketing channels pioneered by such companies as Dell Computer and Gateway 2000. And experiment with the latest marketing innovation of using the Internet as a new sales and distribution channel.

■ *Look at product possibilities.* Search for innovations with product line extensions to maintain an ongoing presence in your existing markets or to gain a foothold in an emerging segment. Harnessing new technology might broaden your customer base and leverage your company's expertise.

■ *Explore opportunities to cut costs for you and your customers.* Investigate such areas as strengthening quality assurance and introducing new warranties related to product performance and reliability. Also look for possibilities to replace products or systems, improve internal and external operating procedures, and discover new product applications.

To fully benefit from your look at the market, you should familiarize yourself with these components: *market and product segments, and customer needs and behavior.*

Market and Product Segments

Segmentation means splitting the overall market into smaller submarkets or segments that have more in common with one another than with the total market. Subdividing the market helps you to identify and satisfy the specific needs of individuals within your chosen segments and thereby strengthen your market position. Segmentation also allows you to concentrate your strength against the weakness of your competitor and improve your competitive ranking.

Examples abound of companies concentrating on segments: Snap-On Tools Corp. serves professional mechanics only; White Rock Corp. products concentrate on smaller segments or niches that have little interest to Coca-Cola or Pepsi Cola; Measurex Corporation initially built a strong foundation for computer-based process control equipment in a single industry; Godiva Chocolates, priced at over $20 a pound, aims at an affluent "me" generation; Women's Health Centers of America, Inc. serves female patients only; Honda Motor Co., Ltd. originally focused on selling high-quality, small motorcycles to an entirely new type of customer, the suburban middle-class male.

Thus, selecting segments depends on a group of variables, including knowledge of *customer needs* and *competitor capabilities*. Grasping the significance of each will add greater precision to selecting viable segments, especially so as you develop your Business Portfolio in SMP Section 4.

Customer Needs and Behavior

If you maintain an ongoing customer analysis that accurately defines the needs and wants of customer groups and individuals, you satisfy a primary ingredient of successful segmentation. Specifically, analyzing customer needs requires you to:

- *Categorize segments.* Begin by adding structure to your view of the market. This approach allows you to properly allocate marketing and sales resources for the greatest impact. For example, categorize your segments by one or more of the following: geographic location, demographics, product attributes, market size, common buying factors, shared distribution channels, and any other categories that are unique to your industry.
- *Determine purchase patterns.* Next, analyze purchasing variables so you can develop customized packages of benefits that will increase your chances of success — by segment and key customers. For example, divide customer purchase patterns into two categories: *regular use* and *infrequent special application* of your product.

    Review how customers perceive your product benefits in terms of *price/value, convenience,* or *prestige factors.* Rank customer loyalty as *nonexistent, medium,* or *strong.* Examine customer awareness and readiness to buy your product as *unaware, informed, interested,* or *intending to buy.* Finally, evaluate your buyers by *product quality, delivery, guarantees, technical services,* or *promotional support.*

Choosing Market Segments

With your SMP projecting a market-driven focus, segmentation ranks as an essential part of your analysis. And concentration in one or more segments is the essence of a competitive strategy. Therefore, in doing your own customer analysis in both the strategic and tactical sections of your SMP, you should know which criteria to use in choosing market segments, what factors to use in identifying a market segment, and how to develop a segmentation analysis.

Therefore, segmentation is particularly applicable in developing your portfolio in Section 4 of the SMP. Use the following criteria to guide your thinking in selecting market segments:

- *Measurable.* Can you quantify the segment? For example, you should be able to assign a number to how many factories, how many farm acres, or how many people are within the market segment.
- *Accessible.* Do you have access to the market through a dedicated sales force, distributors, transportation, or warehousing?
- *Substantial.* Is the segment of sufficient size to warrant attention as a segment? Further, is the segment declining, maturing, or growing?
- *Profitable.* Does concentrating on the segment provide sufficient profitability to make it worthwhile? Use your organization's standard measurements for profitability, such as return on investment (ROI), gross margin, or profits.
- *Compatible with competition.* To what extent do your major competitors have an interest in the segment? Is it of active interest or of negligible concern to your competitors?
- *Effectiveness.* Does your organization have sufficient skills and resources to serve the segment effectively?
- *Defendable.* Does your firm have the capabilities to defend itself against the attack of a major competitor?

Answering those questions will help you select a market segment with good potential for concentrating your resources and with sufficient information for customer analysis. Once you have chosen a market segment, then use these criteria to test its viability.

But how do you select a segment? You can identify market segments by dividing a market into groups of customers with common characteristics.

Categories for Segmenting Markets

The four most common ways to segment a market is by demographic, geographic, psychographic (behavioral), and product attributes. Each of these factors, particularly when used in combination with the others, represents an opportunity or identifies a need that can be satisfied with a product. Table 5.2.1 defines each of the categories.

Table 5.2.1   Categories for Segmenting Markets
Geographic Region, city, or metro size, population density, climate
Demographic Age, family size, gender, income, occupation, education, religion, race, nationality, social class
Psychographic Lifestyles, personality
Product Attributes Benefits preferred, buying readiness status, usage rate, loyalty ranking, attitudes toward product or service

Let's examine these segmentation categories in greater detail:

Geographic Segmentation

Geographic segmentation is relatively easy to perform because the individual segments can be clearly delineated on a map. It is a sensible strategy to employ when there are distinct differences in climatic conditions or cultural patterns.

Internationally, blocks or clusters of countries can be approached in a similar fashion, particularly if they share the same language and cultural heritage. For instance, in most of Latin America the same advertising media are often appropriate for several countries. While there are numerous cultural differences in many of those countries — as well as in other parts of the world — there are common problems that share several common features, known as *cultural universals*. These include economic systems, marriage and family systems, educational systems, social control systems, and supernatural belief systems.

Domestically, you can segment by region; by state, county, or county size; by city size, by population density, or by other geopolitical criteria. However, such segmentation is effective only if it reflects differences in need and motivation patterns. Many firms, for example, adjust their advertising efforts to as small an area as a county.

Demographic Segmentation

Along with geographic information, demographic variables are among the longest-used segmentation factors. They owe their popularity to two facts: (1) they are easier to observe and/or measure than most other characteristics and (2) their breakdown is often closely linked to differences in behavioral patterns. Demographic factors include age, sex, family size, stage in the family life cycle, income, occupation, education, religion, race, nationality, and social class.

Psychographic Segmentation

The most exciting form of segmentation results from the application of psychographic variables, such as life-style, personality, user status, usage rate, spending behavior, and marketing factor sensitivity. Banks, car manufacturers, and liquor producers, to name a few, employ the advantages of psychographic segmentation. It is a branch of market segmentation that is still evolving and promises great vitality in the future.

2.3 DETERMINING PATTERNS OF CUSTOMER BEHAVIOR

A central component of market segmentation deals with patterns of customer behavior. In turn, to connect behavior with practical application raises these questions:

- How is a customer likely to think, behave, and make decisions regarding your products and services?
- How can you use that information to reach and attract potential customers?
- What impact does behavior analysis have on customer analysis and, therefore, on the selection of strategies?

It takes diligent research to understand customer behavior and translate the findings into market entry and product development strategies for SMP Section 3 Growth Strategies and Section 8 Tactics. Here are planning guidelines to follow that are particularly applicable to those SMP sections:

- Locate the optimum product/market entry point through a systematic probe of customers' behavior and competitors' positions.
- Maintain growth with a continuous flow of new products, applications, and value-added services.
- Quantify existing products by sales, profits, market share, position in the market, and any other pertinent criteria that permit you to appraise market performance.
- List new markets in which your existing products can be sold.
- Identify new products that can be sold to existing customers. New products may include any new systems you have licensed, or private-

labeled or modified products with wrap-around services that customers perceive as new.

■ List new products for new markets. While this is the riskiest of the steps, it allows you to test emerging segments that have opened up through expanding applications of technology, government regulations, or unique requirements tied to customers' behavior.

Understanding the Behavioral Cycle

The problem for the marketer is that consumers act rarely, if ever, from a single motive. Rather, multiple and even conflicting motives govern most behavioral acts. For instance, the purchase of a car may be influenced by the motives of prestige, comfort, safety, and economy. It is unlikely that all these motives will point to the same choice.

Therefore, consumers have to assign priorities to their motives to decide which ones are more important. As a manager, try to determine your customers' motives and priorities, and be able to trigger them properly with your advertising, packaging, and other elements of the marketing mix.

Consumer Behavior

How a consumer behaves toward a product is an attempt to decrease or eliminate tension. As such, a response may take three major directions: the consumer (1) decides to purchase and use your product, (2) determines that he or she needs more information and so begins a search effort, or (3) decides to drop the whole matter and take no action.

Once a purchase has been made, the consumer compares expectations and fulfillment in a process called *feedback*. The outcome of this comparison affects future behavior. A single positive experience produces satisfaction that leads to reinforcement. In turn, continued reinforcement results in the formation of a habit, which is an ideal situation because it means repeat purchase of your product and results in brand loyalty. A negative experience, on the other hand, may wind up in the consumer changing brands, avoiding an entire product category, or creating a negative morale situation.

Using the Behavior Model

Two tables will help you apply the information produced by analyzing consumer behavior. Table 5.2.2 shows you how to respond to selective and repetitive forms of consumer behavior. It outlines the nature and result of the consumer's experience, and then gives you the appropriate marketing action to take in order to gain or retain consumer loyalty.

Table 5.2.2 Experience Patterns and Marketing Action

	Consumer		Company	
Type of Experience	Nature	Result	Appropriate Marketing Action	Reasoning
Single positive	Satisfaction	Reinforcement	Free samples, direct-mail couponing	Build loyalty
Repeated positive	Continued satisfaction	Habit formation	Cents-off campaign, advertising, other uses	Strengthen loyalty
Single negative	Dissatisfaction	Adjustment	Explain, repair, replace	Convert to loyalty
Repeated negative	Continued dissatisfaction	Avoidance	Refund, substitute, cross-couponing	Convert to other product

Table 5.2.3 is helpful in developing the tactical portion of your SMP. It reviews the different factors related to behavior and tells you how to influence consumers in each of these areas. For example, regarding motives, the chart counsels you to investigate how consumers choose the brand they will use, and then to use this information in designing your product and promotion.

2.4 EXAMINING UNFILLED WANTS AND NEEDS

The third component of looking at your market is determining the unfilled wants and needs of various customer segments. This area also impacts SMP Section 2 Objectives, Section 3 Growth Strategies, and Section 4 Business Portfolio. The analysis, however, goes beyond simply identifying these wants. It specifies ways to fulfill them by examining how consumers adopt a new product and how you can communicate your offerings to them.

With the customer as the centerpiece behind market success, consider using the following eight steps of a customer satisfaction program for your own operation:

1. *Define customer requirements and expectations.* Begin by establishing continuous dialogue through personal customer contact to define their current and future expectations. Then match customer

Table 5.2.3 Applying the Behavioral Model	
Factor	*What You Should Do to Influence Consumers*
Stimuli	Test, in a competitive environment, how much attention your stimuli create (e.g., product design, advertising, packaging)
Sensations	Unless you can create sensory impressions, no action is likely to follow; stimuli must stand out from their environment to be distinguishable
Needs and predispositions	Look at your product design and/or advertising as you consider the most pressing current need(s) or most positive predispositions
Perception	Ask consumers what your advertising and packaging tell them about your product
Personality	Consumers try to match personality profiles of the products they buy with their own; make sure that yours has a clear-cut profile; it cannot be all things to all people
Social factors	Include acceptance by others in your advertising
Image	Unless you can create a positive image for your product, consumers are unlikely to buy; ask them how they view your product and adjust its image, if necessary
Information search	Provide informative and persuasive booklets, free for the asking
Motive	Investigate what ultimately makes consumers choose one product over another; build this argument into your product and advertising
Decision making	Make the decision atmosphere easy and pleasant; for instance, offer financing or other special incentives for making a decision before the specified date
Behavior	At this point, your product package is probably the most powerful influence on consumer behavior, the "silent salesperson" on the store shelf; make sure that it encourages purchase and consumption
Goal orientation	Explain how your product gives desired results
Feedback	Find out who is repurchasing or abandoning your product and why

expectations against promises made in the sales presentation. The feedback often falls into such basic areas as orders being shipped complete and on time and complaints being handled rapidly and to the customer's satisfaction.

2. *Maintain a system of customer relationship management.* Ongoing customer contact is a key component of the program. It means assigning permanent customer contact people, such as customer service, sales, and technical service to selected customers. Each contact person is then empowered to initiate actions to resolve customers' problems. Other features of customer relations include toll-free telephone lines and online "expert systems" that connect customers to information on inventory, production, and technical problem-solving assistance. Your overall goal: achieve a preferred supplier status with 100% conformance to expectations.

3. *Adhere to customer service standards.* All quality plans, product performance, and customer relationships are driven by customers' standards. Most often those standards are measured by the time it takes to handle complaints, the number of on-time shipments compared to previous time periods, and the amount of invoicing errors, freight claims, and product returns. Once indexed, the information is forwarded to a steering committee made up of various functional managers for evaluation and action.

4. *Make the commitment to customers a company ritual.* A commitment means guarantees that include: stock orders shipped the same day received, technical service teams sent to customers' locations when needed, specialized training provided to customers' employees, products that conform to data supplied by customers, and a 24-hour "hot line" for support services.

5. *Resolve complaints to achieve quality improvement results.* Empower customer-contact personnel to resolve customer problems on the spot. In particular, sales reps should follow up complaints and make a formal report to a Customer Satisfaction Committee.

6. *Determine what constitutes customer satisfaction.* Develop an index to measure customer satisfaction. With customer feedback as the input, assemble information from various sources, such as: direct customer contact, customer audits, independent surveys, quality assurance cards with shipments, suggestions, inquiries, and complaints.

7. *Customer satisfaction results.* Circulate the results so that functional managers can design customer satisfaction objectives for the following year.

8. *Compare customer satisfaction levels.* Contrast your results with those of competitors and with industry standards through formal and informal benchmarking. Then share the results with distributors to help them improve their customer satisfaction ratings.

How Customers Adopt a New Product

Identifying and fulfilling needs and wants with products and services is particularly appropriate in developing SMP Sections 7 and 8.

Table 5.2.4 offers a fertile list of factors to define areas for differentiation and innovation that you can apply to fulfilling your customers' wants and needs. Once defined and solutions provided, the new innovation must be *communicated* to and *adopted* by the customer.

Table 5.2.4 Source of Ideas for Differentiation and Innovation			
Factors			
Product:	*Price:*	*Distribution Channels:*	*Promotion:*
Quality	List price	Direct sales force	Advertising
Features	Discounts	Manufacturers' reps	Customer
Options	Allowances	Distributors	Trade
Style	Payment period	Jobbers	Personal selling
Brand name	Credit terms	Dealers	Incentives
Packaging	Financing	Market coverage	Sales aids
Sizes		Warehouse locations	Samples
Services		Inventory control	Training
Warranties		systems	Sales promotion
Returns		Physical transport	Demonstrations
Versatility			Contests
Uniqueness			Premiums
Utility			Coupons
Reliability			Manuals
Durability			Telemarketing
Patent			Internet
protection			Publicity
Guarantees			

Diffusion and Adoption

When a new product is introduced to the marketplace, two interrelated processes are brought into play: *diffusion* and *adoption*.

Diffusion is the spread of a new idea from your company to its ultimate users or adopters. Adoption, on the other hand, is the decision-making process that prospective users go through after they learn about an innovation. In the final stage of the adoption process the consumer decides whether or not to purchase your new product on a regular basis.

Diffusion: Communication of Innovation

Diffusion — spreading the word about your new product — is initiated by you. But it is only partially under your control because a great deal of it occurs in face-to-face encounters and exchanges between customers, over which you have no direct influence. Thus, it is important to give them every reason to think and speak favorably about your innovation. In this context, it is particularly crucial to understand the nature of innovation and communication.

An *innovation* is an idea perceived as new by customers. This fact has far-reaching implications. First of all, *ideas*, not products, are spread in the diffusion process. Only if you can convince customers to accept the new idea underlying your product will they consider the product itself.

Further, if customers view your new product as being the same as all the others, they will not consider it worth trying. Again, it makes very little difference whether or not your product represents a substantial departure from other products on the market. The only thing that counts is what customers *think* your product is.

What customers perceive is, to a large degree, the outcome of what and how you *communicate* to them. When introducing a new product or service, you must expose your target market to messages that are both informative and persuasive.

Adoption: a Multistage Decision-Making Process

Diffusion of your new idea is a prerequisite for adoption. Only after a customer has learned about the existence, availability, and desirability of your innovation can he or she decide about its adoption.

Information and persuasion are passed on from your firm via the mass media and opinion leaders to individual consumers who, in turn, go through several phases of decision making, as indicated below. Besides that mainstream of information and influence through which consumers first become aware of and interested in your innovation, other sources of communication come into play at different stages of the adoption process.

Therefore, although the diffusion process reaches into every stage of the adoption process by means of communication flow, adoption is essentially an individual matter. In the end, it is the consumer alone who must make the decision after giving due consideration to outside factors.

A consumer adopting your innovation passes through five distinct phases: awareness, interest, evaluation, trial, and adoption.

1. *Awareness.* At the awareness stage, product information flows to the customer with no initiative on his part. He receives it passively, but experiences little emotional response. His information at this point is incomplete in that he may not be sufficiently informed about your availability, price, and features of your innovation.

2. *Interest.* As the information received in the awareness stage is absorbed, a customer may say to himself, "That sounds good. Let me find out more about it." Thus, the interest stage is initiated. It represents a 180-degree turnaround from the nonchalance of the awareness phase. The customer is now turned on, at least sufficiently to investigate the matter further. He conducts an active search for more information.

3. *Evaluation.* Having collected as much additional information as possible, the customer examines the evidence and ponders whether or not to try the product. In the evaluation stage, after weighing the pros and cons of a purchase, the prospect solicits the advice of relevant individuals who are trusted personal sources.

4. *Trial.* During the trial stage, a prospect will test your new product, often by purchasing it on a small scale. Since this usually forces consumers to enter a store, it is the salesperson who potentially becomes the most powerful source of information, sometimes influential even to the point of altering the prospect's original purchasing intention. While many items can be sampled in small quantities, difficulties arise in the case of durable goods that require trial under conditions of normal use, which is all but impossible unless the product is rented or purchased.

5. *Adoption.* When the prospect completes a personal trial of your innovation, your buyer will determine whether or not it has proved to be useful and desirable in a particular situation. If the decision is positive, the customer will adopt — that is, decide to continue using your product. Besides the trial experience, your company and product image as well as his or her social environment will influence this final decision.

Of course, your target market can reject your innovation at any stage. A customer can eliminate your product idea even at the awareness stage as being of no interest. This rejection may well be due to a misunder-standing, if your advertising message was not strong enough.

During the course of his information gathering, the prospect can decide your product is inappropriate or unaffordable. An evaluation of benefits and drawbacks may cause the prospect to reject it as unsatisfactory after the trial period.

Application

The picture of customer reaction to the introduction of your new product is now complete. You can see that potential buyers react differently, though somewhat predictably, in accordance with their psychological and cultural makeup, financial situation, and interactive patterns. And the spread of new ideas via various communications channels is closely related to individual adoption decisions.

The following guidelines will help you internalize the essential concepts:

1. Conducting a customer analysis will indicate how you can manip-ulate the information input at each stage of the adoption process, how you can differentiate between adopter categories, and finally, and most important, how the acceptance of your innovation can be speeded up.
2. If your product is truly news, you may even want to think about a press conference with appropriate fringe benefits for the attend-ees. To trigger adoption in medical circles, pharmaceuticals man-ufacturers frequently encourage an outstanding authority in a particular field (often from a university) to conduct research with a new drug and report his or her findings in a prestigious profes-sional journal. Such a procedure is akin to an independent personal endorsement.
3. While you cannot directly control independent personal sources, you can attempt to either simulate or stimulate personal influence. One approach is to use a highly credible celebrity in your adver-tising as a substitute for the influence of friends. Stimulating per-sonal influence is the approach that suggests, "Ask somebody who knows" — namely, a user of your product.
4. Winning over your dealers' sales personnel is a further crucial step in your game plan. You can motivate them to sell your product more aggressively if you conduct a contest or even pay them a commission. Improving your prospect's own experience with your innovation can provide the ultimate push.

5. It would give a great boost to the adoption of your product if you could identify and persuade likely opinion leaders. Because opinion leadership and mobility are correlated, some firms avail themselves of lists of American Express cardholders, for example, who have used their cards for travel purposes within the past 12 months, and communicate with them via direct mail.

2.5 IDENTIFYING COMPETITOR BEHAVIOR

While customer behavior lets you examine how to attract and satisfy customers, competitor behavior gives you a picture of your competitors' positions in the market. Such a view becomes the focus of the entire SMP process. You can use information of that kind to concentrate on competitors' weak spots or differentiate your product line, with the overall aim of creating your own competitive advantage.

You can view competitor analysis from a variety of perspectives: analyze competitors (1) by how customers select a particular product or choose a company from which they purchase, (2) by how competitors segment their market, (3) by how customers display their various behavioral purchase patterns, and (4) by how competitors develop their strategies against you. In short, competitor analysis can be categorized by *customer selection, competitor segmentation, behavioral purchase patterns,* and *competitor strategies.*

Customer Selection

When you branch into new markets and products, competitors are, in effect, preselected for you. By observing purchasing activities of customers, you can identify your competitors and then group them so that you can examine competitors by such factors as product quality, versatility, accuracy, reliability, speed of access to information, cost, and types of additional services offered.

Further, there are direct and indirect competitors. Looking to other industries, for example, bankers find their traditional depositor customers are placing their savings in a variety of channels that are now competitors to banks. Some insurance policies have an investment component that serves as a savings vehicle. Brokerage houses, mutual funds consisting of stocks and bonds, and government securities are also competitors of banks.

In other fields, Pepsi and Coke battle between themselves as well as with noncola drinks. Airlines also have indirect competitors when their customers select teleconferencing and the Internet to transmit detailed information as alternatives to expensive and time-consuming travel. The filtering-down process continues when airport limousines, hotels, and restaurants feel the effect of such indirect competition.

Competitor Segmentation

Market segmentation has already been discussed in connection with customer analysis, but now we can examine it from another vantage point: how competitors might segment their markets. Your interest is in knowing the various possibilities through which you can be attacked by an existing or new competitor. In addition, such an examination provides insights from which you can develop a counterstrategy.

You should be aware that in addition to competitors segmenting to protect their own positions against inroads of rivals, they could use a set of common buying factors to attack you. Used singly or in any combination, these factors include:

- Performance, quality, service, delivery, and price
- Measurable characteristics, such as customer size, growth rate, and location
- Common sales and distribution channels
- Applications of new technology

Behavioral Purchase Patterns

Why do prospects buy from your competitor rather than from you? What are the behavioral patterns most noticeable in customer behavior? What are the trends as they relate to such factors as product, price, promotion, distribution, research and development, service, and courtesy of salespeople?

It is to your best advantage, as it relates to competitors, to categorize these trend areas so you can consciously look to the behavioral patterns that cause a prospect to purchase from your competitor rather than from you, or vice versa.

See Chapter 4 for a Competitive Advantage Checklist to provide a side-by-side analysis of the key factors that affect purchase considerations.

Competitor Strategies

Of the four components of competitor analysis, you should single out competitors' strategies for major emphasis. Other parts of the analysis are subordinate to those strategies your competitors will use against you.

Strategy means mobilizing every human and functional part of a company, then focusing those resources to achieve corporate, divisional, or product-line planning objectives. Therefore, to identify competitor behavior you have to analyze the total competitor organization and compare it with your own.

In realistic terms, however, the extent of the analysis may be the responsibility of a vice-president of marketing, product manager, marketing manager, or sales manager, and focus only on selected competitors within a target segment. The aim of the analysis is to answer the following questions:

- What are the competitors' marketing objectives as to size, growth, profitability, and market share?
- What are the competitors' current strategies?
- How are they performing?
- What are their strengths and weaknesses?
- What actions can be expected from existing and emerging competitors in the future?

Developing a strengths/weaknesses checklist is one format for analysis. (See Chapter 4.) A second approach is to determine how competitors fit into strategic groups.

2.6 VIEWING THE INDUSTRY

The next part of looking at your market is an industry analysis. It is most applicable as you focus on your firm's strategic direction in SMP Section 1.

An industry is the sum of many parts: sources of supply, existing competitors, emerging competitors, alternative product and service offerings, and various levels of customers from intermediate types such as original equipment manufacturers (OEM) to after-market end users. Within these powerful factors are a range of influences that also affect an industry.

Conducting an Industry Analysis

A key element in taking a strategic focus to your SMP is recognizing the interacting forces that characterize an industry. It proceeds from the broad *level one* analysis of suppliers, existing competitors, emerging competitors, alternative product offerings, and customers to a finite *level two* listing that can be used as a checklist.

Level One Analysis

Suppliers

If a few suppliers in an industry control the flow of materials that result in the control of prices, then a powerful influence is exerted on all the other forces within the industry. Therefore, a review of supplier practices at key stages of the distribution chain will provide you with a clue to future patterns of supplier behavior. In turn, that will push you to develop alternative strategies in SMP Section 3.

Existing Competitors

How do you rate the intensity of competitive actions? Examine the pattern of price wars. Which competitors seem to retaliate first against movements in prices? Review the amount of advertising and identify its themes. Is there a tendency to "knock the competition," or is a more professional approach used? Is there a warlike environment that is changing the character of the industry?

You can also characterize existing competitors within an industry by answering the following questions:

- How would you rank the commitment of most competitors to the industry? Is there a major, average, or minor commitment?
- How diverse are the competitors in shaping their objectives and strategies? Are there some entrepreneurial firms using innovations to increase market share? Are others ready to hold their markets at all costs?
- What is the nature of the products in the industry? Have they reached a commodity status or is there a tendency toward product differentiation?
- Is the industry plagued with overcapacity or undercapacity? What effect would each condition have on the strategies of competitors?

Emerging Competitors

The entry of new competitors over the past 25 years in many U.S. industries — such as steel, automobiles, consumer appliances, textiles, footwear, and high technology — has had a jarring effect on the established companies. Some companies have succumbed to the ravages of aggressive competitors. Others have risen to the threat by reinventing their companies through reengineering, downsizing, and imbuing personnel with the spirit to fight back with new skills to develop competitive strategies.

In viewing your industry there may be a tendency to focus only on existing players. The wrenching lesson is that you must identify and analyze emerging competitors with the same intensity of detail as you apply to existing ones. The job is more difficult when applied to emerging competitors because patterns of behavior are not always visible.

Alternative Product Offerings

Using the lessons from competitor analysis, you should give similar emphasis to alternative products or services. It is appropriate in this type of analysis to employ the knowledge of R&D and manufacturing personnel in your organization who are more likely to know about alternate products.

Outside industry specialists from academia, research organizations, and other industry consultants are also useful sources of information. The auto industry provides a familiar example of how aluminum is replacing steel and how plastics and other space-age materials are increasingly providing an alternative to aluminum.

Customers

Customers are classified at all stages of the buying cycle: from end-use consumers to industrial and commercial buyers as well as to intermediaries such as distributors, wholesalers, and retailers. Each stage represents a force within an industry that warrants investigation.

Answering the following questions will provide you with insights about the influences or power of customers:

- Do customers tend to dictate buying terms because of large volume or concentrated purchases?
- Are customers knowledgeable about costs of raw materials and manufacturing and do they use such information as bargaining power?
- Is there a threat of key customers using backward integration to take over the suppliers' functions?
- Is there sufficient product differentiation or can customers simply switch from one supplier (domestic or foreign) to another?

Level Two Analysis

Industry analysis continues with level two. This aspect of the analysis contains a more detailed breakdown that you can use as a checklist:

Current demand for product: *Indicate,* in quantitative terms, the demand or usage of your product in sales, dollars, units, pounds, number of users, share of market, or whatever measurement provides a reliable indication of demand.

Future potential for product: *Use* a time frame of 3 to 5 years (the period covering the strategic sections of your SMP) to forecast the potential for your product, and try to use the same unit of measurement as that used for determining current demand.

Industry life cycle: *Identify,* even in broad terms, the stage the industry is at in its life cycle — for example, introduction, growth, maturity, or decline.

Emerging technology: *Identify* specific technology that is currently available or may be in use even on an experimental basis with competitors. Determine where the technology is coming from and who holds patents or copyrights.

Changing customer profiles: *Use* segmentation techniques (identified earlier in this chapter) to track any emerging changes in demographics, geographics, or psychographics.

Frequency of new product introductions: *Monitor* the introduction of new products to establish if there is an industry pattern that can serve as a standard for your own level of product development.

Level of government regulation: *Determine* if government regulation is increasing or declining and assess the impact on your industry.

Distribution networks: *Indicate* if there are any innovations in the use of distributor channels. For example, is there emphasis on pushing the product through distributors, or pulling the product through the channel by influencing the end user, or perhaps eliminating distributors entirely. Also determine if there is evidence of forward integration in which producers are acquiring distributors.

Entry and exit barriers: *Assess* the ease or difficulty of entering and exiting an industry. Entry barriers include amount of capital investment needed, extent of economies of scale, access to distribution channels, and opportunities for product differentiation.

Exit barriers include: types and value of fixed assets, length of time needed in market through labor contracts, leases, services and parts provided to customers, and government regulations.

Marketing innovation: *Determine* if there are innovations involving areas such as electronic ordering systems, computer-driven diagnostic systems, interactive product demonstrations, new promotional incentives, Internet advertising (E-commerce), and sales force utilization.

Cost structures: *Evaluate* the impact of economies of scale on costs and profits as they relate to manufacturing, purchasing, R&D, marketing, and distribution. Determine specifically the impact on costs of the current movement to automation and its potential impact on your industry.

Summarizing: Industry analysis helps you define many factors in your industry, such as customer profiles, existing and emerging competitors, products, and technology.

By giving you a picture of the overall industry from all these vantage points, industry analysis lets you look at industry trends so you can stake out opportunities for growth. Such an analysis benefits you in preparing SMP Sections 1, 4, and 6.

2.7 SCANNING THE ENVIRONMENT

The final part of looking at your market concerns the environment and its impact on business opportunities. Scanning the environment permits you to look outward within a framework of adding credibility to your SMP Section 1 (Strategic Direction).

Also, the value of looking at environmental influences opens fresh possibilities as you focus on new markets and products in SMP Section 4 (Business Portfolio). The following is a sampling from principle categories.

Conducting an Environmental Analysis

Demographics

What potential do the following circumstances hold for your SMP?

1. World population is expected to reach 6.2 billion by the year 2000. Although much of the population growth will occur within poor countries, there will be potential markets for foods, medicines, machines, clothing, agricultural products, and various low-technology products.
2. The U.S. population is projected for very slow growth to 264 million by the year 2000. Environmental issues are contributing to the slowdown in the birth rate and the movement to smaller families, the increasing number of women working outside the home, and improved methods of birth control. Possible areas of growth include convenience items, new types of foods, quantity and styles of clothes, and number of automobiles per family.

Economics

What potential do the following circumstances hold for your SMP?

1. With the continuing intensity of competition from the Pacific Rim and Europe, there is tremendous pressure on U.S. firms to stay competitive. Although there has been a revitalization of U.S. manufacturing during the 1990s, many firms still buy finished products abroad — resulting from the ongoing trends of reengineering, downsizing, and outsourcing. In turn, these trends reflect in the

new lean organizations, such as Du Pont, Dow Chemical, Xerox, General Motors, and AT&T.

2. The various economic cycles have an impact on consumer spending patterns. During downturns in the economy the basics of food, housing, and clothing require a good part of household income. During rising economic periods, such products as transportation, medical care, and recreation take on an increasing proportion of expenditures. It is especially important to utilize economic forecasting if your business is income sensitive. With sufficient forewarning, you can take the steps necessary to exploit the economic cycle or to guard against its negative effect on your operation.

Natural Resources

What potential do the following circumstances hold for your SMP?

1. U.S. government reports indicate that diminishing supplies of oil, coal, and various minerals could pose a serious problem; that the quantities of platinum, gold, zinc, and lead are not sufficient to meet demands.

   And by the year 2050, several more minerals may be exhausted if the current rate of consumption continues. Diminishing supplies of other resources, such as wood and water, are continuing to pose problems in many areas of the world. While firms that use these resources face cost increases and potential shortages, for other firms there is the exciting prospect of discovering new sources of materials or alternative synthetic products for natural resources.

2. The availability and cost of energy continue to be major factors for the future economic growth of the U.S. and other countries around the world. In the meantime, an intensive search continues for alternative forms of energy, with investigations taking place to harness solar, nuclear, wind, and other forms of energy. Some firms are searching for ways to make practical products using alternative forms of energy, such as the joint venture between automobile companies and electric utilities to come up with a reliable electric automobile.

Technology

What potential do the following circumstances hold for your SMP?

1. The often quoted statistic that 90% of all the scientists who ever lived are alive today sums up the accelerating pace of technological change. Only in the past few years has technology resulted in a tremendous number of new high-tech products, with audio and video links from workplace to home to other distant locations. New technological advances are changing the way workers are handling their jobs.

2. The U.S. still leads the world in research and development expenditures, with Japan a close second. The U.S. is reported to have 12,000 academic, government, and industrial laboratories. Research continues in such areas as cancer cures, chemical control of mental illness, household robots, new types of nutritional foods, clones, and other types of spectacular products. Organizations are forming joint ventures with either U.S. or foreign organizations to bolster their research and development capability.

Legislation

What potential do the following circumstances hold for your SMP?

1. Businesses are in various stages of regulation and deregulation. Some of the businesses that have entered into the deregulation phase are airlines, banks, utilities, and insurance companies. Yet these, too, are constantly being watched for possible infractions of the law. In general, legislation has a number of purposes: (1) to protect companies from one another with respect to competition; (2) to protect consumers from unfair business practices; and (3) to protect the larger interest of society against unscrupulous business behavior.

2. Within the political and legal environment, the number of public interest groups is increasing. These groups lobby government officials and put pressure on managers to pay more attention to minority rights, senior citizen rights, women's rights, and consumer fights in general. They also deal with such areas as cleaning up the environment and protecting natural resources.

Cultural Values

What potential do the following circumstances hold for your SMP?

1. Cultural values also come and go. The three basic components of culture (things, ideas, and behavior patterns) undergo additions,

deletions, or modifications. Some components die out, new ones are accepted, and existing ones can be changed in some observable way.

2. Society holds a variety of values. Some are classified as primary beliefs and values and tend to be long lasting. These values relate to work, marriage, charity, and honesty. They are usually passed on from parents to children and are reinforced within the institutions of schools, churches, businesses, and government.

Summarizing: in conducting your environmental analysis, focus on six categories of environmental factors: demographics, economics, natural resources, technology, legislation, and cultural values. The scenarios provided should help you focus on the major environmental events that might affect the overall direction of your SMP.

PART 3: LOOKING AT YOUR COMPANY

3.1 LOOKING AT YOUR COMPANY

Developing an ingenious SMP is one thing; implementing it is quite another consideration. Looking at the innards of your company enables you to examine its capabilities, as well as your ability to implement the SMP. As you analyze your company's strengths and weaknesses, also match your strong points against those weak spots of competitors so that you can mount an effective competitive attack.

It is this type of precision analysis that allows you to determine what state of readiness your operation is in to win against competition. To get a complete picture of your organization, you need to evaluate it along the following lines:

- *Performance* relates to organizational structure, people, culture, systems, resource utilization, innovation, and productivity. It examines the ability to react to aggressive competition, to defend existing markets, and to attack new markets.
- *Strategic priorities* concern the long-term effects on strategic direction, commitment to quality, customer orientation, and human resource development.
- *Cost analysis* relates to achieving competitive advantage.
- *Portfolio* reviews markets and the strengths of business units in each market.
- *Financial resources* studies the availability of cash within different competitive scenarios.
- *Strength/weakness* surveys areas of distinctive competencies and types of unique assets.

Let's examine these six factors in greater detail.

3.2 YOUR COMPANY'S PERFORMANCE

Looking at your company begins with a thoroughgoing examination of the organizational structure of a company, division, business unit, or department. It is within that unique structure that business life exists and where the relationships with those of the same level, with superiors, or subordinates interact.

It is also within the organizational unit that the SMP consisting of product, promotion, pricing, and distribution strategies emerges. It is where leadership is exercised, which influences the individual attitudes and collective morale of individuals within the group.

Various schools of thought extol the merits of either a highly structured or loosely run operation. With either form, organizational structure and culture do exist. You need to shape your own company and then evaluate its effectiveness in supporting your SMP — with its long-term objectives and strategies.

Organizing for Marketing

Organization involves the structuring of various elements to achieve a smooth interplay between people (positions) and the work they perform (activities). These are the two basic elements that you can structure within a company.

Organization by positions is called *structural organization* (or chain of command), while organization by activities is labeled *process organization*. Structural organization identifies the authority and responsibilities associated with each job. Since this job-related package normally changes very little over time, it can be considered static. When converted into a diagram, it takes the form of an organization chart.

In contrast, the main objectives of a process organization are to streamline the accomplishment of specific tasks and to facilitate control over the progress of a project. Thus, it should be clear that the nature of a process organization is dynamic — that is, task-related — and, therefore, subject to review and possible change.

Basic Organizational Alternatives

The product–market mix of your firm, as well as the competitive situation in the marketplace, may have changed dramatically over the years. Whatever the present structure, it probably warrants review for its resourcefulness, flexibility, efficiency, and ability to compete in a global environment. Only an organization that is fully in tune with the market will realize its potential.

In trying to evolve the optimum organizational setup to achieve competitive advantages, you should examine the four major alternatives open to most firms: *functional organization, geographic organization, product organization,* and *market organization.*

Functional Organization

A functional organization of the marketing area works best for small- to medium-size companies. It assigns responsibilities and creates positions to conform to the various functions to be performed, resulting in a horizontal division of labor, which in turn results in specialization.

The basic strength of this approach lies in assigning the ultimate responsibility for the marketing function with a single individual. Functional organization is the only setup in which there is no duplication or paralleling of functions. Within a functional framework, the responsibility of each manager thus extends to the entire product and market mix.

As a firm grows, however, this kind of functional setup can become unwieldy and cumbersome, unable either to respond quickly or pay proper attention to specific products or markets. Concentration of functional responsibility in one person, initially a virtue, now becomes a drawback. To avoid dilution of effort, further specialization and more individualized attention to products and markets take priority. If you want to continue to achieve optimum results, duplication of functions is the price that inevitably has to be paid for growth.

Geographic Organization

Some managers choose to organize their marketing effort along geographic lines. A geographic subdivision can be organized easily because territorial borderlines are usually drawn along geopolitical boundaries. Also, the sales effort is readily integrated into the marketing effort, since territories are already defined. However, geographic organization doesn't preclude you from defining different forms of buying behavior within a segment.

Product Management Organization

Product management becomes necessary when the complexity of the product mix threatens to overtax the functional system, resulting in a dilution of effort that leaves many products virtually unattended. The advent of product management brings order and focus to this disarray by clearly lodging responsibility for the fate of a specific product or product line with a single individual, ensuring it the attention it requires. This approach fosters individualized marketing programs for each product or product line — and often results in aggressive internal competition for funds and sales force time.

The responsibilities of a product manager are far reaching. He or she must:

- Provide for the assigned product line a continuing series of programs and projects designed to improve market position and profitability

- Mold the marketing effort according to changing consumer demands
- Coordinate the activities of the firm's functional units with a view toward achieving short- and long-range product objectives
- Act as an intelligence center for all relevant information concerning the product line
- Analyze market potential and develop marketing strategies
- Generate communications campaigns
- Stimulate interest in and support of the product line among the sales force and distributor network

The main advantage of the product management system is that every product or product line has its own advocate whose personal career is directly dependent on the success or failure of the line administered.

Market Organization

Focusing too strongly on an individual product or line may well detract from the main mission of your firm — namely, to serve the needs of its target customers and those of its existing products. Thus, many firms are revamping their organizations to become customer oriented instead of product oriented.

Whatever is lost in product expertise in such a reshuffling effort is gained in market expertise. Each market manager becomes a specialist in the particular needs and problems of a specific group of customers. In many other respects, market organization is comparable to product organization: marketing managers also have to develop annual and long-term sales and profit plans and do not have their own support systems, either.

Therefore, they must rely on much the same set of tools as their product manager counterparts. As for the smaller firm where there is no individual with a marketing title, then the owner or general manager acts as the chief marketing executive.

Choosing the Right Setup

Given such a range of choices, it is not easy to decide on the optimum solution for your firm. The following guidelines should prove helpful:

- While a company with a small number of product lines can do well with a functional organization, a wide range of lines requires product management.
- If your product mix is fairly homogeneous, you can rely on a functional organization, whereas a heterogeneous collection of products warrants product management.

- Highly technical and complex products require product expertise, which is the cornerstone of the product management system.
- Mostly homogeneous markets can be served by a functional or product setup, while heterogeneous markets demand a market organization that responds to their unique needs and buying patterns.
- The size of your firm is another factor. If it is of small or medium size, a functional organization is likely to work well for you. The geographic dispersion of your markets should also be considered. If they are regional, or otherwise fairly concentrated, a product or market setup is a good choice. But if they are dispersed over a large area, you should look into the advantages of a geographic setup.

3.3 YOUR COMPANY'S STRATEGIC PRIORITIES

Your look at the internal workings of your company continues with an examination of how your firm, and in particular how your group, looks at its long-term strategic priorities — as defined in the strategic direction, objectives, strategies, and business portfolio of your SMP.

The level of market orientation is the focal point from which strategic priorities emerge. For instance, does a customer-driven mentality exist in your organization, or is it just given lip service? How much commitment is given to product quality and long-term market development?

You need to understand what makes your company tick. Success in the marketplace doesn't just happen. It usually evolves over years of absorbing hard-won skills, nurturing them into competencies to fit the explosive movements in your industry and, in turn, shapes your firm's core competencies into strategic priorities.

Consumer-Oriented vs. Product-Oriented Concepts

As you develop your SMP, keep in mind that the consumer-oriented concept of marketing is a far cry from the old product-oriented philosophy, whereby the producer developed a product without input from the ultimate buyer and then used promotional pressure to persuade the consumer to buy it. In contrast to this one-way approach, the consumer-oriented concept is cyclical in nature, putting the consumer at the beginning and the end of the marketing process.

The product-oriented concept is shortsighted and usually distorts efforts to develop strategic priorities. It focuses on the needs of the seller and thus leaves a company vulnerable to the inroads of competitors who may be more sensitive to consumer needs and desires. Table 5.3.1 contrasts the differences between the two concepts.

Table 5.3.1 Characteristics of the Two Concepts of Marketing	
Product-Oriented	*Consumer-Oriented*
Focus on product	Focus on consumer
Emphasis on volume	Emphasis on profit
Insignificant marketing research	Thorough marketing research
Engineering self-guided	Engineering guided by marketing
Primarily interested in production economies	Primarily interested in providing need satisfaction
Aiming for short-term gains	Aiming for long-term relationships
Management engineering oriented	Management marketing oriented

Accordingly, marketing research is a key element of consumer-oriented marketing. Based on consumer preferences and problems that have been researched, a company can specify with some confidence what features an upcoming product should include.

Instead of trying to create markets for products, you are now attempting to provide products for markets.

The entire thrust of your firm is now aimed at discovering and exploiting market opportunities. This reorientation is accompanied by another remarkable change: *companies are no longer married to technologies and existing products, but rather to consumers and their evolving wants and problems.*

Characteristics and Benefits of Consumer-Oriented Planning

Following this examination of the primary concepts of consumer-oriented marketing, now let's take a closer took at its operational characteristics and impact. Table 5.3.2 highlights ways in which the concept penetrates every facet of your marketing effort, and lists the benefits derived from its application.

By using such a systematic approach, you can pinpoint and improve areas of weakness. You may want to convert the specific action suggestions into a personal checklist.

Implementing Consumer-Oriented Marketing

How can you implement a new marketing concept if your firm is still using the old product-oriented approach? Table 5.3.3 presents an action program that you can include in your SMP for implementing the consumer-oriented concept. The result column gives information on the benefits of each step in the program.

**Table 5.3.2   The Consumer-Oriented Marketing Concept
and Marketing Behavior**

Area	Action	Benefit
Organization	Set up a separate marketing function under a vice-president who reports directly to the company president	Stresses importance of marketing and puts it on equal footing with other functional areas, such as engineering and production
Strategic Marketing Planning (SMP)	Base the SMP on systematic marketing research; try to project technological and market trends sufficiently far into the future; set objectives and communicate basic assumptions and objectives	Keeps corporate effort truly attuned with markets; provides adequate lead time for developing programs, products, and facilities for future markets; creates a common framework for the SMP that becomes clearly goal oriented
Control	Institute tight feedback system to check results of the SMP	Keeps your "ear to the ground" and enables timely corrective action
Research on consumer behavior	Investigate consumer wants, needs, desires, problems, habits, views, satisfactions, and dissatisfactions	Establishes necessary communications link to consumer to fine tune marketing effort
Legal aspects	Examine legal ramifications of planned marketing activities	Determines legal requirements and framework for your marketing effort
Global marketing	Adjust marketing effort to specific environments	Makes marketing more suited to particular circumstances and likely to be more successful
Marketing strategy	Identify target markets that are emerging, neglected, or poorly served	Pinpoints specific needs and wants in order to serve them better which, in turn, breeds loyalty

Table 5.3.2   The Consumer-Oriented Marketing Concept and Marketing Behavior (Continued)

Area	Action	Benefit
Product	Base product specifications on marketing research; make package appealing and distinctive; select memorable, meaningful brand name	Keeps product design in line with consumer wants and problems; makes "silent salesperson" on the shelf easily recognized and persuasive; suggests important quality of product and is remembered
Pricing	Set prices in line with market value of product, as perceived by consumers	Ensures optimum salability because product is neither underpriced nor overpriced in consumers' eyes
Promotion	Stress benefits that consumer will derive from product instead of glorifying its features; position product properly with respect to competition; aid your dealers through displays, point-of-purchase materials, and generous advertising	Gives consumers good, convincing reasons to buy your product over others; gives product clear-cut profile in consumers' minds; generates consumer business and dealer loyalty
Selling	Advise your customers on how they can derive the most profit from your product instead of overloading them with stock; train your dealers in product knowledge and sales techniques	Makes your salespeople welcome because they bring profits; makes knowledgeable dealers do better, long-term business

Table 5.3.2 The Consumer-Oriented Marketing Concept and Marketing Behavior *(Continued)*		
Area	*Action*	*Benefit*
Distribution	Be selective in choosing distributors; have them fit distribution policy objectives; give your dealers adequate support in terms of product availability and service	Associates your product with the right kind of outlet; gives dealers good reasons to buy from your company

You can use the table as a checklist for actions performed and benefits to be derived. (In your SMP, you might find it helpful to use the left-hand margin to indicate who will perform the action and the time frame for its accomplishment.)

The action program provides a comprehensive overview and permits further details to validate and support your firm's strategic priorities. Without a vigorous enactment program, the "good idea" of the consumer-oriented marketing concept, initially greeted with great enthusiasm, becomes too easily diluted, neglected, and ultimately abused. It is easy to bask in the self-congratulatory, ivory-tower atmosphere of new-product ingenuity and, in the process, forget the most important element — the consumer.

The consumer-oriented marketing concept brings you back to the basics of sensitivity to consumer needs. Periodic reapplication of this action program can provide your company with invaluable survival insurance. That means, tune in to the dynamics of your marketplace because needs and problems change, as do attitudes and habits.

Catering to these changes differentiates your product in a consumer's mind from those of your competitors', thus creating a firm niche for it in the marketplace. Failure to recognize or regard these changes could spell disaster for your product and your company.

3.4 YOUR COMPANY'S COSTS

The third component of looking at your company focuses on costs. If you conduct a cost analysis to maintain a balance of costs and expenditures that are synchronized with your SMP objectives, you don't have to compromise between market share and profitability goals.

Here are practical guidelines, with implications on how to maintain a balance among market share growth, costs, and profitability:

Table 5.3.3   An Action Program for Implementing the Consumer-Oriented Marketing Concept

Step	Result
1. Find out what your ultimate buyers like/dislike about your product and the way in which it is marketed	Provides invaluable assessment of what you are doing right/wrong
2. Determine which changes and/or new products they would like to see	Shows how you can protect your business and make more money
3. Examine the differences that consumers perceive between your product and its better-selling competitors, if any	Enables you to evaluate and, possibly, correct your competitive positioning
4. Draw up a plan aimed at improving consumer satisfaction and profits	Setting objectives and aiming to achieve them is the only way to grow systematically
5. Ensure top-level and full organizational support	New marketing programs can only be successful if they enjoy the full support of the entire organization
6. Initiate appropriate modifications and/or development projects	A steady flow of tailor-made new products emerge
7. Test consumer reaction to new product(s)	You "feel out" probable large-scale reception of your new product and can make final adjustments
8. Launch new product(s) in market	Full-scale presentation and availability of your innovation to your target market
9. Follow up with consumer research to find out whether or not the changes you instituted paid off	Feedback permits you to modify current situation and streamline future activities
10. Keep attuned to evolving trends in the marketplace	Helps you foresee changes and deal with them early

1. While large expenditures are required to build market share, it takes less promotional expenditures as a percentage of sales to maintain market share.
2. Look at the criteria you use to evaluate market share. If you serve a segment rather than an overall market, there are implications for costs and profitability. For instance, examine market share based

on customer type, region, and the type of support provided through on-site technical service, overnight delivery, price contracts, guaranteed product performance, and so on.

3. It is less expensive to defend market share by investing in value-added services and differentiated products than it is to buy back market share after being pushed out by competitors.

4. Examine the following components that contribute to increases in market share and determine what actions would impact your cost structure and profitability:

- *Customer penetration.* What would increase the total number of customers who would buy your product by segment, compared to reaching the overall market?
- *Customer loyalty.* What would increase the purchase of your product compared to your customers' total purchases from all vendors of the same product?
- *Customer usage.* How could you raise the quantity of your customers' purchases, compared to the average-size order from competitors?
- *Price selectivity.* What would determine the profitability of your product at the average price charged, compared to the average price charged by all companies selling the product? (For meaningful comparisons, express all changes as percentages.)

To have a broader decision base from which to select a strategy, you will need to understand cost from the standpoints of the *experience curve* and *sales forecasting.*

Experience Curve

Understanding the experience curve gives you an added dimension to look at costs as they relate to strategy options in SMP Section 3 (Growth Strategies) and Section 8 (Tactics) for your own company, as well as for your competitors.

Much of the work on the experience curve began in the mid-1960s when the Boston Consulting Group (BCG) and others conducted thousands of cost studies. The results showed that each time the cumulative volume of a product doubled, the total value-added costs — including administration, sales, marketing, distribution, in addition to manufacturing — fell by a constant and predictable percentage.

Further, the cost of purchased items usually fell as suppliers reduced prices as their costs fell, also due to the experience effect. This relationship between costs and experience is called the *experience curve.*

Key Factors Causing the Experience Curve

Knowing that costs will be reduced by a fixed percentage each time production doubles is only part of the equation. The other parts are in knowing which factors contribute to the experience curve and then consciously incorporating those factors in planning your strategy.

Some of the key factors include *labor productivity, work methods, production and technology efficiency,* and *product design and materials.* Let's examine each:

Labor Productivity

Labor productivity goes beyond the factory floor to the white-collar jobs of middle management. During the 1980s and 1990s, there was a widespread trend to downsize and wipe out layers of employees, with the aim of reducing the organization into a "lean and mean" operation.

In place of permanent workers, contingency or temporary workers were used on an as-needed basis, followed by an expanded use of outsourcing. These actions further reduced labor costs in such areas as employee benefits. Concurrent with the downsizing of organizations, continued productivity encouraged middle managers to become more innovative and entrepreneurial in planning and strategy development.

Work Methods

Paralleling labor productivity was the critical look at the methods workers used to complete a task. Outside consultants used reengineering techniques to examine and make recommendations about such methods. That approach also focused on problem solving, with teams of workers using techniques from the numerous total quality programs, along with fresh applications of new technology to redesign and simplify work operations. Most importantly, the work methods had an overall effect of bonding with customers to strengthen relationships.

Production and Technology Efficiency

Tremendous progress has been made in factory automation with the use of robots, computer-aided design (CAD), computer-aided manufacturing (CAM), and integrated manufacturing techniques. While some companies faltered initially and did not experience cost reductions, the evidence became clear that such factory automation significantly reduced costs to the point that in many instances unit costs of manufacturing dropped below that of the most inexpensive Asian labor. Executives at one of IBM's fully automated manufacturing plants claimed that it could produce computer printers at a lower cost and at a higher quality than those it previously purchased from Asian sources.

Product Design and Materials

Greater efficiency through experience is gained when product design and manufacturing work together. Also contributing to efficiency is the use of new space-age materials, such as ceramics, and new lightweight metals and epoxies. However, for an increasing number of U.S. companies, the efficiencies may not be realized completely if the trend continues toward separating product design from manufacturing through the shifting of production to overseas locations.

Strategy Implications

The implication of the experience curve is that it is prudent to accumulate experience faster than competitors do. One approach to accumulating experience suggests pursuing a first-into-the-market strategy and going for a large share of the market.

Another is to be a follow-the-leader into a market, assess the mistakes of the leader, and move rapidly to dominate an emerging, neglected, or poorly served market segment. If you can accumulate experience faster than competitors, with the corresponding reductions in costs, then you have the advantage of price flexibility to use as a weapon to attack a competitor's position.

The negative side of this scenario could result in becoming a slave to the experience curve by adopting a production-driven mentality rather than a market-driven orientation. For example, if the production-driven approach prevents responding to such changing consumer patterns as demands for just-in-time delivery, accepting orders for short-run customized parts, or reacting to competitors' innovations, then the cost efficiencies will have a negative effect in a changing marketplace.

In summary, the marketing strategy implications of the experience curve are

1. A competitive advantage is possible if you *accumulate greater experience than your competitors.* The resulting cost advantage can be used to plow back investment to achieve additional manufacturing efficiencies to improve products, shore up the marketing effort, or build market share through lower prices. This advantage also serves to unbalance competitors' expansion moves.

If your strategy calls for using a low price to buy market share rapidly, then it is essential that your company gains experience as rapidly as possible, certainly faster than your competitors. Further, the push for market share should begin early in the life cycle of the product.

2. Within the context of identifying competitor behavior, it is important to examine your competitors' experience curves. It is not a simple task and certainly needs the cooperation of your production, purchasing, and financial staff to create examples of different experience curves under a variety of pricing scenarios.

3. Experience curves can be used to forecast costs, which in turn can be used to set prices. However, costs and prices are usually calculated on the basis of a reasonably accurate sales forecast. The major quantitative contribution marketing people can make to these calculations is to provide a reliable sales forecast.

Sales Forecasting

Company sales normally result from the interaction of your company's marketing effort with marketing opportunities. Add to that any constraints imposed by the competition and the general economic climate. Taking all these contributing factors into account, it is' the task of forecasting to furnish a set of alternative sales potentials derived from various market scenarios, along with the probable effect on sales under each condition.

As a manager, you can use these sales potentials as a frame of reference in developing your objectives in SMP Sections 2 and 7 and in assessing your marketing opportunities in Section 6. Estimating sales also helps in evaluating the payoffs of your marketing strategies under a variety of conditions. You can then deploy company resources to take full advantage of the opportunities open to you.

A well-managed forecasting program will make projections in time to allow you to alter your SMP and develop alternative objectives and strategies before a negative situation is too far gone. Such a program can also provide you with frequent comparisons of actual-to-forecast figures so you can revise your tactics during the forecast period.

Forecasting Techniques

Although various computer models are available to do sales forecasts, time and budget restrictions often bar their use. Rather, executives usually rely on a set of relatively simple, quick, do-it-yourself techniques that substantially reduce the time and money required in forecasting. There are a number of such forecasting techniques that, along with subjective judgment, add precision to sales estimates. However, it is advisable to use multiple approaches for arriving at estimated sales. If they all yield similar results, you can place great confidence in your figures.

The following nonmathematical forecasting techniques can be roughly subdivided into (1) judgmental methods, involving the opinions of various kinds of experts such as executives, salespeople, and informed outsiders; and (2) market surveys using buyer surveys and market tests.

Judgment from the Extremes

Judgment from the extremes involves asking for an expert's opinion as to whether or not future sales are likely to be at an extremely high or extremely low level. If the expert's reaction is that neither seems probable, the range between the extremes is successively reduced until an approximate level of expected sales is reached. Resulting in a range rather than a single-figure estimate, this approach is appropriate in situations where experts feel incapable of giving one-level forecasts.

Group Discussion Method

As a quick check on figures arrived at by other methods, the manager frequently feels that a number of specialists should be invited to participate in forecasting. Most often, the team meets as a committee and comes up with a group estimate through consensus. This group discussion method has the advantage of merging divergent viewpoints and moderating individual biases. You should, however, guard against the potential disadvantage of one or more individuals dominating the discussion, or offering superficial responses where there is a lack of individual responsibility.

Pooled Individual Estimates Method

While the pooled individual estimates method avoids the potential pitfalls of group discussions, it also lacks the benefits of group dynamics. A project leader simply merges separately supplied estimates into a single estimate, without any interplay with or between the participants.

Delphi Technique

An increasingly popular method for forecasting is the Delphi technique, which overcomes the drawbacks of both group discussion and pooled individual estimates methods. In this approach, group members are asked to submit individual estimates and assumptions. These are reviewed by the project leader, revised, and fed back to the participants for a second round.

Participants are also informed of the median forecast level that emerged from the previous round. Domination, undue conservatism, and argument are eliminated because of the written, rather than oral, procedure, and the group members benefit from one another's input. After successive rounds of estimating and feedback, the process ends when a consensus emerges.

Jury of Executive Opinion

As mentioned, the experts consulted in one or more of these methods typically are recruited from one of three pools: executives, salespeople, and informed outsiders. A jury of executive opinion is often composed of top-level personnel from various key functions such as sales, production, and finance.

The major advantage of this type of source is that forecasts can be arrived at quickly. This advantage is, however, easily outweighed by the disadvantage inherent in involving people in the estimating process whom, in spite of their high rank, are relatively unfamiliar with the forces that shape marketing success.

Composite of Sales Force Opinion

The composite of sales force opinion approach collects product, customer, and/or territorial estimates from individual salespeople in the field. Since they are in constant contact with customers, salespeople should be in a position to predict buying plans and needs. They may even be able to take into account probable competitive activity.

Few companies simply add up the estimates of their sales force to compute the sales forecast. Since sales quotas are frequently based on these estimates, a salesperson will tend to be conservative or pessimistic in estimating sales. This tendency can be partially corrected by rewarding accuracy and distributing company data, industry trends, and records showing the accuracy of past forecasts.

Outside Experts

When it comes to outside experts, any knowledgeable source could be consulted — for example, trade associations or economists. Marketing researchers and industry consultants are another valuable resource, together with dealers and distributors. However, it is generally difficult to assess the degree of familiarity with industry conditions and evolving trends by such outsiders. Thus, they should be used with caution and only in a supplementary capacity.

Consumer Surveys

The judgmental methods just described involve estimates by people who are not themselves the ultimate buyers. Some observers consider this fact a weakness and suggest getting the word directly from "the horse's mouth."

Surveys of consumer buying intentions are particularly appropriate when past trends (such as energy consumption) are unlikely to continue or historical data (as for a new product or market) do not exist. This technique works best for major consumer durables and industrial capital expenditures, since these types of buying decisions require a considerable amount of planning and lead time, and the respondents are able to predict their own behavior with reasonable accuracy.

Test Marketing

The problem of accuracy can be remedied by using the test-marketing approach whereby a new product, or a variation in the marketing mix for an established one, is introduced in a limited number of test locations. The entire marketing program that is scheduled on a national basis is put into effect, scaled down to the local level, but otherwise identical in every detail, including advertising, pricing, packaging, and so forth.

The new marketing effort now has to compete in a real sales environment. Purchases are actual, not hypothetical. If carefully chosen and monitored, test markets provide a significant minipicture of the full-scale reaction to the planned change. On the basis of actual sales results in the test markets, sales forecasts are simply scaled up by appropriate factors (Table 5.3.4).

3.5 YOUR COMPANY'S PORTFOLIO OF PRODUCTS AND MARKETS

Used in SMP Section 4, your company's business portfolio consists of formal models that provide a systematic approach to assessing a competitive position and determining investment levels. In practice, portfolio analysis is used for self-contained organizational units — divisions, strategic business units (SBUs), departments, and product lines — in which you make investment decisions on a market-by-market or product-by-product basis.

Table 5.3.4 Comparison of Nonmathematical Forecasting Methods

Method	Nature	Benefits	Drawbacks
Judgmental			
Judgment from the extremes	Successive narrowing of high/low range	Range instead of single figure	Depends on individual estimating
Group discussion	Group consensus estimate	Merges divergent views, moderate biases	Domination by one individual, superficiality
Pooled and individual estimates	Averaging of individual estimates	Avoids group discussion pitfalls	Lacks group dynamics
Delphi technique	Successive written rounds of estimating with feedback from other participants	Eliminates domination, conservatism, superficial response	Lacks group dynamics
Jury of executive opinion	Top-level committee	Quick	Unfamiliar with market conditions
Composite of sales force opinion	Adjusted estimates from individual salespeople	Front-line expertise, motivational tool	Bias due to impact on compensation, unfamiliar with economic trends
Outside experts	Merging of outside opinions	No bias due to personal interests	Difficult to assess degree of expertise
Market Surveys			
Consumer surveys	Consumer interviews about buying intentions	Directly from "the horse's mouth"	Hypothetical behavior
Test marketing	Sale in limited number of cities	Actual sales results	Costly, time-consuming, exposes strategy to competitors

Your job is to seek out the information needed for these portfolio approaches and determine which approach suits your business. The results can help in systematically analyzing your situation and in developing competitive strategies.

The following section describes three of the more popular models used in portfolio analysis and which can apply to your business: *BCG Growth-Share Matrix, General Electric Business Screen,* and the *Arthur D. Little Matrix.*

BCG Growth-Share Matrix

With a technique developed by the Boston Consulting Group, this classic model has proven highly useful in assessing a portfolio of businesses or products. BCG Growth Share Matrix (Figure 5.1) graphically shows that some products may enjoy a strong position relative to those of competitors, while other products languish in a weaker position.

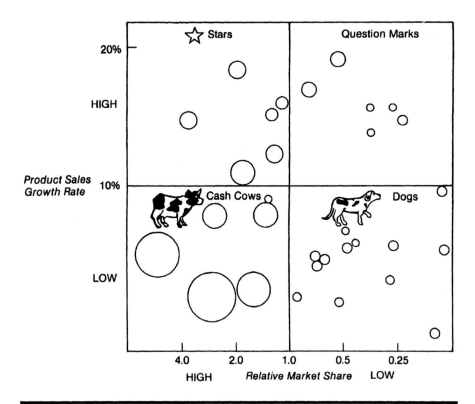

Figure 5.1   BCG Growth–Share Matrix

Also, each product has its own total strategy, depending on its position in the matrix. The various circles represent a product. And from the positioning of these circles management can determine the following information:

- Dollar sales — represented by the area of the circle
- Market share — relative to the firm's largest competitor, as shown by horizontal position
- Growth rate — relative to the market in which the product competes, as shown by vertical position

In addition, the quadrants of the matrix categorize products into four groups:

1. *Stars:* products that have high market growth and high market share. These products need constant attention to maintain or increase share through active promotion, product improvement, and careful pricing strategies.
2. *Cash cows:* products that have low market growth and high market share. Such products usually hold market dominance and generate strong cash flow. The object: retain a strong market presence without large expenditures for promotion and with minimal outlay for R&D. The central idea behind the cash cow is that businesses with a large share of market are more profitable than their smaller-share competitors.
3. *Question marks* (also known as problem children or wildcats): products with potential for high growth in a fast-moving market, but with low market share. They absorb large amounts of cash (usually from the cash cows) and are expected to reach the status of a star.
4. *Dogs:* products with low market growth and low market share, reflecting the worst of all situations. A number of alternatives are possible: maintain the product in the line to support the image of being a full-line supplier, eliminate the product from the line, or harvest the product through a slow phasing out.

As you review the growth–share matrix, note on the vertical axis that product sales are separated into high and low quadrants. The 10% growth line is simply an arbitrary rate of growth and represents a middle level. For your particular industry the number could be 5, 12, or 15%.

Similarly, on the horizontal axis there is a dividing line of relative market share of 1.0 so that positioning your product in the lower left-hand quadrant would indicate high market leadership, and in the lower right-hand quadrant, low market leadership.

The significant interpretations from the matrix are as follows:

- The amount of cash generated increases with relative market share. (This point was borne out in the section covering the experience curve.)
- The amount of sales growth requires proportional cash input to finance the added capacity and market development. If market share is maintained, then cash requirements increase only relative to market growth rate.
- From a manager's point of view, cash input is required to keep up with market growth. Increasing market share usually requires cash to support advertising and sales promotion expenditures, lower prices, and other share-building tactics. On the other hand, a decrease in market share may provide cash for use in other product areas.
- In situations where a product moves toward maturity, it is possible to use enough funds to maintain market position and use surplus funds to reinvest in other products that are still growing.

In summary, the BCG Growth–Share Matrix permits you to evaluate where your products and markets are relative to those of your competitors and what investments are needed relative to such basic strategies as building share for your product, holding share, harvesting, and withdrawing from the market.

General Electric Business Screen

The BCG Growth–Share Matrix focuses on cash flow and uses only two variables: growth and market share. The General Electric Business Screen (Figure 5.2), on the other hand, is a more comprehensive, multifactor analysis that provides a graphic display of where an existing product fits competitively in relation to a variety of criteria. It also aids in projecting the chances for the success of a new product.

The key points in using the GE Business Screen are the following:

1. *Industry attractiveness* is shown on the vertical axis of the matrix. It is based on rating such factors as market size, market growth rate, profit margin, competitive intensity, cyclicality, seasonality, and scale of economies. Each factor is given a weight classifying an industry, market segment, or product as high, medium, or low in overall attractiveness.

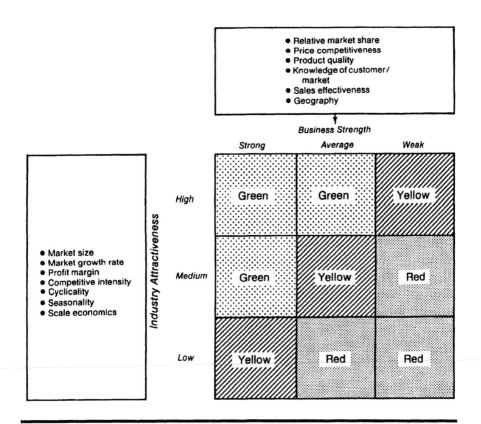

Figure 5.2   General Electric Business Screen

2. *Business strength* is shown on the horizontal axis. A weighted rating is made for such factors as relative market share, price competitiveness, product quality, knowledge of customer and market, sales effectiveness, and geography. The results show the ability to compete and, in turn, provide insight into developing strategies in relation to competitors.

3. Three color sectors divide the matrix: green, yellow, and red. The green sector has three cells at the upper left and indicates those markets that are favorable in industry attractiveness and business strength. These markets indicate a "go" to move in aggressively.

    The yellow sector includes the diagonal cells stretching from the lower left to the upper right. This sector indicates a medium level in overall attractiveness.

    The red sector covers the three cells in the lower right. This sector indicates those markets that are low in overall attractiveness.

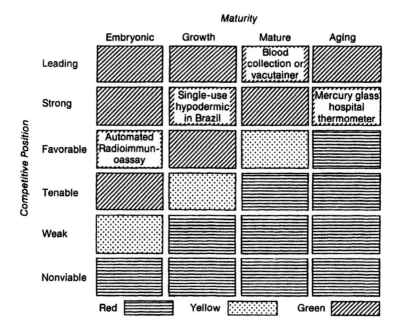

Figure 5.3 Arthur D. Little Matrix Applied to Products

Arthur D. Little Matrix

Another time-tested portfolio analysis approach is associated with the consulting organization, Arthur D. Little Inc. In one actual application, a major manufacturer in the healthcare industry used this approach to analyze how its various products stacked up in market share. In Figure 5.3, some of the company's products are used to demonstrate the function of this matrix.

First, note the similarities of this format to the other portfolio analysis approaches already discussed. The competitive positions of various products are plotted on the vertical axis according to such factors as *leading, strong, favorable, tenable, weak,* and *nonviable*. On the horizontal axis, the maturity levels for the products are designated *embryonic, growth, mature,* and *aging*.

The key interpretations for this matrix are

1. *Nonviable:* the lowest possible level of competitive position.
2. *Weak:* characterized by unsatisfactory financial performance, but with some opportunity for improvement.
3. *Tenable:* a competitive product position where financial performance is barely satisfactory. These products have a less than average opportunity to improve competitive position.

4. *Favorable:* a competitive position that is better than the survival rate. These products also have a limited range of opportunities for improvement.
5. *Strong:* characterized by an ability to defend market share against competing moves without the sacrifice of acceptable financial performance.
6. *Leading:* incorporates the widest range of strategic options because of the "competitive distance" between the given products and the competitors' products.

An examination of the four products shows how this matrix worked during a particular period in the life cycle of those products.

Automated radioimmunoassay (a sophisticated diagnostic product used in laboratories) was considered in its embryonic stage with a favorable competitive position at the time the analysis was prepared. This favorable position offered the manager a range of strategy options as long as the decisions related to the overall corporate strategy.

Single-use hypodermic needles and syringes had a strong competitive position in a growth industry. Here, too, strategy options were fairly flexible and depended on competitive moves as well as on how quickly increases in market share were desired.

Blood collection system (Vacutainers) had a leading competitive position in a mature industry in the U.S. To hold existing market share, the company's strategy centered on product differentiation.

Mercury glass hospital thermometers in the U.S. had a strong competitive position in a declining industry. This product had less price flexibility. However, by using service, repackaging, and distribution innovations, the company attempted to maintain its strong position before giving in to price reductions.

As in the GE Business Screen, a green–yellow–red system is used to indicate strategic options: green indicates a wide range of options; yellow signals caution for a limited range of options for selected development; and red warns of peril with options narrowed to those of withdrawal, divestiture, and liquidation.

You can use this extremely valuable technique to evaluate your own product and market opportunities.

3.6 YOUR COMPANY'S FINANCIAL RESOURCES

Financial analysis is an essential part of looking at your company and is part of SMP Section 9 (Budgets and Controls). It enables you to quantify your strategy decisions. Therefore, this section concentrates on those areas of financial analysis that a general manager or marketing manager needs to understand about the internal condition of his or her company.

Specifically, evaluating financial performance is essential to managing your SMP for superior bottom-line results. Use these common measurements to achieve that goal:

- *Current-to-past sales comparisons.* To measure the performance of sales reps and sales territories, generate periodic reports on the quantities of products sold by product line, the profitability of territories and any quantitative data specific to measuring the overall selling efficiency of your operation.
- *Customer satisfaction evaluation.* This measure is vitally important when long-term relationship marketing is the strategy of choice. Although a rep's likability remains a factor, a more meaningful evaluation should assess outcomes and interests that are important to the customer. These may include being attentive to problems, overcoming technical obstacles, and meeting delivery schedules.
- *Qualitative evaluation of sales reps.* Use this measure to determine the reps' knowledge of your products, customers, competitors, territory, the economy, and any other issues that are important to making a sale. Individual characteristics, such as dress, speech, and personality, also become part of the evaluation.

What follows are the broader measurements of a financial analysis.

Financial Analysis

There are several approaches to calculating return on investment (ROI) depending on how "investment" is defined in your company. The most often used is:

Return on Investment

$$ROI = \frac{Net\ Income}{Investment} \times 100\%$$

Return on Sales

$$ROS = \frac{Net\ Income}{Total\ Sales} \times 100\%$$

Cash Flow

$$CF = (Net\ income + depreciation) - (Change\ in\ plant\ and\ equipment) - (Change\ in\ working\ capital)$$

In some organizations, the term *cash flow* is used to identify cash flow from operations only, and does not include cash flow arising from balance sheet changes, as noted in the equation.

Market Share Analysis

While not used in traditional financial analysis, market share is useful because of its financial implications to ROI. Before a calculation can be made, you need to determine which of the four measures of market share will be used:[1]

- The company's overall market share in sales units or dollars, expressed as a percentage of total industry sales.
- The company's served market stated as a percentage of the total sales to its served market. The served market is that segment that can be reached and served by the company's marketing effort. It is particularly useful if your strategy aims to expand on a segment-by-segment rollout to other geographic regions or customer categories.
- The company's market share expressed as a percentage of the combined sales of the three largest competitors. This measure is especially valid when three or four companies command the major share of the market.
- The company's market share simply tracked as a percentage of sales of the leading competitor's sales. This measure is effective when the industry is fragmented with very small competitors and your growth is measured against the dominant competitor.

Marketing Expense-to-Sales Analysis

One of the key financial ratios to watch is marketing expense-to-sales. When you are monitoring different strategies in situations such as either defending market share or aggressively pursuing market share, it becomes a platform for projecting the financial impact of future strategy approaches.

The components of this ratio comprise sales force-to-sales, advertising-to-sales, sales promotion-to-sales, marketing research-to-sales, and sales administration-to-sales. The ratios can be monitored either through a chart, which graphically shows deviation from budget, or from the more typical periodic budget variance reports.

---

[1] The list is adapted in part from Philip Kotler, *Marketing Management: Analysis, Planning, and Control, 9th ed.* (Upper Saddle River, NJ: Prentice-Hall, 1997, p. 767). See Professor Kotler's book for greater detail.

Break-Even Analysis

Another key financial consideration is the minimum sales revenue necessary to cover costs. This revenue is the product of two factors: *quantity* and *price*. The quantity factor is crucial here because it represents the number of units that must be sold just to recover costs. This quantity is called the *break-even* quantity.

To get the most out of break-even analysis, your cost accounting system must be able to separate each relevant cost category into its fixed and variable components. On a total cost level, the terms *fixed* and *variable* refer to whether or not the amount varies with the output. A cost item is considered fixed if its total amount is unaffected by the number of units produced — for example, advertising expenditures.

Variable cost, on the other hand, refers to items that are dependent on output. The most obvious examples are direct material and direct labor. These costs can be determined on a per-unit basis. Unlike fixed costs, they are not incurred when there is no production. In marketing, salesforce commissions are an example of a variable cost.

3.7 YOUR COMPANY'S STRENGTHS/WEAKNESSES

This last component of looking at your company, strengths/weaknesses, is actually an integration of input from both your company and your market analyses and is vitally important to SMP Section 1 (Strategic Direction). It provides an excellent resource for examining the strengths and weaknesses of your own firm compared to those of your competitors.

Companies now appraise their strengths/weaknesses and core competencies as they consider entering emerging markets, revitalizing mature markets, developing value-added products, and responding rapidly to shifting customer buying patterns.

The resulting new product ideas, product enhancements, and applications of technologies into other industries, emerging markets, and existing markets are added to SMP Section 4 (Business Portfolio).

If specific skills are identified as vital to your success, but do not exist internally, you have the rationale to locate outside alliances. At this stage, what may appear on the surface as a portfolio of disorganized products without a cohesive base, is in fact a well-ordered group of products built from basic strengths.

One special benefit of building a grouping of various strengths is that you can take a fresh look at so-called mature products — which, in effect, is admitting you've run out of product ideas. Whereas working with core competencies, you can use a building-block approach to bring about continuous product and service improvements.

The strengths/weaknesses analysis questionnaire presented in Chapter 4 consists of 100 questions that serve as a Marketing Audit. They contribute to the total competitive analysis in two ways:

1. They look at marketing operations and key environmental factors affecting your company.
2. They assess your company's competencies and strategic marketing capabilities and determine what strategies can be used to increase competitive advantage.

By using the Marketing Audit, you should be able to identify what makes your company or division or product outstanding. It helps you compare your overall distinctive competencies and specific strengths with those of your competitors. Similarly, you also pinpoint the weaknesses that would prevent you from achieving a competitive advantage.

Summary of Looking at Your Company

Essential to developing an effective SMP are six basic components to looking at your company that, taken together, will give you a reliable picture of your organization.

1. Performance helps you evaluate the organization of your company or business unit. Whether you organize by function, geography, product, or market will depend on the size of your firm, your product mix, and the character of the market.
2. Strategic priorities give you a more focused look at how well you are pursuing a *customer-oriented* strategy that puts the needs and wants of customers first. They highlight the essential lesson that you provide products for markets, rather than attempting to create markets for products as the preferred approach to exploiting profitable market opportunities.
3. Costs have two components: first, the experience curve shows you that as cumulative production (or experience with a product) increases, costs decrease. You can assess your experience by looking at labor productivity, work methods, production efficiency, and product design and materials.

   Second, you should engage in *sales forecasting* in order to predict and, therefore, control future levels of sales. Both of these factors give you a way to evaluate and manage costs.
4. Portfolio takes place in an organizational unit, such as a division, SBU, or in most small businesses. It helps you assess your com-

petitive position systematically in order to determine investment levels. The three popular portfolio models include BCG Growth–Share Matrix, General Electric Business Screen, and Arthur D. Little Matrix.

5. Financial resources offer a range of quantitative techniques for identifying the financial implications of strategies. The major techniques include ROI, ROS, cash flow, market-share analysis, marketing expense-to-sales ratio, and break-even analysis.

6. Strengths/weaknesses summarizes both the internal and external aspects of your analysis. It examines your strong and weak points in comparison with those of your competitors, so that you can concentrate in areas of the highest potential for market expansion.

PART 4:
INTEGRATING MARKETING INTELLIGENCE INTO YOUR SMP

Contents	
HELP TOPICS	*Applies to SMP in*
4.1 Integrating Marketing Intelligence Into Your SMP Information, Intelligence, and Decision Making The World Wide Web Marketing Research vs. a Marketing Intelligence System Developing a Competitor Intelligence System Application of the Competitor and Marketing Intelligence Systems	Sections 1, 3, 4, 5, and 6

4.1 INTEGRATING MARKETING INTELLIGENCE INTO YOUR SMP

You cannot expect to develop a competent SMP without a workable marketing intelligence system. Action without information leaves results to chance, as opposed to planning your course and attempting to control the outcome. Strategic marketing planning and the development of tactics require an effective and efficient information system.

Scores of U.S. companies are discovering that an ongoing marketing intelligence system can turn into a potent strategic weapon. By using information outputs, organizations can better support their basic products, offer new value-added services that distinguish them from their competitors, and create new products and businesses that extend their markets. As management guru Peter Drucker points out, "In the next 10 to 15 years, collecting outside information is going to be the next frontier."

Use the following framework for acquiring and organizing marketing information:

- *Use information from your internal records.* The most basic information should include reports on sales by segment, prices, inventory levels, customer activity, and so on. By analyzing this information, you can spot significant opportunities.
- *Develop a market intelligence system.* While internal records supply results data, a marketing intelligence system provides in-depth information to aid decision making in such areas as setting advertising budgets, determining market saturation, assessing competitors' strategies, and measuring customer satisfaction.
- *Systematize your approach to pursue marketing intelligence along four pathways:*
  1. Overall exposure to information from newspapers, trade publications, and your sales force where there is no special purpose in mind other than keeping current.
  2. Controlled exposure to a clearly identified area of information by talking informally to customers, suppliers, distributors, and other outsiders.
  3. Informal research to obtain information for a specific purpose by attending trade shows, reading competitors' published reports, attending their open trade meetings, talking to their former employees, collecting competitors' ads, and so on.
  4. A planned effort to secure specific information; this form of market intelligence is gathered through (a) syndicated-service research firms, such as A.C. Nielsen, that supply periodic trade information; (b) custom marketing research firms; (c) specialty-line marketing research firms that sell specialized research service to others; and (d) online services such as America OnLine that offer information at a modest cost.

To find new places to grow, utilize as many of the above sources as possible and organize the information into an intelligence system to capture the opportunity.

Information, Intelligence, and Decision Making

Your SMP must rely on precision information. Given the highly volatile environments, instinct and market intelligence must be combined for effective business management. While it is not easy to work through the quantitative language often accompanying sensitive intelligence, the alternative of "flying by the seat of your pants" is hardly promising.

The purpose of an intelligence system is to improve, not replace decision making. For example, the intelligence delivered by an information system will guide you in allocating scarce resources in a manner that will optimize profits. For that reason, the cost of acquiring intelligence is justifiable as long as it continues to improve decision making.

Such a system can accomplish the following:

- Monitor competitors' actions to develop counterstrategies
- Identify neglected or emerging market segments
- Identify optimum marketing mixes
- Assist in decisions to add a product, drop a product, or modify a product
- Develop more accurate strategic marketing plans

The World Wide Web

The colossal development in setting up a marketing intelligence system is the dynamic expansion of the World Wide Web. With it, you can gain access to broad, multi-industry coverage of virtually every major sector of the business world.

You can locate company and industry overviews, management practices, regulatory decisions, and executive changes. You can access information on industry trends, market share and size, mergers and acquisitions, new products and technologies, facilities and resources, sales and earnings performance, and R&D activities.

Important, too, is that the World Wide Web provides you with a barometer of popular culture. The databases enhance your search for trends in the following areas:

- Research on ways in which consumer products are marketed to specific ethnic groups
- Lifestyle trends and changing attitudes among aging baby boomers to products related to fashion, entertainment, education, cosmetics, food and nutrition, personal fitness, and home computing

- Demographic information about users of various products and services associated with travel, toys, religion, personal finance, automobiles, and music

You can also develop a well-defined set of strategies that combines isolating your competitor's weaknesses and using your core competencies to greater advantage. You can do this by:

- Researching market needs, customer values, and technologies that will support your business over the next 3 to 5 years
- Selecting a favorable position consistent with your capabilities
- Enhancing products and services to satisfy customers' needs and place you in a more favorable position

What You Can Expect from Your System

No marketing intelligence system can replace competent and effective line management, but it can help you develop a first-rate SMP, run your business more efficiently, and measure performance on a day-to-day basis. Used properly, a system can track progress toward long-term strategic goals and alert you to significant structural and performance changes in your business as well as relevant environmental developments.

Table 5.4.1 summarizes what your system can and cannot do for you.

Marketing Research vs. a Marketing Intelligence System

Marketing research provides vital input into a marketing intelligence system, but it is not a substitute for total marketing intelligence. At times there can be misunderstanding and legitimate confusion between the two systems. For your purposes and to clearly distinguish for senior management the differences between marketing research and a marketing intelligence system, see Table 5.4.2.

Developing a Competitor Intelligence System

The urgency for acquiring competitor intelligence and the magnitude of the search earn it a distinct place in marketing intelligence. As already stressed, competitor intelligence results in competitive strategies, which is the essential output of your SMP.

Perhaps its importance is best described by the monitoring activities of four U.S. companies overseas. In the 1980s, IBM, RCA, 3M, and Corning

Table 5.4.1   Capabilities and Limitations of a Marketing Intelligence System

Can Do	Cannot Do
1. Track progress toward long-term strategic goals 2. Aid in day-to-day decision making 3. Establish a common language between marketing and "back office" operations 4. Consider the impact of multiple environments on a strategy 5. Automate many labor-intensive processes, thus effecting huge cost savings 6. Serve as an early warning device for operations or businesses not on target 7. Help determine how to allocate resources to achieve marketing goals 8. Deliver information in a timely and useful manner 9. Help service customers 10. Enable you to improve overall performance through better planning and control	1. Replace managerial judgment 2. Provide all the information necessary to make an infallible decision 3. Work successfully without management support 4. Work successfully without confidence 5. Work successfully without being adequately maintained and responsive to the user community

Table 5.4.2   Difference Between Marketing Research and a Marketing Intelligence System

Marketing Research	Marketing Intelligence System
1. Emphasizes handling external information	1. Handles both internal and external data
2. Is concerned with solving problems	2. Is concerned with preventing as well as solving problems
3. Operates in a fragmented, intermittent fashion on a project-to-project basis	3. Operates continuously and is a system
4. Tends to focus on past information	4. Tends to be future oriented
5. Is not always computer based	5. Is a computer-based process
6. Is one source of information input for a marketing intelligence system	6. Includes other subsystems besides marketing research

Glass first set up offices in Japan to monitor competitor activities and emerging technologies.

Further, to show how ferociously businesses are working to get information on competitors, according to one reliable source approximately 50,000 electronic bugging devices are now hidden in the offices and meeting rooms of U.S. corporations, with 10,000 more planted every year, usually by rival corporations. In addition, estimates show that corporate spending on electronic surveillance is already at $50 million a year and is growing by 30% annually.

Assembling reliable market intelligence helps you in the following ways: you can develop defensive strategies to counter competitive moves. What's more, you can design offensive strategies that move you into new market segments by feeding information to product developers about customer trends and problems.

For example, GTE developed an information system to monitor competition in its various product categories. Their system answers the following questions, which you may wish to modify for your own use:

1. What are our competition's current strategies?
2. How are they performing? (By sales, ROI, market share?)
3. What are their strengths and weaknesses relative to GTE?
4. What action might they take in the future that would affect the company?

GTE's Competitive Information System then attempts to collect the following information about all major competitors:

Competitor's plans	Distribution facilities and strategy
Competitor's organization	Pricing strategy
Product strategy	Regulatory strategy
Production strategy	Major events
New product development	Product-line strategy
Investment strategy	

Answers to the four questions, combined with the information contained in the above categories, create a profile that will offer insight into likely competitive actions.

Used as a source of competitor analysis, the step-by-step process leads to effective strategies about:

1. *Competitors' size* — categorized by market share, growth rate, and profitability.

2. *Competitors' objectives* — both quantitative (sales, profits, ROI) and nonquantitative (product innovation; market leadership; and international, national, and regional distribution).

3. *Competitors' strategies* — analyzed by internal strategies (speed of product innovation, manufacturing capabilities, delivery, marketing expertise) and external strategies (distribution network, field support, market coverage, and aggressiveness in defending or building market share).

4. *Competitors' organization* — examined by structure, culture, systems, and people.

5. *Competitors' cost structure* — examined by how efficiently they can compete, the ease or difficulty of exiting a market, and their attitudes toward short-term vs. long-term profitability.

6. *Competitors' overall strengths and weaknesses* — identified by areas of vulnerability to attack as well as areas of strength that can be bypassed or neutralized.

Finally, the primary lesson you can derive about market intelligence:

There is no reliable way to develop competitive strategies without accumulating and accurately interpreting market intelligence.

Responsibility for the competitor intelligence model sits squarely on the shoulders of the marketing executive — or with any executive in charge of devising competitive strategies. In order to understand the flow of data, you need to examine the following intelligence-gathering procedure.

Collecting Field Data

The sales force represents one of the most valuable sources of competitor intelligence. When salespeople are trained to observe key events and oriented to believe their input fits into the competitive strategy process, these men and women are first-line reporters of competitor actions.

Communications with salespeople can be maintained by periodically traveling with them, by conducting formal debriefing sessions to gain detailed insights behind the competitor actions, and by creating or expanding a section of the sales force call reports to record key competitor information.

Another valuable source is the use of reverse engineering. That is, technical people and other product developers tear down a product and examine its components for methods of production, quality, and other details. Then a purchasing agent and financial analyst calculate the costs of duplicating the product in order to provide insights into the competitors' operations.

Collecting Published Data

There are numerous sources of published information, from small-town newspapers, in which a competitor's presence makes front-page headlines, to large-city or national newspapers and magazines that provide financial and product information about competitors. Monitoring want ads in print and over the Internet provide clues to the types of personnel and skills being sought.

Also, speeches by senior management of competing companies provide valuable insights into other firms' future plans, industry trends, and strategies under consideration. At times it is astonishing how much sensitive information is provided in speeches that are given at a variety of trade shows and professional meetings and that subsequently get into print.

Assembling the Data

Using tailored forms, individuals attending such key events as trade shows can observe and report accurately on competitors' activities, pricing, new products, or special promotions.

Cataloging the Data

The varied sources of data come together at this point in the system. Depending on the facilities available to you, the data should be organized and maintained by a secretary or, more appropriately, by a marketing analyst, manager of marketing intelligence, or librarian.

Summary Analysis

The first four procedures are mechanical ways of collecting, compiling, and cataloging data. The analytical and creative aspects now apply as you begin to synthesize the data to detect opportunities. It is appropriate to call in key functional managers from finance, manufacturing, and product development to assist in the analysis.

Communications

There are various approaches to communicate the synthesized information: oral reports at weekly staff meetings and the increasingly popular competitor newsletter in the form of print or by e-mail.

Competitor Analysis for Strategy Formulation

As has been mentioned elsewhere, the whole purpose of looking at your market, your company, and establishing a competitor intelligence system is to develop competitive strategies and improve the quality of your SMP.

Application of the Competitor and Marketing Intelligence Systems

Your specific job in applying competitor intelligence is to provide accurate information on your competitors' strengths and weaknesses, so that you can attack those weaknesses. The aim: to dislocate and unbalance the competition. You thereby gain your objectives without costly market confrontations that may result in using your resources with little or no gain.

Above all, when going outside your prime markets, use Competitive Intelligence (CI) to determine your competitors' strategies. Consider the following criteria of CI:

1. CI must be *accurate*. Critical decisions affecting expenditures of money, human resources, and time are at stake.
2. CI must be *timely*. Events have time cycles. Past a certain point, an opportunity may not occur again — or competitors may seize the opportunity.
3. CI must be *usable*. Data without application becomes irrelevant.
4. CI must be *understandable*. Information that cannot be interpreted with relative ease by the average manager and then applied to developing strategies and tactics is nearly useless.
5. CI should be *meaningful*. If it cannot be translated into scenarios of strategies, it's just nice-to-know information.

While it is in your best interest to become the driving force behind installing a marketing intelligence system, your most important role is to know where to apply the information. For instance, looking to such key issues as withdrawing from an existing market or expanding into a new market can be viewed through (1) market segmentation analysis, (2) product life-cycle analysis, and (3) new product development.

For *market segmentation analysis,* marketing intelligence systems can be used to:

■ Identify segments as demographic, geographic, and psychographic (life-style), as well as by product attributes, usage rates, and buyer behavior
■ Determine common buying factors within segments

- Monitor segments by measurable characteristics — for example, customer size, growth rate, and location
- Assess potential new segments by common sales and distribution channels
- Evaluate segments to protect your position against competitor inroads
- Determine the optimum marketing mix for protecting or attacking segments

At the introduction stage of a *product life cycle analysis,* system output can be used to:

- Determine if the product is reaching the intended audience segment and what are the initial customer reactions to the offering
- Analyze the marketing mix and its various components for possible modifications — for example, product performance, backup service, and additional warranties
- Monitor for initial product positioning to prospects — that is, to determine if customer perceptions match intended product performance
- Identify possible points of entry by competitors in such areas as emerging or poorly served segments, product or packaging innovations, aggressive pricing, innovative promotions, distribution incentives, and add-on services
- Evaluate distribution channels for market coverage, shipping schedules, customer service, effective communications, and technical support
- Compare initial financial results to budget

At the growth stage, system output can be used to:

- Analyze product purchases by market segment
- Identify emerging market segments and any new product applications
- Conduct a competitor analysis and determine counterstrategies by type of competitor
- Adjust the marketing mix to emphasize specific components; for example, change product positioning by shifting from a pull-through advertising strategy directed to end users to a push advertising program aimed at distributors
- Decide on use of penetration pricing to protect specific market segments
- Provide new incentives for the sales force
- Monitor financial results against plan

- Provide feedback on product usage and performance information to R&D, manufacturing, and technical service for use in developing product life cycle extension strategies

At the maturity stage, system output can be used to:

- Evaluate differentiation possibilities to avoid facing a commodity-type situation
- Determine how, when, and where to execute product life cycle extension strategies — for example, finding new applications for the product to new market segments
- Expand product usage among existing market segments or find new users for the basic materials of the product
- Determine potential for product line extensions
- Continue to monitor threats at market segments and to total market share on a competitor-by-competitor basis; then use competitor intelligence to develop strategies to protect market share
- Evaluate financial performance, in particular profitability (if all went well, you should be in a "cash cow" stage of the cycle)

At the decline stage, output can be used to:

- Evaluate options such as focusing on a specific market niche, extending the market, forming joint ventures with manufacturers or distributors, and locating export opportunities
- Determine where to prune the product line to obtain the best profitability
- Monitor financial performance as a means of fine tuning parts of the marketing mix
- Identify additional spin-off opportunities through product applications, service, or distribution networks that could create a new product life cycle

For *new product development,* marketing intelligence system output can be used as a preliminary screening device to:

- Identify potential market segments as an idea generator for new product development
- Determine the marketability of the product
- Assess the extent of competitors' presence by specific market segments
- Develop a product introduction strategy from test market to rollout
- Develop financial performance

PART 5:
APPLYING MARKETING RESEARCH TO YOUR SMP

Contents	
HELP TOPICS	*Applies to SMP in*
5.1 Applying Marketing Research to Your SMP	Sections 2, 4, 5,
5.2 Market Research Guidelines	6, and 7
5.3 Generating Primary Data	
Experimentation	
Observation	
Interviewing	
5.4 Focus Groups	
5.5 Image Research	
Developing an Image	
Researching an Image	
Guidelines to Image Management	
5.6 Generating Secondary Information	
Industry Studies	
Trade Associations	
Periodicals and Directories	
Suppliers of Commercial Marketing Research Data	
Reducing the Risk of New Market Entry	
5.7 The World Wide Web — a Boon to the SMP	
Summary	

5.1 APPLYING MARKETING RESEARCH TO YOUR SMP

When you use market intelligence to plan competitive strategies, marketing research provides the primary input to reduce the risks inherent in decision making. Such research is invaluable during every phase of the marketing process, from the onset of a new product or service idea through the stages of its evolution and market life, and, finally, to the decision to discontinue the product or service.

Marketing research acts as the primary tool for bridging the communications gap that enables managers to stay in touch with their markets. Better and more successful strategy decisions can be made when based on facts rather than hunches. These facts are the output of marketing research, which act as a listening post between your company and the customer.

Marketing research is the mechanism to improve the effectiveness of your marketing decisions by furnishing accurate information about consumer needs or problems through which you can base your recommendations.

Further, marketing research is the systematic gathering, processing, and analyzing of relevant data to develop your firm's long- and short-term objectives in SMP Sections 2 and 7, as well as to clarify potential marketing opportunities in Section 6. Ideally, your marketing research efforts should be *systematic, comprehensive,* and *objective.*

They should be systematic because an unplanned undertaking cannot be interpreted quantitatively. They should be comprehensive because having only some of the truth can be misleading. And they should be objective because research is worthless if it is not reproducible and aimed at discovering the truth.

To justify the expenditure of time and money, consider the following benefits of market research. You can:

- Single out market segments for growth and expansion, as well as protect an existing market position against competitors' inroads
- Shift emphasis in your product, price, promotion, and distribution mix to target special groups of buyers with greater precision
- Generate reliable customer feedback so product developers can coordinate their efforts to improve the usage, performance, and reliability of the product
- Avoid the threat of your product facing an indistinguishable commodity situation by accurately defining differentiation strategies

- Suggest meaningful options for growth as you evaluate market data and pinpoint viable export markets
- Target poorly served customer niches as fresh opportunities to accumulate incremental sales
- Reverse a sales decline, polish a tarnished product image, or reestablish customer relationships

5.2 MARKET RESEARCH GUIDELINES

Reliable market research comes from two major sources: *primary data* and *secondary data*. For you to gain the optimum use of feedback, market research must be

1. *Accurate* — at stake are critical decisions affecting expenditures of money, human resources, and time.
2. *Timely* — events have cycles that, once past, may not occur again or whose opportunities pass to competitors as they seize the moment.
3. *Usable* — data that cannot be applied is irrelevant. It must fill the gaps of information in your SMP.
4. *Understandable* — information is virtually useless if it cannot be internalized and interpreted with relative ease by the average manager and then used to develop strategies and tactics.
5. *Meaningful* — if the information lacks importance, if it is not significant but is merely nice-to-know information, then the primary purpose of market research to survival and growth is missed.

You can obtain the data needed for marketing research either by turning to existing information (secondary data) or by generating your own (primary data). Initially, you should avoid a primary research study for reasons of time and cost. Instead, many marketing questions can be answered satisfactorily by utilizing secondary data. Only if this avenue proves inadequate should you consider primary research.

5.3 GENERATING PRIMARY DATA

If you come up with "what if" questions, secondary data are no longer useful. They cannot address the issues of new product information, reactions to advertising, the impact of alternative pricing approaches, or the effect of a package change, among others. It then becomes unavoidable to generate your own data for the specific research purpose at hand.

You have three major methods at your disposal that have been refined to a high degree of sophistication: *experimentation, observation,* and *interviewing.*

Experimentation

Experimental research aims to discover the impact on changes of two variables that, in turn, can help you optimize your marketing mix (product, price, promotion, and distribution). It involves the creation of artificial situations in which all variables except the one to be tested are kept constant.

The one experimental variable is deliberately manipulated to test its effect on the outcome, usually measured in terms of sales. An example of an experiment is a test-marketing setup in which different prices are charged for the same product in different cities to test the direct effect of price on sales.

To be meaningful, experimentation requires controlled situations, either in the field or in the laboratory. If influences from uncontrollable variables are found (for example, dealer display), the data can be adjusted accordingly.

To ensure the reliability of the experimental research, it is always advisable to employ *control groups,* in which no changes are introduced. For best results, the experiment must be designed and tailored to meet the specific needs of your project.

Observation

Should you want to know the reactions of consumers to your product, packaging, advertising, or some other aspect of your marketing mix, observation can supply the input. Researcher and marketing manager would personally watch a test to get a firsthand look at the consumer's reaction to an intended change before implementing it on a large scale.

Observation involves recording the behavior of people. Sometimes it is done without the knowledge or consent of the subjects, thereby allowing them to behave uninhibitedly.

The content of an observation can be recorded either by a person or by an electronic device. For example, you could personally observe the behavior displayed by consumers in selecting toys. In contrast, a surveillance camera and lie detector are examples of electronic devices used to record consumer reactions.

Auditing and visual assessment, often referred to as "looking" research, is another kind of observation. By generating a count of the merchandise most recently moved through the nation's supermarkets, observation research gives you a capsule overview of the competitive framework for your product at a particular point in time.

As in experimentation, observation can be carried out either in the marketplace (traffic counts) or in a laboratory setting (eye movement studies). Whatever the circumstances, use observation to find out what people do. Its big limitation is, of course, that it cannot tell you why they do what they do.

Interviewing

Interviewing is asking questions of selected respondents who might possess valuable insights and would represent the group under investigation. Such survey research can be conducted formally or informally, structured or unstructured, and disguised.

If informal, the results cannot be extended to the underlying population. If structured, a formal questionnaire is used. And if disguised, the true purpose of the research is concealed from the interviewee. An example of an informal questioning technique is the focus group interview, while a mail questionnaire is a formal technique.

Interview research that you conduct can extend over a period of time to monitor changes in your competitive environment. Or it can provide a one-time snapshot of your market highlighting; for instance, the impact of a particular advertising campaign. As with the other two methods, you can interview either in the field (in shopping malls, offices, or homes) or in the laboratory (inviting selected consumers into a research facility).

A key rule in interviewing is to ask only necessary questions, because every additional question takes time, increasing the risk of consumer refusal. You should therefore refrain from asking questions that interest you personally, but contribute little to the understanding of the subject at hand.

Three Approaches

Depending on the nature of your research task, the amount of money and time available, and the accessibility of the target group to be surveyed, conclusive interview research may take one of three forms:

1. *In-person interview:* interviewer questions the respondent face to face (a) in the privacy of the interviewee's home or office, or (b) in a central location by intercepting the consumer in a shopping mall or on the street.
2. *Telephone interview:* interviewer conducts survey over telephone (a) in a local market or (b) nationwide over telephone lines.

3. *Mail interview:* survey questionnaire is mailed to selected respondents and returned by mail.

In choosing one approach over another, look not only at your budget and time frame, but also the likely rate of response and response bias. The rate of response is the ratio of those who respond to the total number of people contacted.

Response bias, on the other hand, is the distortion inherent in the answers given, due to misinterpretation of the questions or deliberate misrepresentation. You will want to keep the rate of return as high, and the response bias as low, as the constraints of time and budget will allow.

Table 5.5.1 represents a comparison of the three interviewing techniques on the basis of a variety of criteria. It is designed to assist you in examining their relative merits and choosing the approach best suited to your particular research objectives.

In-Person Interviewing

In-person interviewing produces not only a relatively high rate of response, but also an unusually high proportion of usable responses. It is the most flexible of the techniques. For instance, it can respond spontaneously to the unique conditions of each interview and also incorporate a variety of visual cues such as environmental situations, facial expressions, gestures, and body language.

Also, it allows for follow-up questions to clarify and specify answers given. Once a respondent agrees to interview in this mode, a considerable amount of time can be spent and extensive information obtained. However, in-person interviews are the most expensive questioning technique and can be rather time consuming to complete because they involve travel.

All things considered, in-person interviewing is, in most instances, the best research method because it combines flexibility with depth and visual monitoring.

Telephone Queries

Since about 95% of the households in the U.S. have telephones, lack of accessibility is not a serious problem. For various reasons, however, an increasing number of residential hookups are not listed. This difficulty can be overcome through random dialing.

Phone interviewing is the least time consuming of the three questioning techniques. You can survey a relatively large number of people within a

Table 5.5.1   Comparison of Relative Strengths and Weaknesses of the Three Principal Interviewing Techniques

	In Person	Telephone	Mail
Flexibility in data collection	Most flexible; can use visual aids, depth probes, various rating scales; can even alter direction of interview while still in progress	Fairly flexible, although visual aids and extensive rating scales cannot be used	Least flexible, but pictures and rating scales that do not require investigator assistance may be incorporated into a questionnaire; too many open-minded questions reduce response rate
Quality of data obtainable	Fairly extensive data may be obtained, subject to respondent–investigator rapport	Generally limited by short duration of interview	Long questionnaire adversely affects response rate and is not recommended
Speed of data collection	Process of personally contacting respondents is time consuming	Data available almost instantaneously; ideal for ad-recall and similar studies	Delays result from slow and scattered returns
Expense of data collection	Generally most expensive	Less expensive than in-person interview	Least expensive, depending on return rate
Investigator bias	Respondent investigator interaction may significantly modify responses	Investigator bias, while present, is less serious than with in-person interview	No investigator bias

Table 5.5.1 Comparison of Relative Strengths and Weaknesses of the Three Principal Interviewing Techniques *(Continued)*

	In Person	Telephone	Mail
Lead time for respondents	Need to respond quickly to questions may result in incomplete or inaccurate data	Same problem as with in-person interviews	Respondents have time to think things over and do calculations to provide more detailed and accurate information
Sampling considerations	In-person interviews require detailed addresses of all respondents; problem may sometimes be overcome by using area and systematic sampling procedures	Problems resulting from imperfections in telephone directory may be controlled to some extent by using "random digit dialing" or other computerized procedures	Mailing list is required; samples generated from unreliable lists introduce substantial selection bias
Nonresponse bias	Refusal rate is generally somewhat higher than with telephone interview	Callbacks can reduce nonresponse bias and are fairly inexpensive	Nonresponse bias could be very serious in cases where those who return the questionnaire differ substantially from those who do not
Sequence bias	No serious problem; investigator can record any changes respondents make to previous questions as interview progresses	Same problem as with in-person interviews	Respondents can see entire questionnaire and modify their responses to individual questions

Anonymity of responses	In-person, eye-to-eye contact may stifle frank interchange on sensitive issues	Obtaining frank responses is a problem, although less so than in in-person interview situations	Frank responses on sensitive issues can be obtained by guaranteeing anonymity
Identity of respondents	Easily available for future reference	Name and telephone number are available for future reference	May not be available in many cases; questionnaire may even have been filled out by someone other than intended respondent
Field control	Difficult and expensive	Centralized control is no problem; better quality data result	Generally not a problem
Difficulty of reaching certain segments of population	The very rich are hard to reach, and investigators dodge very poor areas; most working men and women cannot be reached during normal working hours	Nontelephone-owning households cannot be reached; most working men and women are unavailable unless interviews are conducted in the evening and on weekends	Individuals with a low literacy level cannot be reached
Geographic coverage	Generally limited by cost considerations	Telephone facilities permit wide coverage at reasonable cost	Geographic coverage is no problem
Investigator assistance	Easily available to explain instructions, provide help with unfamiliar terms and research procedures	Available, although not to the same extent as in in-person interviews	Not available; instructions may be misinterpreted; incomplete answers or blanks are fairly common

short period of time. This makes the telephone query particularly suitable for measuring customer reaction to your product and that of a competitor.

With telephone interviewing, the response rate is good and callbacks are easy. Also, travel is eliminated and interviewer bias is reduced. However, you cannot ask intricate or intimate questions over the phone without the risk of people hanging up on you.

All things considered, because of ease of administration, speed of response, flexibility, and wide coverage, phone interviews are rapidly gaining in popularity among marketers.

Mail Surveys

Although it is the slowest technique in the fieldwork stage, and the most susceptible to internal questionnaire bias, mail survey research offers the most cost-effective method available. It has the great advantage of generating input from many people at relatively little cost. No interviewing staff is required, and no training or travel expenses are incurred.

Probably the most serious problem with mail surveys is motivating people to fill out the questionnaires. If the response rate is less than 20%, it will raise questions about how truly representative your results are with respect to the underlying population. Since respondents tend to differ from nonrespondents, you cannot remedy the situation simply by increasing the size of your sample.

To increase your response rate, you should follow up your original sample by sending them another copy of your questionnaire with a different cover letter. This action tends to increase returns significantly.

In spite of some handicaps, mail surveys are widely used because they can reach thousands of participants at a reasonable cost, offer wide geographic coverage, and can address issues that would otherwise be too sensitive.

5.4 FOCUS GROUPS

Focus group interviews are a flexible, versatile, and powerful tool for the decision maker. These interviews can furnish you with valuable information on a variety of competitive and marketing problems in a short span of time and at a nominal cost. But you have to keep in mind their limitations. Focus groups are a *qualitative* research technique and should not be a device for head counting.

The results of focus group interviews cannot be projected to your target market at large. They may not even be representative and, certainly, cannot replace the quantitative research that will supply you with the necessary numbers.

Yet the interviews can improve the quality of your quantitative research significantly. When there is no time for a well-planned formal project, you can call upon this technique to supply factual and perceptual input for making reasoned decisions, which otherwise would have to rely exclusively on executive speculation.

Focus group interviewing involves the simultaneous interviewing of a group of individuals — physicians, homemakers, police officers, purchasing agents, or any other group of potential buyers or specifiers representative of your market. A session is usually conducted as a casual roundtable discussion with 6 to 10 participants. Fewer than 6 poses the danger of participants feeling inhibited. More than 10 could result in some members not being heard. The idea, of course, is to get input from everybody.

Although the length of a focus group interview varies, an average session lasts about 2 hours. By holding focus group interviews in various cities around the country, in a week you can collect a good geographic cross section of opinions. Thus, focus groups offer a quick and relatively inexpensive research technique.

Use focus group interviews to:

- Diagnose your competitor's strengths and weaknesses
- Spot the source of marketing problems
- Spark new product lines
- Develop questionnaires for quantitative research
- Find new uses for your products
- Identify new advertising or packaging themes
- Test alternative marketing approaches
- Streamline the positioning of your product

The key figure in a focus group interview is the moderator who introduces the subject and keeps the discussion on the predetermined topic. The moderator could be you or someone employed by an outside marketing research firm. The job of moderator is not an easy one, and much preparation is necessary, but the information obtained can be substantial and well worth the effort.

The focus group interview does not follow a strict question-and-answer format. Rather, questions presented by the moderator serve essentially as catalysts for effective group discussion. Typically, answers point out areas that merit deeper probing by the moderator through ad-lib questioning.

A successful session leads to thoughts and ideas that were not anticipated. Consequently, it is crucial that the moderator create an atmosphere conducive to spontaneity and candor. This format allows for flexibility and enables the moderator to pursue leads suggested by participants.

5.5 IMAGE RESEARCH

The consumer and the industrial purchaser buy an image as well as a product or service.

An image is the complex of attitudes, beliefs, opinions, and experiences that make up an individual's total impression of a product, service, or corporation.

An image represents a "personality" with which the prospective buyer either can or cannot identify. How your company, product line, or service is perceived in the marketplace should take center stage in your SMP priorities. Toward this end, you should conduct image research.

Developing an Image

An image evolves from a multitude of factors. It can be outcomes of a company's own efforts as well as those of its competitors. It can result from the choice of corporate or brand name, the symbolism used, or any other part of the entire marketing effort, including product design, pricing, and distribution. The symbolism may include logos, slogans, jingles, colors, shapes, or packaging.

Therefore, if you want to strategically shape the image of your product, Table 5.5.2 offers some useful insights and guidelines. It presents a dozen image ingredients that are under your control and briefly highlights their respective roles in determining the overall image of your product.

Table 5.5.2 Marketing Mix and Product Image	
Controllable Image Ingredients	*What They Can Do*
Design	Provides esthetic appeal
Color	Sets a mood
Shape	Generates recognizability
Package	Connotes value
Name	Expresses central idea
Slogan, jingle, logo	Create memorability
Advertising, personal selling	Communicate benefits
Sales promotion	Stimulates interest
Price	Suggests quality
Channels of distribution	Determines prestige
Warranty	Establishes believability
Service	Substantiates product support

Researching an Image

In view of their largely emotional nature, images are best researched by using projective techniques that present the respondents with a stimulus (such as a cartoon character) and ask them to interpret it. While ostensibly talking about this stimulus, the interviewees will unknowingly project their own feelings into the interpretation, thus revealing a true image that could not be obtained by straightforward questioning.

The three projective techniques most frequently used in marketing research are *sentence completion, word association,* and *picture association.*

Sentence Completion

This test is made up of 10 to 20 sentence fragments that give only a partial direction of thought and encourage the respondents to complete the sentences in any way they think appropriate. The statements should be balanced with respect to personal ("I think CitiBank is ...") and neutral ("Aim toothpaste is ...") direction.

An equal balance should be achieved between negative ("The worst thing about the Lincoln Town Car is ...") and positive ("The thing I like best about the Lincoln Continental is ..."). The major benefit of this technique is that respondents express their own feelings in their own words. Sentence completion tests can be administered either by personal interview or by the pencil-and-paper method.

Word Association

This test is a high-pressure technique that presents an interviewee with key words, terms, or names one at a time and insists on the respondent's immediate reporting of whatever comes to mind upon hearing a given word. In order to avoid second guessing, the subject is not granted any time for reflection or deliberation.

A brief series of about five responses per trigger word is generally registered. The main advantage of this method is that it produces spontaneous association. This technique must be administered by means of personal interview.

Picture Association

This test presents respondents with drawings or photographs of different people representing potential product users. The interviewees are asked to identify the prospective users of products A, B, and C. The interviewer then probes for characteristics of the pictured people, thus developing a personality profile of the perceived typical user of a particular product, which reflects its image.

The prime payoff of this approach is that it elicits a wealth of uninhibited information that would otherwise be impossible to obtain. Like the word-association test, picture associations are best administered by personal interview.

Guidelines to Image Management

Here are some of the key questions that you may want to ask yourself with respect to your image management responsibilities and efforts:

- What do we know about the image of our company/product/service in the eyes of actual or potential buyers?
- Do we have any image at all? Are we well-enough known?
- Is our image positive or negative?
- Is the perceived image accurate or inaccurate? Are we better than our reputation?
- What does our name suggest? Is it appropriate? Have we outgrown it?
- How does our image compare with that of our competition?
- What are our perceived strengths and weaknesses?
- How can we improve our image?

Favorable images serve to attract investment, talent, and buyers. A company's image can make products stand out that are otherwise indistinguishable. Mostly, however, good images lead to a competitive edge.

5.6 GENERATING SECONDARY INFORMATION

The following listings represent the major sources of information open to you, either through direct access, service organizations, or over the Internet.

Federal Agencies
- Securities and Exchange Commission
- Bureau of Economic Analysis (Department of Commerce)
- Bureau of the Census (Department of Commerce)
- Internal Revenue Service
- Department of Agriculture
- Civil Aeronautics Board
- Patent and Trademark Office (Department of Commerce)
- Consumer Products Safety Commission

- Federal Home Loan Bank Board
- Federal Reserve System
- Department of Health and Human Services
- Department of Education
- Department of Labor

State Agencies
- Division of Banking
- Department of Commerce
- Department of Consumer Services
- Department/Division of Economic Development
- Department of Environmental Regulation
- Department of Food and Drugs
- Department of Insurance
- Division of Labor/Industrial Relations
- Department of Occupational Regulations
- Division of Purchasing
- Division of Securities
- Bureau of Workers' Compensation

Some of the more important government publications that are issued by these various federal and state agencies are

- *Statistical Abstract of the United States:* provides summary data on demographic, economic, social, and other aspects of the American economy.
- *County and City Data Book:* presents statistical information for counties, cities, and other geographic units on population, education, employment, income, bank deposits, housing, and retail sales.
- *U.S. Industrial Outlook:* projects industrial activity by industry and includes information on production, sales, shipments, and employment.
- *Marketing Information Guide:* offers a monthly annotated bibliography of marketing information.

Other publications include the *Annual Survey of Manufacturers, Business Statistics, Census of Manufacturers, Census of Population, Census of Retail Trade, Wholesale Trade, Selected Service Industries, Census of Transportation, Federal Reserve Bulletin, Monthly Labor Review, Survey of Current Business,* and *Vital Statistics Report.*

Industry Studies

A variety of broad industry studies are conducted by organizations such as Frost & Sullivan Inc., Arthur D. Little Inc., Stanford Research Institute, and a number of Wall Street securities firms. It should be noted that many of these studies do attempt to make broad generalizations. You should carefully examine these reports to be sure of applications for your particular organization.

Trade Associations

There are a variety of directories (published by Gale Research Company, for example) of trade associations covering virtually every product or business category.

Periodicals and Directories

- *Business Periodicals Index:* lists business articles appearing in a wide variety of business publications
- *Standard and Poor's Industry Surveys:* updates statistics and analyses of industries
- *Moody's Manuals:* offers financial data and names of executives in major companies
- *Journal of Marketing, Journal of Marketing Research, Journal of Consumer Research*
- *Advertising Age, Chain Store Age, Progressive Grocer, Sales and Marketing Management, Electronics, Architectural Record, Plastics*
- *Business Week, Fortune, Forbes, Harvard Business Review* (general business magazines)

Suppliers of Commercial Marketing Research Data

A. C. Nielsen Co.: provides data on products and brands sold through retail outlets, on television audiences, on magazine circulation, and on Internet banner ads.

Market Research Corporation of America: provides data on weekly family purchases of consumer products, on home food consumption, and on retail drug and discount retailers in various geographic areas.

Selling Areas Marketing Inc.: offers reports on warehouse withdrawals to food stores in selected market areas (SAMI reports).

Simmons Market Research Bureau: provides annual reports covering television markets, sporting goods, and proprietary drugs with demographic data by sex, income, age, and brand preferences.

Other research sources: Audit Bureau of Circulation; Audits and Surveys; Dun & Bradstreet; National Family Opinion; Standard Rate and Data Service, Inc.; and Starch/Inra/Hooper, Inc.; and Information Access Company (available only on the World Wide Web).

Reducing the Risk of New Market Entry

To reduce some of the risk before entering a new market, use the techniques of market intelligence and market research covered in these Help Topics. Overall, the central methods for gathering market intelligence include the following:

- *Competitive audits*: measures market share and finds out how competitors "stack up" against each other in product quality, performance, delivery, price, and distribution, as well as any other areas of particular significance to your industry and to prospective customers
- *Customer satisfaction studies*: after you have made your initial entry, tracks your company's performance over a period of time and measures progress (or lack of it) toward becoming a better supplier
- *Testing new products at the conceptual stage*: avoids investment in products with no or very little acceptance in the marketplace; prioritizes those that do have a chance

5.7 THE WORLD WIDE WEB — A BOON TO THE SMP

Perhaps the biggest breakthrough in conducting commercial marketing research is the World Wide Web and its easy-to-use browser interface. The Internet is now a viable platform for online research services, database producers, and primary publishers of all types.

- Corporate directories identify and screen customers, prospects, competitors, and provide quick profiles of particular firms and their lines of business, management structure, staffing levels, and sales.
- Detailed financial reports help assess the financial health of an individual company, as well as overall industry trends.
- Press releases highlight new product announcements, staffing changes, and quarterly financial results.
- Trade journals and general business publications provide a wealth of information, including company profiles, case studies and analyses, interviews with executives, industry surveys, and overviews on emerging technologies.

Table 5.5.3 Market Research on the Internet	
Company activities and events	Professional business activities
Industry trends and overviews	International trade
Economic/demographic information	Company stock performance
Management theory and practice	Editorials
Legislative/regulatory information	Biographies
Product evaluation and reviews	Financial exchange information
Executive changes and profiles	

Table 5.5.3 describes typical examples of multi-industry coverage advertised by one online service.

Altogether, the World Wide Web opens up an unparalleled source for detailed information on industries, companies, company individuals, competitors, and consumer behavior that can add greater precision to your SMP.

Summary

There is an overwhelming amount of information available for input into a marketing intelligence system. Yet, as a practical matter for many managers, there is not enough time or money to conduct all forms of marketing research. The prudent approach for determining what specific research to undertake is to look at your SMP and identify any gaps of information and what additional information is needed to make intelligent decisions.

PART 6:
SELECTING MARKET
STRATEGIES

Contents	
HELP TOPICS	*Applies to SMP in*

6.1 Selecting Market Strategies
6.2 Market Size
6.3 Market Entry
  Entry Options
6.4 Market Commitment
6.5 Market Demand
6.6 Market Diversification
  Horizontal Diversification
  Vertical Diversification
  Lateral Diversification
  Diversifying Globally
	Sections 2, 3, 4,
	6, 7, and 8

6.1 SELECTING MARKET STRATEGIES

To look at your market in its totality is especially relevant as you develop your portfolio of markets and products in SMP Section 4. Meaning, first consider the size of the market and types of segments that interest you. Also determine what market entry procedures you intend to use, the amount of commitment of resources you intend to make, the level of product demand, and what opportunities there are to diversify.

Second, decide if you want to participate in a particular market. If so, how much of it do you want? How are you going to hold on to it? And how are you going to manage the market for long-term profitable growth? Let's consider all of these issues.

6.2 MARKET SIZE

Once you determine the size of the market you can handle successfully against competition, then concentrate your selling power in a form that offers the greatest chance of success. Avoid spreading out your marketing efforts that may result in becoming vulnerable to competitors. When growth opportunities become available, branch out to additional markets — as long as those opportunities conform to your strategic direction.

In addition to the above guidelines, refer to the detailed discussion of segmentation under Analyzing Customer Groups in Help Topics. Review how to segment a market and how to apply segmentation criteria. There are a variety of strategy applications from single-market concentration, to product specialist, to market specialist, to selective target niches, and to total market coverage.

For example, you may have identified a poorly served, neglected, or emerging market niche and introduced a dedicated product or service. Having established a foothold in a niche, you have a series of choices:

1. You can become a product specialist and expand your product line.
2. You can serve as a market specialist serving, for example, the banking industry with a diverse grouping of products and services.
3. You can choose a highly selective niche strategy concentrating in areas of most favorable opportunities.
4. You can select full market–product coverage. For example, Seiko watches started in a single niche and spread into full market coverage with 2400 models of watches.

An example of the reversal of the process, from full market to niche strategy, is again the banking industry. Deregulation of banking in the early 1990s phased out interest rate ceilings and permitted the tightly regulated banks to compete aggressively. As a result, many banks began to change over from full service and pursue a strategy of segment marketing.

Citibank pushed its automatic teller machines to increase share of *consumer* deposits. Republic National Bank (Dallas) specialized in the energy business. Madison Bank & Trust Co. (Chicago) specialized in services for the *commuter*. Riggs National Bank of Washington, D.C. geared its services to *trade associations* based in the capital.

These examples illustrate a radical change in strategy from offering full service to dominating a market segment and competing vigorously for market share within a confined specialty.

6.3 MARKET ENTRY

The overriding issue of market entry deals with deciding on a strategy of *first-in, follow-the-leader,* or *last-in* to the market with a new product or technology.

A first-in strategy has the potential advantage of identifying a company as the market leader. Often, the companies that decide on the follow-the-leader and last-in strategies must conform to the market leader. In those situations, managers have several options: they can create a competitive advantage by using product differentiation, price incentives, promotion originality, service add-ons, or distribution innovations to overcome the leader's advantages. They also have the choice of targeting poorly served or emerging market segments left vacant by the first-in competitor.

Entry Options

- *First-in strategy:* the first-in strategy enjoys the advantage of locking up key distributors and customers and possibly gaining a reputation of market leader. To further support that notion, a McKinsey study showed that being first to introduce a new product, even if it is over budget, is better than coming in later, but on budget. The downside is that rushing to the market before the product is thoroughly debugged can result in a negative image.
- *Follow-the-leader strategy:* here, a firm might time its entry with the competitor. Both companies would gain from the promotional impact of advertising the product category, and they would share the overall promotional costs of the launching.
- *Late entry:* delaying a product launch until a competitor has already entered has some clear-cut advantages: at the outset, the first-entry company will have borne the cost of educating the market. The late entrant also can avoid product flaws and take the time to appraise the size of the market, profile the buyer, and target still-viable segments that remain untapped.

To a great extent, your market entry strategies are *preset* at the time of product launch. By grasping the full significance of the first-in, follow-the-leader, or last-in strategy choice, you will gain additional insight as you make market decisions and develop and refine your SMP.

Ultimately, the decision in market entry depends on your resources, your ability to sustain a competitive edge (particularly if you are first-in), and your long-term objective as it relates to amount of market share and your position in the market.

6.4 MARKET COMMITMENT

Company priorities and resources determine the degree of commitment to a market. Consider if heavy involvement should characterize the major thrust of your growth strategy. Or, if less involvement is the best course of action, to protect your other market commitments.

There are two dimensions to market commitment: yours and that of your competitors. Competitive strategy requires that you use your strengths against the weaknesses of the competitor. Therefore, through a side-by-side analysis determine how much commitment will be given to key areas such as: extent of new product development, amount of market share desired, and willingness to sustain an aggressive promotional effort against competitors.

You also need to know your competitors' pattern of behavior and how they are likely to respond to your level of commitment. And, finally, you need to consider how and what you communicate to the marketplace (your customers and competitors) about the amount of commitment you will make, i.e., major, average, or limited.

6.5 MARKET DEMAND

Managing market demand is a key factor to successful performance. You need to know at what point to prune markets if demand slackens, when to concentrate on key markets when demand increases, and how soon to harvest profits should sales plateau and cash flow is needed.

The following guidelines will help you align your product introductions with your market demand strategy:

1. *Selecting markets.* Whether domestic or international markets, be certain the markets you select align with a long-term demand strategy. Then determine your capabilities to sustain a steady product flow of new or enhanced products. In addition, determine the commitments of competitors to match or exceed your product introductions.

2. *Entering markets.* Study the markets for points of entry. That is, determine geographic locations of available distribution networks and their capacity to handle your products. Also evaluate what product advantages you can tout, such as lower price, more features, or some other value-added benefits that are strong enough to displace competitors' products in favor of yours.

3. *Building market share.* Depending on your resources, explore the potential of a rolling strategy: (a) producing your product as a private brand; (b) followed by establishing your own brand name; (c) then continuing with product improvement, product upgrading, and supporting services.

4. *Protecting market share.* This strategy assumes the best defense is an offense. Begin with continuous observation of competitors' products and strategies. Then monitor how customers judge your products and observe their changing needs. Lastly, recognize that timing new product introductions are not isolated activities, but are integral parts of your total market demand strategy.

Managing market demand requires flexibility, good timing, and extensive use of competitive analysis. For example, Chrysler Corp. used a pruning strategy during its period of revitalization in the early 1980s. It pulled out of European markets and then selected key markets with the successful K cars, while harvesting profits during the succeeding years.

Though obviously simplified, the execution of the strategy through a 5-year period can be recorded as one of the greatest turnarounds in business history. Thus, the applications of market demand strategy connect directly to the strategies of concentration and segmentation as they relate to expanding or contracting your presence in a selected market.

6.6 MARKET DIVERSIFICATION

You should be aware of opportunities to add new businesses that relate to existing production or distribution capabilities (horizontal diversification), or about opportunities to add another stage of production or distribution to existing operations, one that either precedes or follows the ultimate path to the consumer (vertical diversification), and also the possibility to diversify into unrelated businesses using new technology and marketing strategies (lateral diversification).

Therefore, market diversification presents many opportunities for middle- and upper-level managers to exercise innovation and entrepreneurial thinking. Let's consider the three categories of diversification in more detail.

Horizontal Diversification

Procter & Gamble and Borden are experts in horizontal diversification. Originally a soap company, Procter & Gamble has long since expanded horizontally into such diverse products as cake mixes, potato chips, coffee, paper products, toothpastes, deodorants, and detergents. Borden's product mix ranges from American cheese and reconstituted lemon juice to glue and adhesive tape.

What these companies have discovered is that great economies can be derived from using the same sales force to sell new product categories to the same retail outlets, simply by applying already developed marketing skills. Because it involves building on an existing strength, either in technology or in marketing, horizontal diversification is the most promising and least risky of the market diversification strategies.

Vertical Diversification

Hart Schaffner & Marx, the manufacturer of such famous clothing brands as Hickey-Freeman and Christian Dior, acquired a chain of retail stores in the early 1980s to add to its existing stores. This type of vertical diversification has attracted a variety of companies.

Some large retailers that produce some of the goods they sell practice another form of vertical diversification. For instance, Sears makes some of its own appliances, or has large ownership interests in manufacturers. A&P makes much of its own baked goods. In the industrial sector, Ford has long owned its steel-making facilities.

Vertical diversification (or integration) in some instances increases the level of risk because the management of one level of business (retailing) may not have enough expertise at another level (manufacturing).

Lateral Diversification

Lateral diversification is the most extreme form of diversification because it usually represents a complete departure from current operations. The only connection is that the same parent owns diverse businesses. The resulting group is called a conglomerate and was made popular in the 1960s by such corporate names as LingTemco-Vought, ITT Corporation, Litton Industries, Inc., and Gulf + Western, Inc.

While this form of diversification still occurs through holding companies, the current trend is more restrained, and the business portfolio (SMP Section 4) is developed with greater attention to the overall strategic direction of the company.

Diversifying Globally

Finally, where you wish to diversify globally, or move into another stage of business, there are additional issues you will also deal with in developing your SMP. Use the following guidelines:

1. Don't distance yourself from customers, regardless of the types of alliances you form. In global markets, where possible, set up indigenous operations staffed with the nationals of each country.
2. Don't permit distributors to shoulder the entire load of contacting prospects, selling your products, and servicing the customer. Take the time to learn the intricacies of distributing to local markets. (This point is as true of domestic markets as it is for global ones.)
3. Watch the actions of your competitors. Identify territories where foreign competitors buy a distributor as a quick way to enter a market and circumvent barriers to market entry.

PART 7: SELECTING PRODUCT/SERVICE STRATEGIES

Contents	
HELP TOPICS	*Applies to SMP in*
7.1 Selecting Product/Service Strategies	Sections 2, 3, 4,
7.2 Positioning	6, 7, and 8
Developing a Positioning Strategy	
7.3 Product Life Cycle	
Measuring the Product Life Cycle	
Strategies Throughout the Life Cycle	
7.4 Product Competition	
7.5 Product Mix	
7.6 Product Design	
7.7 New Products/Services	
Categories of New Products	
Combined Approach for New Product Categories	
Steps in the Evolution of a New Product	
7.8 Product Audit	
Establishing a Product Audit Program	

7.1 SELECTING PRODUCT/SERVICE STRATEGIES

Reviewing your products offers a dual opportunity.[2] First, you tune in to the changing needs and wants of customers. Second, you decide how and when to remove losing and marginal products.

The seven major areas of product considerations — positioning, product life cycle, product competition, product mix, product design, new products, and product audit — provide a systematic framework for reviewing your products and developing competitive strategies.

7.2 POSITIONING

Al Reis and Jack Trout popularized *positioning* during the 1980s as "Not what you do to a product. Positioning is what you do to the mind of the prospect. That is, you position the product to the mind of the prospect."

Professor Philip Kotler (Northwestern University) says, "Positioning is the act of designing the company offer and image so that it occupies a distinct and valued place in the target customers' minds."

What follows, then, is to find out how customers perceive your product by examining the image it projects and the needs it satisfies. Next, monitor those perceptions through observation and research. If they are undesirable, change them. Then locate an open position in the market and in the customer's mind. Occupy that new position and protect it against competitive inroads.

To consider the broader aspects of positioning, use the following guidelines:

1. *Keep focused.* Position your products in those niches where there is an above average chance to rank among the leaders. Where possible, avoid the commodity segments. Ideally, find a technology, product design, distribution system, or service that differentiates you and leads to a favorable position compared to that of competitors.
2. *Establish flexible work teams.* Cross-functional teams now create the vital linkage between customer and successful product development. To succeed, however, teams must have a clear definition of how the company wants to be positioned and be able to implement the desired position through the SMP.

---

[2] For the purpose of simplicity, the term *product* is used to cover services as well. Today, banks, insurance companies, and other organizations routinely refer to their offerings as products.

3. *Solve customers' problems.* The extent to which you are able to solve customers' problems and thereby make your customers more competitive, the greater chance you have for survival and long-term growth. Therefore, look for new product applications, value-added services, and new market segments that were overlooked in the initial stages of product development.

4. *Look globally.* Trade barriers continue to crumble. Push your product ideas and technologies wherever they apply in the world. However, follow the principles indicated above. That is, make sure you are positioned to offer a specialty or customized product that will satisfy local needs, and not use foreign markets as a means to unload a standardized product.

The primary goal of positioning, then, consists of a two-pronged strategy: create a long-term desirable position for your product in the customer's mind and secure a strong advantageous position against your competition.

Developing a Positioning Strategy

If the picture of your market reveals an undesirable position for your brand, the following procedure may help you improve your situation in the marketplace:

■ *Step 1:* identifying the actual position of your product invariably requires individual consumer interviews, generally in the form of a questionnaire. (See the section on marketing research techniques.)

■ *Step 2:* the easiest way to select an ideal position is to accept the current position of your brand if it commands a strong position in its field. A second method is to select a position that nobody else wants.

■ *Step 3:* in attempting to achieve an ideal product position, your firm has two principal options. It can (1) move its current product to a new position, with or without a change in the product itself, or (2) introduce a separate, new product with the necessary characteristics for new positioning and leave the current product untouched or possibly withdraw it from the market.

Once you discover that the position of your product is far from ideal, your advertising has its job cut out for it. Together with the other elements of your promotional mix — namely, personal selling, publicity, and sales promotion — your advertising will have to shoulder the burden of creating a new position for your product.

■ *Step 4:* after developing several alternative strategies for achieving your ideal product position, select one of them to implement in the marketplace. In making your decision, be guided by your company's overall objectives, resources, and capabilities. Consider, too, how long and how firm a commitment your company is willing to make, and how much money it is ready to put behind such a commitment.

Achieving a lasting and favorable position is an expensive, time-consuming proposition. Unless your company's management is firmly committed to this strategy, it is best not to tamper with the position of your brand. You might do more harm than good if the effort is half-hearted, or is terminated halfway into the program.

■ *Step 5:* while tracking your competition, monitor the impact of your positioning on the customer's mind, where it counts most. Follow-up research must examine and compare the actual position of your product with its desired ideal position. After all, it is possible that your program will not produce the intended results. In this event, a review of your strategy may be necessary.

7.3 PRODUCT LIFE CYCLE

The product life cycle has particular relevance for SMP Section 1 (Strategic Direction), with specific application in Section 4 (Business Portfolio). Also, the various strategies that extend the sales life of products are the pillars for successful growth (Figure 5.4).

You will find that these life cycle extenders are the safest and most economical strategies to follow. To identify the best extension opportunities, seek the cooperation of product developers and manufacturing, finance, distribution, marketing, and sales personnel.

The product life cycle offers a reliable perspective for observing a "living" product moving through dynamic stages, influenced by outside economic, social, and environmental forces — as well as by inside policies, priorities, and resources.

For many companies, monitoring the life cycle curve often prevents the severe consequences of allowing a product to reach a commodity status, where price is often the solitary weapon in the marketing arsenal. Consequently, the classic product life cycle model remains a highly effective framework for devising marketing strategies at various stages of the curve.

Examples abound of organizations successfully extending the sales life of their products. The classics include nylon, Jell-O brand gelatin desserts,

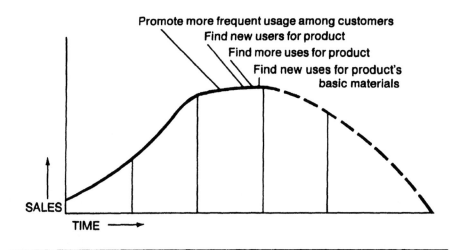

Figure 5.4   Strategy Application for Extending the Life Cycle of a Product

and Scotch brand tape. All have had average life cycles of more than 60 years and are still going strong.

Measuring the Product Life Cycle

If the product life cycle is of any strategic value to you and your firm, you have to determine where in the life cycle your product is at any given time. You can determine the stage of your product category's life cycle by identifying its status on the three curves shown in Figure 5.5.

These curves are

1. Market volume, expressed in units to avoid any distortion resulting from price changes.
2. Rate of change of market volume.
3. Profit/loss, illustrating the differences between total revenue and · total cost at each point in time.

Successful management of the life cycle of your product requires careful planning and thorough understanding of its characteristics at the various points of the curve. Only then can you respond quickly and advantageously to new situations, leaving competitors in your wake.

Strategies Throughout the Life Cycle

As shown in Table 5.7.1, different conditions characterize the stages of the product life cycle. This fact suggests continuous monitoring and

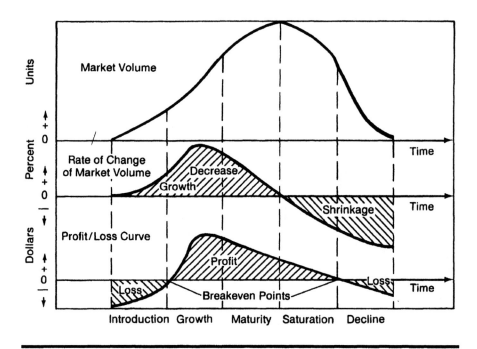

Figure 5.5 Curve Trends Used to Measure Life Cycle Position

appropriate changes in your tactical approach, if you are to optimize results. These changes include adjustments in your marketing mix — that is, the particular combination of marketing tools that you use at each stage (Table 5.7.2) and which apply to SMP Section 8 (Tactics).

Introduction

In the introduction stage, it is the task of the pioneer to create primary demand — namely, demand for the new product category. Creating

Table 5.7.1 Identifying the Position of Your Product in the Life Cycle			
Life Cycle Stage	*Sales Volume*	*Rate of Change of Sales Volume*	*Profit/Loss*
Introduction	Slow growth	Increasing	Loss
Growth	Rapid growth	Increasing/decreasing	Very high profit
Maturity	Growth	Decreasing	Decreasing profit
Saturation	Stagnation	Negative	Decreasing profit
Decline	Decrease	Negative	Loss

Table 5.7.2   Strategies Throughout the Product Life Cycle

Life Cycle Stage	Product	Pricing	Distribution	Promotion
Marketing Mix Elements				
Introduction	Offer technically mature product, keep mix small	"Skim the cream" of price-insensitive innovators through high introductory price	"Fill the pipeline" to the consumer; use indirect distribution through wholesales	Create primary demand for product category; spend generously on extensive and intensive "flight" advertising
Growth	Improve product; keep mix limited	Adjust price as needed to meet competition	Increase product presence and market penetration	Spend substantially on expansion of sales volume
Maturity	Distinguish your product from competition; expand your product offering to satisfy different market segments	Capitalize on price-sensitive demand by further reducing prices	Take over wholesaling function yourself by establishing distribution centers and having your own sales force call on retailers	Differentiate your product in the minds of prospective buyers; emphasize brand appeal
Saturation	Proliferate your mix further; diversify into new market	Keep prices stable	Intensify your distribution to increase availability and exposure	Maintain the status quo; support your market position
Decline	Prune your mix radically	Carefully increase prices	Consolidate your distribution setup; establish minimum orders	Reduce advertising activity to reminder level

primary demand is an educational process that involves activating people's needs and focusing them on the product in question.

Initially, keep the product mix small to provide a clear focus and keep costs under control. Also, confine the mix to just a few variations that reflect the underlying concept of the entire category.

Your channel decisions are crucial because they lock your firm into long-term commitments to a selected group of middlemen that cannot be changed easily, if at all. The degree to which you know how to secure maximum availability of your product in the right outlets can make or break your participation in the ongoing growth of a new market.

If you have an established sales force and ongoing business relationships with prospects, you still have to sell them on the merits of your innovation, which is no easy task. To this end, you have to motivate your sales force with a dramatic show that gets the adrenaline flowing.

Also essential is the support given your product in the form of advertising. Anything less than generous funding and an all-out advertising effort will reduce the chances for survival of the product. Giving a new product lukewarm advertising support is generally tantamount to signing its death warrant.

As for price, you can set it fairly low. A strategy called penetration pricing aims at creating a mass market and discouraging competitive imitation through low unit profits and large investment requirements. Or, you may consider a skimming strategy that starts out with a comparatively high price and attempts recovery of the initial outlays for development and market introduction, before competitive pressure erodes your temporary advantage.

Growth

In the growth stage, you will want to modify your basic product to take care of any problems discovered through initial consumer reactions. However, if the product is selling well, the product mix can remain small.

With channels of distribution, your goals will include persuading current channel members to buy more and to sign up new channel members.

Your salespeople will continue to sell along the same lines as before, building upon the emerging success story of your innovation. Your advertising emphasis is likely to shift somewhat from creating product awareness to expanding market volume. Prices soften as price-cutting competitors enter the market.

Maturity

Moving into the maturity phase now turns into a fight for market share against other competitors. At this time, it pays to redesign your product to make it more distinctive and easier to differentiate from competitive offerings. It is also advisable to adopt a strategy of market segmentation to satisfy the unique needs of these fairly homogeneous groups within the market.

Consider your channel strategy as it relates to effective market coverage, costs, and control. If you employed the services of wholesalers in your introductory thrust, think about eliminating some and shifting support to the remaining ones to push your product harder and cut costs.

Your advertising has to communicate and enhance your drive to differentiate your product. It should put heavy emphasis on brand appeal to presell the product, so that the prospect recognizes and prefers your product even in a competitive environment. The effectiveness of your promotional efforts, however, is likely to decrease sharply as demand becomes less responsive to promotion because of growing brand loyalty and resultant market resistance.

Since actual differences between substitute products are very slight and price sensitivity of demand is high, price variations between your firm's products and those of your competitors gain in importance. Prices will tend to drop further, but stabilize toward the end of the stage as a result of cost pressures. Insofar as your company has been able to create brand loyalty among its buyers, you can permit price adjustments when necessary without losing a substantial amount of sales.

Saturation

As your product enters the saturation stage of its life cycle, typically a no-holds-barred fight develops for market share. Because market volume has ceased to improve, the growth of individual firms' sales volume is achieved at the expense of competitors.

In your product strategy, attempt to differentiate further by offering even more choices. Because of the limited growth potential, it will pay to pursue a strategy of diversification. For instance, it might be worth moving into international markets where your product could be at the introduction or growth stages of a new life cycle.

Your channel strategy remains unaltered in the saturation phase. You should attempt to gain even more intensive distribution and thereby maximize availability and exposure. Toward this end, your salespeople will have to make a well-planned, concerted effort to obtain more trade cooperation.

Your advertising strategy at this point is to maintain the status quo. Little new ground can be broken, so advertising of the reminder or reinforcement type is needed. Elasticity of demand reaches its highest point at this stage. This fact is of little strategic consequence, however, since most possibilities for cost reduction have been exhausted.

Decline

With consumer interest on the wane, competitors drop out of the market in droves. If you are still in the market, you will trim your product offerings, vigorously weed out weak products, and concentrate on a few unchanged items.

Similarly, you will attempt to reduce distribution cost by consolidating warehouses and sales offices, as well as establishing minimum orders to discourage small shipments. Your sales effort will tend to be low key, with emphasis on retaining as much of your market as you can. Advertising support will diminish to the low-budget, infrequent-reminder type. Your prices will stay right about where they are.

Finally, studies show that the classic product life cycle pattern just described conforms reasonably well to reality. Therefore, as you develop your SMP, take note of the strategies at each stage of the product life cycle and incorporate them into the appropriate sections of your plan.

7.4 PRODUCT COMPETITION

Also relevant to SMP Section 4 (Business Portfolio) is to gain a larger share of a total market, by introducing additional products as competing lines or as private labels. The additional products provide a solid front against competitors. Overall, the strategy aims at generating higher revenue than does the use of only a single product.

To develop competing products, however, be certain you apply a differentiation strategy so that you don't cannibalize sales from one line to another. Here are useful guidelines:

- *Features and benefits:* select salable features and benefits that complement the basic functions of the product. Start with your basic product. Then envision adding unique features and services; ideally, ones based on users' expectations.
- *Performance:* relate this factor to the optimum level at which the product operates — including quality.

- *Acceptance:* measure this characteristic by how close the product comes to established industry and customer standards or specifications.
- *Endurance:* relate this factor to the expected operating life of the product.
- *Dependability:* measure this attribute to the probability of the product breaking or malfunctioning within a specified period.
- *Appearance:* look at numerous considerations ranging from image, function, look, or feel. Different from performance, appearance integrates the product with all its differentiating components, including packaging.
- *Design:* combine the above differentiating components into this factor. While design encompasses the appearance, endurance, and dependability of the product, particular emphasis is placed on ease of use and appropriateness to the function for which it was designed.

Procter & Gamble, with its array of brands of detergents and other product categories, is the master at executing a product competition strategy. Likewise, Becton Dickinson, the large healthcare firm, produces its famous brand of Ace bandages as the premium brand. It also makes a competing brand, the lower-priced line of Bauer & Black bandages.

You have to be careful with competing brands, though, to be sure there is a minimal amount of grabbing sales from one product to another. The intent is to segment and position your product with as much precision as possible.

Care must be taken because the supplier shoulders a high-risk position should the relationship deteriorate. In its worst-case scenario, such a firm could be out of business overnight. One possible remedy is to have a long-term supply contract with the customer — or open an alternative channel of distribution.

7.5 PRODUCT MIX

The intent here is to evaluate the profit advantage of a single product concentrated in a specialized market. Then, for growth and protection from competitors, also consider a multiple-product strategy, which could include add-on products and services.

In doing so, keep in mind the definition of a new product. A product is new when it is *perceived* as new by the prospect or customer. Therefore, new products can cover a range of innovations — from minor change to new to the world — if the changes are perceived as new. For example, *new* could mean modifying products for specialized applications, or developing new forms of packaging, or devising a convenient system for storage and retrieval.

Further, you can give the impression of *new* by adding value through improved field technical assistance, computer-linked inventory systems, and technical/advisory telephone hookups. The following checklist can get you started on developing your product mix:

- *Step 1:* review your company's strategic direction (SMP Section 1) or overall product line objectives (SMP Sections 2 and 7). You thereby guard against venturing into line extensions that do not relate to your core business.
- *Step 2:* define your market by sales and profit volume, customer usage, purchasing patterns, anticipated market share, and investment required.
- *Step 3:* determine product development requirements, such as using existing company technology, obtaining new technology, licensing finished products, or subcontracting an entire project.
- *Step 4:* evaluate competitive offerings. Determine how to differentiate your new product to avoid a direct confrontation with look-alike products.
- *Step 5:* determine the position of proposed product. Will it be positioned to *defend* a market niche or be placed on the *offensive* to secure additional market share? Will it be used as a *probe* to enter an emerging market or as a *preemptive* attack on competitors to discourage their entry?

The product mix strategy overlaps with other considerations, such as those already discussed for market dimension, market entry, and market commitment strategies. As always, you should also orient your competitive thinking to your competitors' product mix and how you intend to position your product line to them.

7.6 PRODUCT DESIGN

To deal with product design decisions, instill a mindset within yourself and those with whom you work that keeps your customers' needs in the forefront of product development and service. Sustaining such an attitude is one part of the success formula. The second, and more critical part, is to install a systematic approach that permits you to learn about your customers' business.

Here's one system that works. Explore customers' needs and problems in two broad categories that would appeal to their self-interests: *revenue expansion* and *cost-reduction* opportunities. To conduct the analysis, ask the following questions:

Revenue expansion opportunities:
- What approaches would reduce customer returns and complaints?
- What processes would speed up production and delivery to benefit your customer?
- How can you improve a customer's market position and image?
- How would adding a name brand impact your customers' revenues?
- What product or service benefits would enhance your customers' operation?
- How can you create differentiation that would give your customers a competitive advantage?
- How would improving reordering procedures impact revenues?

Cost-reduction opportunities:
- What procedures would cut customers' purchase costs?
- What processes would cut customers' production costs?
- What systems would cut customers' production downtime?
- What approaches would cut customers' delivery costs?
- What methods would cut customers' administrative overhead?
- What strategies would maximize customers' working capital?

Several of those areas reach beyond the traditional role of marketing. Therefore, use your planning team to interpret findings and translate them into product design solutions.

Finally, implementing the process is a sticky problem, particularly when it comes to involving nonmarketing individuals into actively thinking about such areas as customers' needs, market growth, and competitive advantage. There is no easy solution.

For starters, however, enlist the assistance of the senior executives in your group or company. Have them brief those nonmarketing personnel on the benefits of paying attention to market-driven issues for the welfare of their company as well as their personal career growth — and even survival. If that doesn't do the trick, you might recommend that an orientation seminar be used to help instill the appropriate attitudes.

7.7 NEW PRODUCTS/SERVICES

In this category, you take into account strategies related to product innovation, modification, line extension, and diversification, each of which requires changing the product either slightly or extensively. Also, as you

	Table 5.7.3 Categories of New Products		
Category	*Definition*	*Nature*	*Benefit*
Modification	Altering a product feature	Same number of product lines and products	Combining the new with the familiar
Line extension	Adding more variety	Same number of product lines, higher number of products	Segmenting the market by offering more choice
Diversification	Entering a new business	New product line, higher number of products	Spreading risk and capitalizing on opportunities
Remerchandising	Marketing change to create a new impression	Same product, same markets	Generating excitement and stimulating sales
Market extension	Entering a new market	Same products, new market	Broadening the base

consider new products, look at the opportunities for remerchandising and market extension. These strategies don't alter the product, but permit a perception of a "new" product.

Categories of New Products

New products come in many different forms. This diversity can be reduced to varying degrees of technological and marketing newness. In terms of increasing degrees of technological change, you may want to distinguish among modification, line extension, and diversification.

For increasing degrees of marketing newness, you can differentiate between remerchandising and market extension. Table 5.7.3 presents the differences between these five categories of new products and points out the benefits of each.

Combined Approach for New Product Categories

Rarely will the five categories of new products presented here be used separately. They lend themselves to combined applications for maximum impact. Moreover, you will probably want to avail yourself of a package approach if you wish to maintain steady growth in a rapidly changing environment.

Line extension, for example, is often used with remerchandising or market extension. Diversification is often combined with market extension. The use of one category does not preclude the application of other approaches at the same time, possibly within the same market. What remains essential, though, is that the prospective customer perceives a difference worthy of consideration.

Steps in the Evolution of a New Product

A new product results from a process called new product evolution. The steps are presented in Table 5.7.4, together with their respective results.

Initiative

New products don't emerge from thin air. Rather, the initiating force is likely to reside with some astute individual within your organization who perceives a product concept and triggers the process that results in a profitable addition to your product mix.

Numerous external or internal factors (discussed in these Help Topics) can inspire a new product initiative. They may reflect market, technological, competitive, or company developments. In any case, they constitute the motivating forces behind the evolutionary process.

Some companies even retain the services of an elite group of planners to speculate about such future scenarios. Yet, there are more basic approaches for obtaining significant insights into market trends. One is to carefully examine consumer preferences and life-styles, competitive new product activity, distribution patterns, and — most basic of all — sales and profit data.

Technological developments can be just as stimulating. For example, new applications of lasers, glass fibers, and superconductors offer a host of opportunities for the imaginative manager. And there is the immense potential of technology transfer. That is, applying to one field the technology developed in another. For example, Rockwell International Corp., a major space contractor, used technology developed for the U.S. space program in designing anti-skid devices for truck braking systems.

Events within your firm may also be the source of a new product initiative. These may include employees' suggestions about improving existing products or developing entirely different ones, or purchasing problems involving limited availability of key materials or price increases may motivate a rethinking process.

Table 5.7.4 The Process of New Product Evolution	
Process Steps	*Results*
Initiative	
1. Initiating forces	Get action under way
2. Perception and identification of problem or opportunity	Realize and pinpoint nature of challenge
Decision Making	
1. Definition of objectives and criteria	Set frame of reference
2. Start of comprehensive marketing research program	Feed decision maker relevant information on continuous basis
3. Examination of market data	Provide factual input
4. Idea generation	Map out alternative courses of action
5. Screening	Weed out unpromising alternatives
6. Business analysis	Subject surviving proposals to in-depth scrutiny
7. Product development	Convert ideas into products
8. Market testing	Examine market acceptance
9. Finalize marketing program	Prepare for rollout
10. Pilot production	Fill the pipeline
Execution	
1. Full-scale launch	Begin market introduction
2. Product life cycle	Analyze sales and profit changes
Control	
1. Continuous feedback of results	Compare planned and actual figures
2. Corrective action	Keep on course

Decision Making

The sequence of new product evolution begins with goal setting and ends with initial production. In between is a series of crucial steps that will determine the success of your venture in the marketplace. Close attention to each of the following steps is essential:

Defining objectives and criteria — well-defined objectives not only give direction and orientation to your effort, but they serve as a measure of actual achievements. Typically, new product objectives involve growth targets with outcomes measured by increases in sales volume and market share. However, they often remain nonoperational, since they are interpreted by criteria.

Research and examination of market data — while it is the role of objectives and criteria to guide the evolutionary effort and keep it on course, it is the job of ongoing marketing research to supply the decision maker with the relevant facts. The task, then, is to hook up with the consumer and establish communication links that keep the evolutionary process going efficiently and on course.

The body of data generated in the first round of this marketing research program is then screened for usable information capable of triggering dynamic thinking. The following process, attributed to consultants Booz, Allen & Hamilton, is a reliable product development system you can emulate:

Phase 1: Idea generation. Once a database has been established, idea generation begins. At this early stage, many ideas are necessary for an ultimate yield of one successfully commercialized product. Booz, Allen & Hamilton put this ratio at 58:1. Scrutiny becomes more and more rigorous as a product idea advances from its source. All the more reason to generate as many ideas as possible at the outset.

Tap a wide range of sources for product ideas: internal sources such as top management, research and development people, marketing personnel, and other employees. Also use a variety of external sources such as consumers, middlemen, competitors, scientists, inventors, research labs, and suppliers. The techniques employed in activating these sources range from brainstorming to various surveying methods.

Phase 2: Idea screening. Assuming you have generated a wealth of new product ideas, they should then be subjected to a screening procedure. This step aims to weed out unpromising ideas before they become costly in time, effort, and money. Thus, the goal at this step is to eliminate from further consideration as many ideas as possible. Two thirds to three quarters of the original ideas vanish at this point.

The focus now is to examine questions of feasibility and profitability. Neither of the two, after all, can exist without the other: feasible products that are not profitable are simply giveaways; profitable products that are not feasible are fiction.

Phase 3: Business analysis. The few chosen ideas that pass the screening test enter the business analysis stage. They now receive in-depth scrutiny. The purpose of this step is to advise top management whether it should authorize certain proposals as development projects. Therefore, a careful impact statement has to be developed for each concept, with thorough projections of what would happen if it were adopted and converted into a real product.

Management must know the consequences to your firm in terms of required technological know-how, production and sales force utilization, image, morale, and — most of all — finances. Testing the product concept through market research can help you assess consumer reaction and preference at this point.

Phase 4: Product development and market testing. Once a particular idea has tested well and has received top management's blessing, it is assigned to personnel for conversion into a tangible product. Here, your technical and production people go to work with clear-cut specifications spelled out by you on the basis of several rounds of marketing research. They will develop rough drafts that will then be laboratory tested and refined, until they have developed a product that is completely debugged and ready for full-scale production.

Of course, before you begin full-scale production, you have to test a sample quantity among users, asking them to try your product at your expense and then suggest changes to improve its performance or enhance its appeal. This procedure — product testing — is intended to help you modify and finalize the product design.

Phase 5: Final marketing program and pilot production. Completion of market testing enables you to put the finishing touches on your marketing program by adjusting certain elements of your marketing mix for maximum effectiveness. This adjustment permits you to get ready for a full-scale rollout.

Of course, you first have to go through pilot production; that is, produce enough merchandise to satisfy initial demand. This step completes the decision-making phase of new product evolution.

Phase 6: Execution and control. Once you complete the internal development and external testing of your new product, you are ready to launch its full-scale market introduction. Your revised introductory program should now set in motion the start of the life cycle of your product.

As no one is all knowing and even the best planning cannot foresee all possible events, continuous feedback to monitor the effectiveness of your product strategy is necessary. This feedback enables periodic comparisons between planned and actual figures. In turn, you can take corrective action to keep your program on course.

7.8 PRODUCT AUDIT

Knowing when to pull a product from the line is as important as knowing when to introduce a new one. Consider such internal requirements as profitability, available resources, and new growth opportunities. Examine external factors of sales force coverage, dealer commitment, and customers' needs to determine if a comprehensive line is required.

One easy-to-install procedure with direct impact on profitability is the *product audit*. Just as regular physical examinations are essential to maintain the good health of the body, likewise, products require regular examination to determine whether they are healthy, need repromotion, or should be allowed to phase out.

Begin your product audit by setting up a Product Audit Committee (see details below). The product audit can assist you in accomplishing the following:

1. Determine the long-term market potential of your product.
2. Assess the advantages and disadvantages of adding value to the product.
3. Alter the market position of your product compared to that of a competitor's comparable product.
4. Evaluate the chances of your product being displaced by another product or technology.
5. Calculate the contribution of your product to your company's financial goals.
6. Judge if the product line is filled out sufficiently to prevent your customers from shopping elsewhere.

In addition to the above criteria, consider such issues as availability of money and human resources, assessment of new product and market growth opportunities, and even the effective use of your executives' time. Also, add such factors as your firm's willingness to sustain sales force coverage, dealer commitment, and ongoing eagerness to respond to changing customers' needs.

Finally, phasing out weak products or exiting a market requires careful consideration of your company's obligations. For instance, there may be significant costs related to labor agreements, maintaining capabilities for spare parts, contractual relationships with dealers and distributors, financial institutions, and so on. In sum, the product audit provides a practical approach to the profitability and the decision-making process.

Establishing a Product Audit Program

The first step in establishing a regular product evaluation program is to create a Product Audit Committee. The committee may consist of members of the planning team or a separate group.

This core group, comprised of the top people in the marketing, finance, engineering, and purchasing departments, should control decision-making authority about the design of the company's product mix. Depending upon the dimensions of the product mix and the significance of the products or developments involved, the Product Audit Committee should meet monthly and every product should have at least an annual review.

How does such a committee operate? To do justice to each product and to have an objective basis for product comparisons, a common rating form should be used. For products that appear dubious and, thus, demand careful evaluation, you can use a product audit form using a simple 1-to-5 scoring system using the above six criteria.

Phasing out weak products, following the decision to drop them, requires careful consideration of your company's obligations to the various parties affected by the decision. Supplier and customer notification and an adequate stock of replacement parts may be necessary.

PART 8:
PRICING STRATEGIES

Contents	
HELP TOPICS	*Applies to SMP in*
8.1 Selecting Pricing Strategies The Pricing Process Pricing Strategies Summary	Sections 3 and 8

8.1 SELECTING PRICING STRATEGIES

Pricing is a component of the marketing mix and thereby is not treated in isolation from the broad objectives you developed in your SMP Section 2, which might include high return on investment or high market share.

Also look at the threat of tough pricing competition, by examining all possible alternatives, such as product improvement, promotion, and distribution strategies, before getting involved in pricing wars. The essential point: pricing must work in harmony with all of these strategies.

The Pricing Process

When pricing new products in your line, ask: can low price and high price be compatible? Do you create a conflict in the customer's mind? What perception or image do customers hold in their minds about your product?

Do give careful consideration to these questions when positioning a product into a new category and devising a pricing strategy. For instance, some organizations recognize image as a precious factor and will create a new name brand within a low-price category, just to avoid conflict rather than run the risk of damaging the image of its upscale product.

In general, it is difficult to regain a premium price position for the same brand once it has been diluted by low-price promotions through mass-merchandising outlets. Therefore, as you shape a strategy for a new product entry, it is wise to maintain ongoing feedback about the market position you want. In turn, the market position you select ultimately has consequences on the image of your product.

The following process increases your chance for success:

1. *Establish your pricing objectives.* These might be to maximize profits, increase sales revenues, increase market share rapidly, or position your product advantageously among competitive look-alike products.
2. *Develop a demand schedule for your product.* Specifically, forecast the probable quantities purchased at various price levels.
3. *Examine competitors' pricing.* This review will determine where you can slot your price to achieve your market objectives.
4. *Select your pricing method.* Use the following strategies for use in SMP Sections 3 and 8.

Pricing Strategies

Skim Pricing

Skim pricing involves pricing at a high level to hit the "cream" of the buyers who are less sensitive to price. The conditions for using this strategy are

- Senior management requires that you recover R&D, equipment, technology, and other startup costs rapidly
- The product or service is unique; it is new (or improved) and in the introductory stage of the product life cycle, or it serves a relatively small segment where price is not a major consideration
- There is little danger of short-term competitive entry because of patent protection, high R&D entry costs, high promotion costs, or limitations on availability of raw materials, or because major distribution channels are filled
- There is a need to control demand until production is geared up

A typical example is the electronics industry, which usually employs skim pricing at the introductory stage of the product life cycle to the point that consumers and industrial buyers expect the high introductory pricing pattern. There are exceptions, however. One was Texas Instruments' introduction of its much-touted solid-state magnetic storage device for computers that has the capability of not losing stored data when power is cut off. Even with the impressive technology, sales were initially disappointing because potential users were not willing to pay the high introductory price and were willing to wait for price reductions.

Penetration Pricing

Penetration pricing means pricing below the prevailing level in order to gain market entry or to increase market share. The conditions for considering this strategy are

- There is an opportunity to establish a quick foothold in a specific market
- Existing competitors are not expected to react to your prices
- The product or service is a "me too" entry and you have achieved a low-cost producer capability
- You hold to the theory that high market share equals high return on investment, and management is willing to wait for the rewards

One of the most striking examples of penetration pricing occurred in the early 1980s in the fast-growing market for computer printers, a market pioneered by U.S. manufacturers. At that time the Japanese seized the opportunity and targeted the segment for printers selling for less than $2500. Such companies as Ricoh, Okidata, Shinshu, and Seiki attacked the segment by offering printers at rock-bottom prices and short delivery times. From virtually no U.S. sales in 1979, the Japanese shipped 75% of all units selling for less than $1000 by 1982.

Psychological Pricing

Psychological pricing means pricing at a level that is perceived to be much lower than it actually is; for instance, $99, $19.99, and $1.98. Psychological pricing is a viable strategy and you should experiment with it to determine its precise application for your product. The conditions for considering this strategy are

- A product is singled out for special promotion
- A product is likely to be advertised, displayed, or quoted in writing
- The selling price desired is close to a multiple of 10, 100, 1000, and so on

While psychological pricing more likely applies to consumer products, there is an increasing use of the strategy for business-to-business products and services, as in the example of a machine priced at $24,837. Note in this example that the traditional "9" is not used. Tests by such organizations as Sears reveal that the "9" doesn't have the psychological impact it once had. In various combinations, the "7" has come out on top. In instances where a prestige product or service is offered, a psychological price may be expressed as "one hundred dollars" to give an elitist impression.

Follow Pricing

Pricing in relation to industry price leaders is termed follow pricing. The conditions for considering this strategy are

- Your organization may be a small- or medium-size company in an industry dominated by one or two price leaders
- Aggressive pricing fluctuations may result in damaging price wars
- Most products offered don't have distinguishing features

The most visible example of follow pricing is found in the computer market, in which IBM still holds a strong worldwide position. IBM traditionally set the pricing standards by which its competitors priced their products. However, this situation turned out to be a two-edged sword.

The IBM-compatible computers priced at 20 to 40% below IBM reached such high proportions that IBM was forced to reverse its role and use follow pricing against aggressive competitors as a means of protecting its share of the market. However, IBM's use of follow pricing was a holding action in its broader strategy of attempting to regain leadership with the introduction of new products and systems.

Cost-Plus Pricing

Cost-plus pricing means basing price on product costs and then adding on components such as administration and profit. The conditions for using this strategy are

- The pricing procedure conforms to government, military, or construction regulations
- There are unpredictable total costs owing to ongoing new product development and testing phases
- A project (product) moves through a series of start-and-stop sequences

Cost-plus pricing, unless mandated by government procedures, is product-based pricing. Such an approach contrasts with market-based pricing, which takes into consideration the following: corporate, divisional, or product-line objectives concerning profits, competitive inroads, market share, and market stability; target-market objectives dealing with desired market position, profile of customer segments, current demand for product, and future potential of the market.

Slide-Down Pricing

The purpose of slide-down pricing is to move prices down to tap successive layers of demand. The conditions for considering this strategy are

- The product would appeal to progressively larger groups of users at lower prices in a price-elastic market
- The organization has adopted a low-cost producer strategy by adhering to learning curve concepts and other economies of scale in distribution, promotion, and sales
- There is a need to discourage competitive entries

Slide-down pricing is best utilized in a proactive management mode rather than as a reaction to competitors' pressures. If you anticipate the price movements and do sufficient segmentation analysis to identify price-sensitive groups, you can target those groups with specific promotions to preempt competitors' actions.

Skim pricing, as previously noted with the electronics industry, begins with high pricing and then evolves to slide-down pricing. The downward movement of price usually coincides with such events as new competitors entering to buy market share through low price, and then waits for economies of scale to begin taking effect.

Segment Pricing

Segment pricing involves pricing essentially the same products differently to various groups. The conditions for considering this strategy are

- The product is appropriate for several market segments
- If necessary, the product can be modified or packaged at minimal costs to fit the varying needs of customer groups
- The consuming segments are noncompetitive and do not violate legal constraints

Examples abound of segment pricing. The most visible ones are airlines that offer essentially one product, an airplane seat between two locations. Yet this "same" product may serve different segments, such as business people, clergy, students, military, and senior citizens, each at different prices. Then, there is further segmentation according to time of day, day of week, or length of stay at one destination.

To best take advantage of this pricing strategy, search out poorly served, unserved, or emerging market segments.

Flexible Pricing

Pricing to meet competitive or marketplace conditions is known as flexible pricing. The conditions for considering this strategy are

- There is a competitive challenge from imports
- Pricing variations are needed to create tactical surprise and break predictable patterns
- There is a need for fast reaction against competitors' attacking your market with penetration pricing

As organizations downsize and reengineer to become more competitive, field managers familiar with the dynamics of their respective markets usually are handed greater pricing authority and accountability. The intent is to allow a flexible pricing strategy when appropriate. In contrast, the opportunity to react is missed where there is a long chain of command from field managers to executive levels, with the detrimental effect of consuming excessive response time.

Preemptive Pricing

Preemptive pricing is used to discourage competitive market entry. The conditions for considering this strategy are

- You hold a strong position in a medium to small market
- You have sufficient coverage of the market and sustained customer loyalty (that is, customer satisfaction) to cause competitors to view the market as unattractive

Preemptive pricing, as with flexible pricing, requires close contact with the field. That means tuning into customers, competitors, market and economic conditions, and any other factors that would influence pricing decisions.

Phase-Out Pricing

Phase-out pricing means pricing high to remove a product from the line. The conditions for considering this strategy are

- The product has entered the down side of the product life cycle, but it is still used by a few customers
- Sudden removal of the product from the line would create severe problems for your customers and create poor relations

Phase-out pricing does not mean dumping a product. Rather, it is intended for use with a select group of customers who are willing to pay a higher price for the convenience of a source of supply.

Loss-Leader Pricing

Pricing a product low to attract buyers for other products is called loss-leader pricing. The conditions for considering this strategy are

- Complimentary products are available that can be sold in combination with the loss leader at normal price levels
- The product is used to draw attention to a total product line and increase the customer following; the strategy is particularly useful in conjunction with impulse buying

The loss leader is one of the most common forms of pricing strategy. It is prevalent in all ranges of businesses, from department stores to auto dealers to industrial product lines. You should remember, however, to consider the profitability of the total product line.

Summary

Your overriding purpose in all of the above strategies is to avoid or postpone price wars. You can begin by locating untapped market segments and focusing on product improvements. You can also preempt and discourage new competitors by gradually sliding down prices, thereby making the market seem unprofitable. And you can always price according to the flexibility of demand and your production economies.

Consider six strategies to avoid the dire consequences of a price war:

1. Look for viable acquisitions or possible joint relationships with firms that offer services to complement your own.

2. Devote time and energy to develop value-added services. For instance, initiate emergency delivery, offer private-label packaging, install computerized inventory control systems and ordering procedures, reduce time to resolve complaints, connect a 24-hour hot line for technical assistance, and other customized services.

3. Work jointly with suppliers to find new applications for products that would open up new market niches.

4. Examine opportunities for multiplex marketing. That is, search for opportunities to add new segments with innovative marketing approaches.

5. Make use of new technologies. Look to the immense opportunities to create a competitive edge and unstick yourself from the commodity/price problem. For instance, reach for high performance with computerized order-entry systems or warehouse automation.

6. Hone your marketing efficiency with direct-response, telemarketing, and Internet breakthroughs.

PART 9:
PROMOTION STRATEGIES

Contents	
HELP TOPICS	*Applies to SMP in*
9.1 Developing Promotion Strategies	Sections 3 and 8
9.2 Advertising	
How to Develop a Successful Advertising Campaign	
Making Your Advertising Investment More Productive	
9.3 Sales Promotion	
How to Use Sales Promotion to Stimulate Sales	
Beginning a Sales Promotion Campaign	
9.4 Marketing Over the Internet	

9.1 DEVELOPING PROMOTION STRATEGIES

Promotion is incorporated in SMP Section 3 (Growth Strategies) and Section 8 (Tactics). To develop effective promotion strategies, you need to shape a program that combines advertising and sales promotion (including the Internet) into a totally integrated force. Keeping these activities separate leads to vague advertising and ineffective sales support. Let's begin with advertising and how to develop a successful advertising campaign.

9.2 ADVERTISING

Advertising is but one part of the communications mix, communications is but one part of promotion, promotion is but one component of the marketing mix. Thus, advertising — as with all the other components — is never created in isolation.

Initially, you should know the job you want advertising to accomplish. For example, it can support personal selling, inform a target audience about the availability of your product, or persuade prospects to buy. Then, you can choose media and copy themes to match those objectives. As a result, your advertising becomes realistic, measurable, and results oriented.

How to Develop a Successful Advertising Campaign

If you are responsible for implementing an overall advertising strategy through an advertising department or an outside advertising agency, here are key points you need to know:

- First, advertising is aimed at informing your target audience about the availability and features of your product or service
- Second, once that audience has been informed, advertising should persuade your prospects to buy your offering

In this process, advertising interacts closely and continuously with the other elements of your marketing mix, such as your product, pricing, and distribution. More specifically, it prepares the way for and reinforces personal selling efforts. In turn, its impact is enhanced by sales promotion activities.

Table 9.1.1 details the steps involved in developing an advertising campaign. It shows that continuous marketing research is the foundation of a sound campaign.

Pre-Campaign Phase

Sound planning techniques call for a careful assessment of overall market conditions before formulating an advertising campaign. Here's how:

- *Step 1:* conduct a market analysis that surveys the competitive field. For instance, this analysis should examine the range of competitive offerings and related market trends, their positioning and media choices, and their distribution and usage patterns.

    You will want to find out who competitors' customers are and when, where, and for what purpose they make purchases. This background information will provide the necessary perspective for choosing appropriate promotion strategies.
- *Step 2:* subsequent product research should focus more intensively on your own product. Its principal purpose is to find out from actual or potential users of the product which features they consider desirable and what benefits they associate with its use.

Table 9.1 Developing an Advertising Campaign

Campaign Step	Advertising Activities	Research Activities
Pre-Campaign Phase		
1. Market analysis		Study competitive products, positioning, media, distribution, and usage patterns
2. Product research		Identify perceived product characteristics and benefits
3. Customer research		Conduct demographic and psychographic studies of prospective customers; investigate media, purchasing, and consumption patterns
Strategic Decisions		
4. Set advertising objectives	Determine target markets and identify user profile, exposure goals	
5. Decide on level of appropriation	Determine total advertising spending necessary to support objectives	Investigate competitive spending levels and media cost necessary to reach objectives
6. Formulate advertising strategy	Develop creative approach and prepare "shopping list" of appropriate media	Examine audience profiles, reach, frequency, and costs of alternative media
7. Integrate advertising strategy with overall marketing strategy	Make sure that advertising supports and is supported by other elements of marketing mix	
Tactical Execution		
8. Develop detailed advertising budget	Break down overall allocation to spending on media categories and individual media	

Table 9.1 Developing an Advertising Campaign *(Continued)*		
Campaign Step	*Advertising Activities*	*Research Activities*
9. Choose message content and mode of presentation	Develop alternative creative concepts, copy, and layout	Conduct concept and copy tests
10. Analyze legal ramifications	Have chosen copy reviewed by legal staff or counsel	
11. Establish media plan	Determine media mix and schedule	Conduct media research, primarily from secondary sources
12. Review agency presentation	See entire planned campaign for approval	
Campaign Implementation		
13. Production and traffic	Finalize and reproduce advertisement(s), buy media time and space, and deliver ads	
14. Insertion of advertisements	Actually run ads in chosen media	Check whether or not ads appeared as agreed and directed
Campaign Follow-Through		
15. Impact control		Get feedback on consumer and competitive reaction
16. Review and revision	Adjust advertising execution or spending levels to conditions	Check whether or not changes yielded desired results

Such information will help you make the right positioning decision and formulate effective appeals. In this context, study the usage patterns in depth.

■ *Step 3:* finally, the pre-campaign research should concentrate on the customer. Here, you attempt to develop demographic and psychographic (behavioral) profiles of actual or prospective buyers.

For instance, recognize who are the frequent and infrequent users of your product, how old they are, where they live, how much money they have at their disposal, their educational backgrounds, their occupations, their marital status and family size, and the cultural group they belong to.

You can gain additional insights by looking at consumption patterns. At that point, you can determine who ultimately consumes your product, when, how much, how often, and under what circumstances. Only after all of this preliminary information has been gathered, interpreted, and internalized should the advertising planning be initiated.

Strategic Decisions

Once you assemble and examine the relevant data, then you are ready to make a number of strategic decisions that will guide the detail work that follows. As in all planning activities, the first major decision is to set advertising objectives for SMP Section 7.

Advertising Objectives

You could say that the basic objective of all advertising is to sell something — a product, service, idea, or company. To that end, advertising is effective communication, resulting in positive attitudes and behavior on the part of the receivers of the message that results in increased sales.

However, the objective of increasing sales is too broad to be implemented effectively in an advertising program. Rather, you should formulate more specific aims that nail down with greater precision and measure with accuracy. For example:

- Support a personal selling program
- Achieve a specific number of exposures to your target audience
- Address prospects that are inaccessible to your salespeople
- Create a specified level of awareness, measurable through recall or recognition tests
- Improve dealer relations
- Improve consumer attitudes toward your product or company
- Present a new product and generate demand for it
- Build familiarity and easy recognition of your company, brand, package, or trademark

The list illustrates some of the possibilities and pinpoints the need for precision to derive maximum guidance from objectives. Because objectives imply accountability for results, they often lead to an evaluation of individual or agency performance.

Advertising Appropriation

Having determined where you want to go, you must now decide how best to get there. You can choose from a number of alternative approaches for setting the level of total advertising spending.

- *Affordable method:* ignores your objectives and is simply an expression of how much you think you can afford to spend. This viewpoint makes your level of appropriation subject to whim and may grossly over- or underestimate the amount in relation to your needs.
- *Percentage of sales approach:* probably the most widely used because of its simplicity. That is, it ties your advertising allowance to a specified percentage of current or expected future sales. This procedure, with its built-in fluctuations, not only discourages long-term advertising planning, but also neglects current business needs and opportunities.
- *Competitive parity method:* proposes that your company match competitive spending levels. This simplistic outlook is no more sophisticated or justifiable than the two preceding approaches.
- *Objective and task method:* produces the most meaningful results. You proceed in three steps: (1) define your advertising objectives as specifically as possible, (2) identify the tasks that must be performed to achieve your objectives, and (3) estimate the costs of performing these tasks.

    The sum total of these costs represents your level of appropriation. While this approach does not examine or justify the objectives themselves, it nevertheless reflects a reliable assessment of your perceived needs and opportunities, which you can translate into a workable budget.

Tactical Execution

At this point, tactical execution deals with selecting those appeals most likely to stimulate prospects' purchasing decisions in your favor. Product appeal is defined in terms of price, importance to the consumer, frequency of purchase, competitive edge, and utility.

While the creative process at this stage involves a considerable amount of intuition, the quality and reliability of the data available to copywriters and art directors significantly affect the outcome of their efforts. Therefore, besides selecting appeals, you must choose the basic method by which you want to convey your message. This means considering audience profiles, style, and costs of alternative media.

Making Your Advertising Investment More Productive

Advertising is a key element in a total communications package. In terms of creating widespread awareness and exposure of your product, it certainly is your best buy. Remember, however, no matter how good your agency or advertising department is, you bear the ultimate responsibility for results. Therefore, it pays to be skeptical, independent, and not be intimidated by the creators of your advertising.

You can work more intelligently and effectively with your advertising people, and offer more precise guidance as to what they should stress. The following cardinal guidelines pertain primarily to print advertising:

1. *Be aware of the positioning of your product in the marketplace.* You may choose to offer it as an alternative to an exciting way of doing things or to the competing product in the field. Also, emphasize a major customer benefit that is unique, meaningful, and competitive — and one that can truly and convincingly be delivered by your product.

2. *Maintain a personality for your brand.* Use your advertising to make a positive contribution to the brand image. If you want your ads to command attention and produce results, try for a uniqueness that makes them stand out from the flood of competing messages. It is helpful to use a symbol, logo, or other repetitious element that will be remembered by customers.

3. *Don't bore your audience and don't be impersonal.* Innovate, don't imitate. Start trends instead of following them. The risks are high, but so are the potential rewards.

4. *Be factual rather than emotional.* One powerful way to present factual material is to use a problem-solving approach. Choose a problem that your customer can relate to and show how your product can solve it.

5. *Formulate effective headlines.* Use simple, understandable language. Department store advertising research has shown that headlines of ten or more words sell more merchandise than do shorter ones.

6. *Visually reinforce your advertising with illustrations, particularly of demonstrations.* Also, pictures with story appeal awaken the curiosity of the readers and tempt them to read the text. Photographs almost invariably pull better than drawings. They attract more readers, generate more appetite appeal, are more believable, result in higher recall and coupon redemption, and produce more sales.

7. *Use captions, the capsule explanations beneath pictures, to sell.* Include your product's brand name and the major benefit you promise.
8. *Generate an informative atmosphere.* Giving your ads an editorial appearance is at times more successful than using elaborate "creative" layouts.
9. *Be aware that readership falls off rapidly in ad copy of up to 50 words, but shrinks only insignificantly in copy of 50 to 500 words.* Although relatively few people read long copy, those people generally represent genuine prospects. Studies show that those industrial ads with more than 350 words are read more thoroughly than shorter ones.
10. *Don't replace your advertisements before they have a chance to develop their full potential.* The most basic learning theories stress the importance of *repetition* in affecting behavior. Repeat your winners until their effects start to wear off.

9.3 SALES PROMOTION

Used primarily in SMP Sections 7 and 8, attempt to integrate sales promotion with your advertising and sales force objectives and strategies. Your intent is to use sales promotion to encourage more product usage, induce dealer involvement, and stimulate greater sales force efforts.

Here are some characteristics of effective sales promotion: use sales promotion as an incentive to buy; use advertising to offer a reason to buy. Also, while sales promotion is part of an overall marketing program, it involves a variety of company functions to make it work effectively. Sales promotion permits tremendous flexibility, creativity, and application.

Consider the following applications:

- *Consumer promotions:* consist of samples, coupons, cash refunds, premiums, free trials, warranties, and demonstrations
- *Trade promotions:* include buying allowances, free goods, cooperative advertising, display allowances, push money for sales people, video conferencing, and dealer sales contests
- *Sales force promotions:* employ bonuses, contests, and sales rallies

As indicated with advertising (and all other components of the marketing mix), sales promotion is not a stand-alone activity. Instead, make it a component of the tactical portion of your SMP. Further, establish your sales promotion objectives to support the broader vision of your strategic direction.

Such objectives include:

- Entering new market segments
- Gaining entry into new channels of distribution
- Encouraging purchase of larger-size units
- Building trial usage among nonusers
- Attracting switchers away from competitors
- Building brand loyalty
- Stimulating off-season sales
- Winning back customers

How to Use Sales Promotion to Stimulate Sales

Sales promotion is a potentially powerful tool that is often poorly understood, planned, and applied, leading to considerable waste and inefficiency. Yet, it can be an effective component of most any promotion mix with creative applications from consumer goods to industrial goods and even services. It supplements and complements the more sophisticated advertising and personal selling efforts.

What is sales promotion? It consists of all those promotional efforts of a firm that cannot be grouped under the heading of advertising, personal selling, publicity, or packaging. More precisely,

> *Sales promotion refers to activities or objects that attempt to encourage salespeople, resellers, and ultimate buyers to cooperate with a manufacturer's plans by temporarily offering more value for the money or providing some special incentive related to a specific product or service.*

While somewhat lengthy, this definition points up a number of essential features:

- Sales promotion includes both *activities,* such as demonstrations and contests, and *objects,* such as coupons, premiums, and samples
- Sales promotions may be directed at one or any combination of *three distinct audiences:* a company's own sales force; middlemen of all types and levels, such as wholesalers and retailers (for the sake of simplicity, they will be referred to as dealers); and consumers or industrial buyers
- In contrast with the continuous, long-term nature of the other elements of the promotion mix (legendary advertising guru David Ogilvy said "an advertisement is a long-term investment in the

image of a brand"), sales promotion campaigns are *temporary measures* that should be used with discretion

However, unless used wisely, sales promotion can easily become self-defeating and counterproductive. While there are no hard and fast rules, a brand, for example, that is "on deal" one third of the time or more is likely to suffer image problems. In fact, if yours is a leading brand in a mature market, you should use sales promotion most sparingly because it is improbable that you will gain any lasting advantage from a more generous application.

It is important to remember that sales promotion is costly and should thus be judged from a cost/benefit point of view. So, don't overuse it — even if the temptation is great to yield to external competitive challenges.

Some important external reasons for the increased use of sales promotion include:

- The number of products in the industrial and consumer marketplace has proliferated, leading to intensified competition and the need to create more "noise" at the point of purchase
- There is a need to respond to competitive increases in promotion spending, although clearly accompanied by the danger of escalation into a "war" in which all sides lose
- In a recessionary economy, manufacturers are more willing to use rebates to shrink inventories and improve liquidity, just as consumers are more responsive to sales stimulation measures
- The growing power of and pressure from the trade produce more promotional allowances and support from suppliers
- There is a certain degree of disenchantment with advertising, which many managers feel has declined in efficiency and effectiveness owing to a disproportionate rise in cost and in competing messages

Beginning a Sales Promotion Campaign

To develop a planned approach to sales promotion over a haphazard one, you will find it profitable to follow a series of logical steps for maximum impact and efficiency. This can be achieved only if you make a sales promotion campaign an integral part of your SMP, carefully coordinated with the other elements of your firm's promotion mix and, ultimately, with its marketing mix.

As already stated, sales promotion complements, supplements, and often amplifies other promotional tools; and it should always be used in concert with them. For example, displays that tie in with TV commercials produce more sales than unrelated ones.

The following steps are involved in the evolution of a sales promotion campaign:

1. Establish your objectives.
2. Select appropriate techniques.
3. Develop your sales promotion program.
4. Pretest your sales promotion program.
5. Implement and evaluate your campaign.

Establish Sales Promotion Objectives

While the main purpose of sales promotion is to increase the sales volume of a product or to stimulate traffic in a retail outlet, more specific objectives can be identified, depending upon the type of audience and the nature of the task involved.

For instance, sales promotion efforts directed at your *company's own sales force* aim to generate enthusiasm and zeal. It is important, then, that you offer your salespeople special incentives to excel and provide the desired support.

A second targeted group is your *company's dealers* or *distributors*, without whose active cooperation your entire marketing effort and, more specifically, a sales promotion campaign would falter.

Lastly, while the support and loyalty of your sales force and dealer/distributor network are certainly crucial, a sales promotion campaign would hardly be complete if it failed to *stimulate buyer* action.

Consider these objectives:

■ Identify and attract new buyers
■ Encourage more frequent and varied usage of current products
■ Motivate trial and purchase of new products
■ Educate users and nonusers about improved product features
■ Suggest purchases of multiple and/or larger units of your product
■ Win over buyers of competitive products
■ Reinforce brand loyalty and purchase continuity
■ Create customer enthusiasm and excitement leading to word-of-mouth recommendations and referrals
■ Diminish fluctuations by encouraging off-season usage
■ Counter competitive raiding
■ Generate more traffic at your dealers' outlets

Although sales promotion campaigns represent short-term stimulation, they are most effective when used in a long-term framework. Further, sales promotion objectives cannot and should not be developed in a vacuum, but rather should tie in with overall marketing strategies — in particular, with the total promotion effort. In addition, your sales promotion objectives should be audience specific and should be spelled out in quantitative form to facilitate later evaluation.

Select Appropriate Techniques

Once you have decided which market segments you want to address, you can select specific techniques for motivating the dealer, introducing new products, and promoting existing products.

Motivating the dealer. With dealers (or any intermediary in the industrial, consumer, and service sector) the most powerful language to speak is still money; that is, profit. Among many available techniques, sales promotion to motivate dealers can include buying allowances, cooperative advertising, dealer listings, sales contests, specialty advertising, and exhibits at trade shows.

Introducing new products. Another meaningful way to break down the variety of approaches is to group them according to their major application area. Sales promotion techniques particularly well suited to the introduction of new products include free samples or trial offers, coupons, and money refunds.

Promoting existing products. You may want to use one or more different tools when attempting to promote established brands, such as premiums, price packs, contests and sweepstakes, trading stamps, and demonstrations. These tools aim to attract competitors' customers and build market share, introduce new versions of established brands, and reward buyer loyalty.

Table 9.3.1 will aid your selection process by presenting the pros and cons of these sales techniques.

Develop Your Sales Promotion Program

When deciding on the length of your campaign, you will find yourself at a critical point. If the promotion is too short, neither you nor your target audience will derive sufficient benefit from it. On the other hand, if it is too long, your brand image is likely to be cheapened and the "act now" urgency of your campaign will be diluted.

Table 9.3.1 Advantages and Disadvantages of Various Sales Promotion Techniques

Technique	Advantages	Disadvantages
Free samples	Induce trial Attract new customers Speed up adoption	Expensive Lacks precision Cumbersome
Free trial	Overcomes market resistance	Costly to administer
Door-to-door couponing	Very selective High redemption rate	Time consuming Needs careful supervision Lead time needed
Direct-mail couponing	High targetability At-home coverage High redemption rate	Needed Costly Dependent upon list quality
Newspaper couponing	Quick and convenient Geographically targetable Low cost	Low redemption rate Retailers may balk Requires careful planning
Magazine/supplement couponing	Targeted audience Effective coverage Increases in readership	Can become expensive Consumers neglect to clip Slow redemption rate
Money refund	Generates new business Reinforces brand loyalty	Results can be slow Modest impact
In-or-near-pack premiums	Increases product sales Modest distribution cost	Bonus to loyal buyers Pilferage problem
Self-liquidating premiums	Low cost Boosts brand image	Modest sales impact May be too popular
Price pack	Moves merchandise Keeps up visibility	Not selective May cheapen brand image
Contests/sweepstakes	No purchase required Increases brand awareness	Expensive Modest participation
Trading stamps/ promotional games	No extra expense for consumer Creates store preference	Consumer boredom Expensive
Point-of-purchase displays	Effective stimulation	Requires dealer cooperation

A related issue is, of course, frequency — that is, how often you should promote a given product. Generally, the rules are not too often, not too short, and not too long. Other issues to maximize the effectiveness of your campaign include the following:

Pretest your sales promotion program — having further determined when to run your campaign, make sure your schedule ties in smoothly with the other elements of your SMP. You should also proceed to *pretest your campaign* on a limited scale. This activity will help reassure you that you have chosen the most appropriate device and incentive and are delivering it in the most effective manner.

Implement and evaluate your campaign — once your campaign has been fine tuned and fully orchestrated, put it into effect. If you are introducing a new product, you may want to demonstrate it at a national sales meeting to motivate your sales force to go out and excel. For an established product, you may instead send your salespeople kits that spell out the objectives of your campaign and its operational details, as well as the nature and size of the incentives offered to them, your dealers, and your consumers.

Monitor the progress of your campaign — you can measure the extent of goal attainment and campaign effectiveness in various ways; the essential ones, for example, are product movement or market share figures. But it is here that you must keep in mind the limitations of your sales promotion campaign; namely: *sales promotion is a short-term tool that can support long-term goals only in a supplementary capacity.* It cannot build a consumer franchise. To the contrary, if it is used too often, it can destroy the image of a brand. Thus, it should be used not as a substitute for advertising, but rather as a complementary effort.

9.4 MARKETING OVER THE INTERNET

Spanning the networks of retailers to brokers to manufacturers, a remarkable new marketing tool, the Internet, is transforming the way individuals buy and the methods by which companies conduct business. Its usage is as far reaching as the World Wide Web itself, with applications as sweeping as trading stocks, obtaining information on autos, subscribing to book and music clubs, getting price quotes on mortgages, and purchasing airline tickets.

International Data Corp. predicts there will be 94 million Internet users in the U.S. and 175 million worldwide by 2001. Dataquest says revenues from electronic commerce will rise from about $500 million in 1998 to $100 billion in 2001.

Let's track the workings of a particular transaction where a computer maker is searching for the best price and delivery of a memory chip in an open-market networking system:

1. A computer maker needs 10,000 memory chips to assemble one of its new models.
2. The purchasing department logs on to the Internet network and enters information about the chip. The system shows a list of available chips with price, quantity, and other specifications.
3. The computer maker puts in a price. E-mail messages notify the suppliers and other buyers interested in the same part of the bid.
4. The seller indicates its selling price. The buyer is alerted by E-mail and accepts the price.

The ability to utilize the Internet is not confined to the large organizations — small companies with limited sales resources can establish a home page as a way to communicate a product message, offer special deals, announce a new service, or launch into foreign markets.

Having established your Internet presence, the next step is to market your online service and have customers and prospects visit your site. The following guidelines will assist you in gaining visibility:

■ Promote your web site in all advertising media, including sales promotion brochures, technical manuals, letterheads, and business cards.
■ Display your web address on packages, in-store displays, and counter tops.
■ Use your web address on press releases and any articles written for or about your firm.
■ Develop dedicated promotions that "sell" the recipient on the advantages of visiting your Web site. This goes together with the guidelines of offering genuine information to the visitor.
■ Register with Web search engines, the means by which individuals locate sites that interest them. You can also buy a banner ad in a popular search engine in a particular section in which your company is classified. Interested users can then link or connect to your site, thereby increasing your traffic at a modest cost. The major search engines include Yahoo, Excite, Infoseek, WebCrawler, Alta Vista, Megellan, Lycos, and OpenText.

This exciting promotion medium is still in its infancy. And with the projected revenue growth into the 21st century projected to skyrocket into the billions, establishing a solid presence on the Internet will pay off in sales growth and market expansion.

The bottom line: make the Internet an integral component of your promotion effort in SMP Sections 7 and 8.

PART 10:
DISTRIBUTION STRATEGIES

Contents	
HELP TOPICS	*Applies to SMP in*
10.1 Developing Distribution Strategies	Sections 2, 3, 7,
10.2 Channel Size	and 8
Choosing Channels of Distribution	
Distribution and Market Exposure	
Direct vs. Indirect Distribution	
Function vs. Institution	
Making the Decision	
The Internet	
10.3 Channel Control	
Selecting Distributors	
Evaluating Distributors	

10.1 DEVELOPING DISTRIBUTION STRATEGIES

The ultimate success of your business strategy depends on moving your product to its intended market. Accordingly, you should take considerable care in selecting distribution strategies and considering the far-reaching impact of channel decisions.

Such decisions involve (1) the long-term commitment to the distribution channel, (2) the amount of geographic coverage needed to maintain a competitive advantage, and (3) the possibility of competitive inroads.

10.2 CHANNEL SIZE

Your initial step in developing a channel strategy is to review the categories of products being sold by your company and their market coverage. In your review consider these criteria:

- Specialty products do best with exclusive (restricted) distribution
- Convenience products do best with intensive (widespread) distribution
- Shopping products do best with selective (high sales potential) distribution

Next, determine if existing channels provide adequate market coverage and if there are possibilities for expansion. Enhancing your present distribution network or creating a new one affords a prime opportunity to unseat a channel leader or deter a challenger.

First, begin by tailoring distribution to each major market segment, weighing the following alternatives:

- *Direct selling vs. using distributors.* Consider selling direct. Eliminating the middlemen permits faster, more efficient access to product users. The rapid growth of direct-response marketing through telephone, mail, and the expanding use of the Internet permit flexible response to customers' demands by circumventing traditional space and time barriers. With this in mind, determine whether or not you can deliver service that distributors normally offer.
- *Distributors vs. brokers.* Whereas distributors typically carry inventory and brokers do not, question how each would serve market niches in light of customers' needs for critical delivery schedules, immediate customer assistance, and storage needs.
- *Distributors vs. retailers.* Pinpoint how each of these two options is efficient, taking into account quantities purchased, services rendered, and access to technical backup.
- *Exclusive vs. nonexclusive outlets.* Weigh the pros and cons: exclusivity may constrict the breadth of coverage of a channel, yet provide compensating service and commitment benefits. On the other hand, nonexclusive outlets may broaden overall availability, but impair the level of commitment required for your product line.

Also, look for potential possibilities for enhancing your distribution strategy by infusing value-added services that may provide enough differentiation to save your product from becoming a commodity. For example, strengthen customer relationships by employing value-added services:

- Make use of greater mobility by following customers into growth segments, thereby serving buyers' needs at various locations.
- Develop one-stop shopping that allows buyers to order a variety of related products with ease, convenience, and volume discounts. The combined effect makes it harder for competitors to gain a foothold in the distribution network.
- Centralize the delivery of technical training, customer service, and reliable after-sales support to provide an infrastructure from which to launch into new segments.
- Install a computerized ordering and stocking system to tie customers to the supplier, thereby creating an electronic stronghold from which it is difficult for competitors to disengage a customer.

Choosing Channels of Distribution

There are at least three reasons why distribution channel size should rank high in importance as you develop your firm's SMP.

Channel Dimensions Involve Long-Term Commitments to Other Firms

Once chosen, distribution channels typically develop a great deal of inertia against change. Your choice of a channel type associates your brand in the consumer's mind with a certain kind of store or outlet, thus creating an image that is difficult to alter.

Signing up individual wholesalers or retailers often involves substantial up-front outlays. This money is needed for the following: field training of sales personnel, granting of easy terms for initial stock, advertising and promotional support, and field sales support through missionary salespeople. These and many other investments and commitments would be wasted if you decide to abandon these channel partners.

Remember, too, that it would hardly sit well with the trade if you walked away from your commitments. Your channel partners would also resent any infringement on their franchise if you adopted a multiple-channel strategy for the same brand.

Channel Dimensions Delimit the Portion of the Market You can Reach

Your selection of channel members restricts the kinds and numbers of ultimate buyers you can reach through them. In effect, you could be cut off from that part of the market that does not patronize those outlets. Conversely, your selection of outlets may coincide with your target market, in which case neglecting the remainder of the market is deliberate.

But what if you can't attract the kinds of stores or outlets that cater to the group of consumers you wish to reach? Then you have to settle for what you can get. To avoid this trap, your product, price, and support must satisfy the intermediaries you want to win over.

Channel Dimensions Affect all other Marketing Decisions

The interdependence of marketing mix decisions is most evident when choosing distribution channels. If you choose a pattern of exclusive distribution, your product often becomes a luxury item requiring high prices and high dealer margins. If, on the other hand, you go after intensive market coverage, you characterize your product as mass merchandise, which often necessitates a low-price policy.

Choice of advertising approaches, themes, messages, and media will vary with the distribution channels of your product. Also, product and packaging design must reflect the characteristics of your selected channels.

For instance, merchandise suited for self-service outlets have to be presented differently from goods requiring the advice and explanation of knowledgeable sales personnel. Consequently, don't make channel decisions in a void, since they have repercussions on every other marketing decision you make and thus affect your entire marketing effort.

Distribution and Market Exposure

Adequate market coverage is interconnected to the product being promoted. Depending on the degree of market exposure desired, you can choose from exclusive, intensive, and selective distribution strategies (see Table 10.1).

Exclusive

If you sell a prestige product, you are likely to grant exclusive rights covering a geographic area to a specific wholesaler or retailer, protecting this firm against territorial encroachments by other companies carrying your products. This policy severely limits the number of middlemen handling your products and should be adopted only if you want to exercise substantial control over your intermediaries' prices, promotion, presentation, and service. It results in a stronger commitment on the part of your dealers and, thus, in a more aggressive selling effort.

Table 10.1 Considerations in Choosing Your Degree of Market Exposure			
Distribution Considerations	*Exclusive*	*Selective*	*Intensive*
Degree of coverage	Limited	Medium	Saturation
Degree of control	Stringent	Substantial	Virtually nil
Cost of distribution	Low	Medium	High
Dealer support	Substantial	Limited	Very limited
Dealer training	Extensive	Restricted	None
Type of goods	Specialty	Shopping	Convenience
Product durability	Durable	Semidurable	Nondurable
Product advertising	Yes	Yes	No
Couponing	No	No	Yes
Product example	Automobile	Suit	Chewing gum

Intensive

Intensive distribution is the direct opposite of exclusivity. Popular among producers of convenience items, this policy aims to make these goods available in as many outlets as possible.

As the category name suggests, buyers of such products expect them to be conveniently accessible and will not expend much shopping effort. Products in this category are frequently purchased, low-ticket nondurables, such as cigarettes and chewing gum.

Selective

Selective distribution falls between the extremes of exclusive and intensive distribution. This policy involves setting up selection criteria and deliberately restricting the number of retailers that will be permitted to handle your brand. More than one, but less than all applicants in an area will be selected. This approach implies quality without the restrictions of exclusivity.

Direct vs. Indirect Distribution

A very basic distribution decision that you have to make relatively early in your planning is whether you want to handle the distribution of your product alone or enlist expert help. You must choose either direct distribution or indirect distribution.

Direct Distribution

Direct distribution involves a direct transfer of ownership from the producer to the consumer. This method does not preclude various types of facilitators from entering into the picture. As long as they do not assume title separate and distinct from the manufacturer, the channel still remains direct.

Thus, producers can sell through the mail, over the phone, door to door, on the Internet, through a factory outlet, through their own retail stores, or even through an independent agent, and still be involved in a direct transaction. Direct distribution obviously involves a greater degree of control than indirect distribution, but it cuts a producer off from the widespread coverage that the latter approach can offer.

Indirect Distribution

On the other hand, indirect distribution always incorporates middlemen or resellers, who are basically of two types: distributors and retailers.

In the direct distribution channel there is never a third party who takes title to the goods in question. For indirect distribution, the opposite situation is clearly the case, even though the manufacturer is likely to have a sales force to call on intermediaries of the middleman variety.

Function vs. Institution

In differentiating between direct and indirect distribution, a basic distinction ought to be made between the functions and institutions of wholesaling and retailing. The function of wholesaling is to sell those items necessary for use in the conduct of a business (for example, word processors) or for resale.

The function of retailing, in contrast, is to sell for personal, nonbusiness use. In a retailing transaction the buyer of an item is a consumer who intends it for private use or consumption.

The reason for drawing these rudimentary distinctions between function and institution is that *institutions can be eliminated; their respective functions cannot.* When you first enter a new market, it is generally advisable to go the indirect route, involving wholesalers who can deliver a variety of quick and reliable services at little or no cost.

Later, though, as your product moves into the maturity stage of the life cycle, you may want to eliminate your wholesalers in order to gain more immediate access to your retailers and better control over the selling effort. It is at this point that you often discover that one can eliminate the institution, but not the function of wholesaling (or retailing, for that matter). The question, therefore, is not whether to perform these functions, but who is to perform them.

Making the Decision

When the time comes to make the channel decision for your product, you should consider several factors. Initially, an important consideration is where does the customer expect to find your product or service?

Therefore, the prevailing distribution pattern in the industry is a powerful guide in making such a channel decision. If your current sales force has related experience and appropriate business contacts, you may want to follow established routes.

Other factors you should take into account can be grouped as company, competitive, and customer factors.

- *Companies* that are strong financially have the option of using direct distribution, while weaker firms have to use middlemen. If your product line is broad, you are in a better position than a specialized supplier to consider going direct. And, in keeping with the marketing credo of staying close to the customer, you will want to have fewer intermediaries.
- *Competitive* practices will often encourage you to meet competitors head on in the very same outlets they use.
- *Customer* characteristics include the number of buyers, their geographic location, and their buying patterns. You are better off going direct when you have a limited number of prospects. Again, if they are concentrated in only a few areas, you can send your own sales force out to do the job. Should they buy often and in small quantities, you had better let others handle the selling.

Channel members are a vital link in your effort to satisfy distant customers. By making them your partners and serving their best interests, you will find that they will help you achieve your goals.

The Internet

As discussed in other sections of Help Topics, there is still another factor that is beginning to make a significant impact on channel-related decisions: the Internet. By 2002, businesses are expected to exchange an estimated $327 billion annually in goods and services through that explosive new channel.

As a channel of distribution, doing business via the Internet shows cost savings in the range of 5 to 10% of sales (an average based on the experience of a wide variety of companies in 1998). In more dramatic numbers, some companies reported huge advantages from online business relationships. For instance, chipmaker National Semiconductor Corp. reported saving its distributors $20 million in 1998. Boeing Co. booked $100 million in spare parts orders from airlines in 1 year through its Web site. And networking giant Cisco Systems Inc. booked $11 million in orders each day from resellers, or about $4 billion a year on its Web site.

10.3 CHANNEL CONTROL

Channel control considers four sets of circumstances that dictate the search for new distributors:

1. New marketing efforts — for example, the introduction of a new product or entry into new markets.
2. Desire to intensify market coverage.
3. Need to replace existing distributors.
4. Industry changes or your strategy changes in methods of distribution.

After you've developed a channel control strategy that involves distributors, you need to know how to select and evaluate them. Use the guidelines described in the following sections.

Selecting Distributors

Only with the appropriate distribution mix can you satisfactorily achieve your company's marketing goals.

For instance, as you introduce new products, you may find that your current distributors are ill equipped to sell and service them, or that they already handle competitive products from other manufacturers. Or you may be addressing a new kind of clientele not serviced by your current network. If you enter into new geographic markets, the need for appropriate representation may become self-evident.

As you review your share of the business in a given segment, you may conclude that your firm is underrepresented. Or you may determine that your present distributor network is not going after the business aggressively enough to satisfy you. As a result, you may need to add or replace more distributors in the territory, based on population, sales, buying potential, or other relevant considerations.

By far the most frequent reason for appointing new distributors is the turnover of existing outlets. These changes may be due to natural attrition, the death or retirement of principals, or the sale or collapse of a distributor.

The recent trend toward more specialization or limited-line selling has also led many distributors to drop a certain manufacturer's line.

Often, changes in your distributor mix come about by inadequate distributor performance that leaves the manufacturer, or even both sides, dissatisfied. In some instances, you may try to rekindle an existing relationship, as long as there is a willingness to recognize the dynamic changes of the marketplace, and consequently the changes required in strategy.

Looking at Your Distribution Structure

Rarely should you have to revamp your entire distribution structure. In some situations, however, you may want to add or eliminate an intermediary step in distributing your company's products, requiring the selection of new distributors.

Once you establish a need for a new or additional distributor representation, your next task is to develop a list of candidates. You usually have a number of sources for this list, including your own field sales force, your manager of distributor sales, trade associations, and present distributors and dealers.

Table 10.2 highlights the selection criteria most often mentioned by some 200 leading U.S. manufacturers in a study on this subject. Look at how the numerous considerations are classified and summarized into a limited number of categories that can apply to any distributor selection task. You have the option of modifying or adding criteria to the list to suit your particular needs.

Evaluating Distributors

Once you have secured the services of a sought-after distributor candidate, you must then ensure that your association brings maximum benefit to both parties. You need to perform periodic evaluations designed to keep you continually informed about the relative performance of your various distributors.

These evaluations may be in the nature of current operating appraisals or may take on the form of overall performance reviews. If they are simple and limited in scope, you could conduct them monthly. Thorough analyses, however, should be undertaken only at infrequent intervals: annually, biannually, or even triannually.

If you engage in selective rather than exclusive distribution, the amount of evaluative input that you can obtain from your distributors is quite limited, forcing you to rely mostly on your own records, observations, and intelligence. If your product is a high-volume, low-cost item with

Table 10.2. Criteria for Selecting Distributors

Criterion (Category)	Reasoning
Financial aspects	Only a distributor of solid financial strength and practices can assure you of adequate, continuous representation
Sales organization and performance	The sales strength and record of a prospect is essential to your potential relationship
Number of salespeople (in the field and on the inside)	The general rule: the more salespeople, the more sales and the more effective the market coverage
Sales and technical competence	Salespeople with inadequate technical and sales skills are a liability
Sales performance	A track record speaks for itself
Product lines carried Competitive Compatible Quality level Number of lines	Pick your partners carefully Generally avoid, sometimes okay Tend to be beneficial The higher, the better Will your line get enough attention?
Reputation	You are judged by the company you keep
Market coverage Geographic Industry Intensity of coverage	Exposure means sales Avoid overlap and conflicts Major user groups must be covered Infrequent calls means lost business
Inventory and warehousing Kind and size of inventory Warehousing facilities	Ability to deliver is often crucial You want the right mix and a willingness to maintain adequate stock Storage and handling must be appropriate
Management Ability Continuity Attitudes	Proper leadership spells success You want competent leadership Succession should be assured Look for enthusiasm and aggressiveness

little need for after-sale servicing, you can restrict yourself to a more limited evaluation than in the case of complex systems installations.

If your team is composed of many hundreds of multiline distributors, you will tend to take a closer look at a particular reseller only if its sales trends are way out of line. This procedure is called *evaluation by exception*.

If, in contrast, your firm employs only a moderate number of outlets, your analysis can be more thorough. You may not even need a formal evaluation if you have a close, continuous working relationship.

Whether you are a distributor or manufacturer, here are some broad guidelines:

If You Are a Distributor

Take control of the distribution channel by becoming more than just a conduit for supplying products from manufacturer to customer. Utilize technology to manage customers' inventories, improve delivery times, solve customers' problems, and reduce costs in order processing and shipping.

If You Are a Manufacturer

Recognize that if you decide to bypass the middleman, you will have to deliver the above services. With distributors taking the initiative, it may be a prudent alternative to select a distributor and provide maximum support, even to the extent of supplying capital to purchase or update the distributor's technology. Such an alliance accepts the middlemen not as a weak link in a distribution chain, but as a powerful coupling to activate a marketing strategy.

Regardless of your position in the distribution chain, there are key functions you have to deal with in shaping a distribution strategy:

- *Information:* collect, analyze, and disseminate market intelligence about potential and current customers, competitors, and other forces affecting the market
- *Communication:* combine various forms of communication, including literature, videos, and workshops to attract and retain customers
- *Negotiation:* seek agreement on price, terms of delivery, and other value-added services as they relate to a preferred-customer status and long-term relationships
- *Ordering:* set up procedures for the efficient transmission of ordering information, e.g., using the Internet

- *Financing:* develop the means to fund a managed inventory system
- *Risk taking:* assume the responsibility for risks associated with the expanded role and activities of the middleman
- *Physical possession:* develop a suitable capability to store additional varieties of products for customers and manage increases in inventory turnover
- *Payment:* design an effective system for payment — including the selective financing of inventories for the buyer
- *Title:* develop a system to pinpoint the transfer of ownership from seller to buyer; in some situations, inventory is held at the buyer's location and title changes only when usage occurs

With the backward and forward flow of activities throughout the distribution channel, different participants in the channel assume distinct functions. Therefore, whether manufacturer or distributor, when forming a relationship clearly define the role of each channel member.

PART 11:
CREATING GLOBAL
STRATEGIES

HELP TOPICS	Applies to SMP in
11.1 Creating Global Strategies	Sections 1
11.2 Achieving a Global Perspective	through 4
Overseas Markets Offer Attractive Potential	
11.3 Entry Strategies for International Markets	
Exporting	
Licensing	
Joint Venture	
Wholly Owned Subsidiaries	
Management Contract	
Summary	

11.1 CREATING GLOBAL STRATEGIES

A global marketing perspective goes well beyond geography and, in its broader dimensions, focuses on fresh applications of competitive strategies. Exhibiting a global perspective requires the mind of a strategist and the scope of thinking of a senior-level executive.

It boils down in pragmatic terms to opportunistic thinking. Such thinking is expressed in how you select and target markets and then penetrate for market share leadership (based, of course, on capabilities and resources of your company). Such a perspective is the central aim behind developing your SMP.

11.2 ACHIEVING A GLOBAL PERSPECTIVE

More specifically, a global perspective means acquiring a mindset to assist you in successfully managing a customer-oriented business, such as:

- Exhibiting expertise in competitive strategies
- Encouraging sound strategic marketing planning
- Fostering product innovation
- Encouraging entrepreneurship
- Committing to total product quality
- Driving for product differentiation
- Pursuing target (niche) marketing
- Maintaining a complete global perspective

Applying that orientation must play out against tough barriers, including aggressive competition from an increasing number of countries worldwide. Then, there are the fighting-back attitudes from domestic companies, as well as the growing protectionist feelings from some governments.

Overseas Markets Offer Attractive Potential

There is no denying, however, that international markets present a challenging and steadily growing opportunity for global expansion, particularly as you develop SMP Section 4. It is likely that there are many people and companies around the world in need of what you have to offer, regardless of your industry.

More and more, the world is becoming a global marketplace. To stop your marketing activities at the borders of the U.S., and even other parts of North America, is not only arbitrary, but also shortsighted.

Developed countries, such as the industrial nations of Western Europe, usually place few restrictions on international marketing activities. They also provide an easier place to break into international markets, because they usually have fully developed communications, distribution, and transportation systems, to name but a few facilitating factors.

In developing countries, on the other hand, you will need a more flexible approach, since they tend to be more jealous of their national prerogatives and less advanced in their infrastructure. Nevertheless, their sales potential is quite substantial. It can be tapped successfully if you are willing to adapt.

The entry strategies that follow show the choices available to your firm in its attempt to penetrate markets abroad and to establish a presence in them. While representing alternative possibilities, they also can be thought of as stages in a sequential process of increasing commitment.

1. Products have to be tailored for local markets. Setting up such a strategy requires coordination at many levels. Sometimes termed "mass customization," local marketing involves full cooperation from product developers, producers, and local users in finding applications and solutions to customers' problems.
2. Employ country nationals in key positions, where possible. Cultural, language, and local market barriers are more likely to be overcome by the sensitive responses of management familiar with the local markets.
3. Participate with distributors that can create effective linkages to specific customer groups.
4. Monitor the image your company and product line project to target segments. When completed, the next step is to determine what changes are needed in product quality, performance, or service to improve the image that is consistent with the culture and practices of individual market segments.

11.3 ENTRY STRATEGIES FOR INTERNATIONAL MARKETS

Strategies for entering foreign markets are conveniently classified into five basic categories: *exporting, licensing, joint venture, wholly owned subsidiaries,* and *management contract.*

Table 11.1 presents these approaches in a systematic form for comparison. These alternatives differ from one another in intensity of commitment, amount of investment, extent of control, and degree of profitability.

The choice from among them is often dictated by circumstances such as insufficient funds, inadequate knowledge of a foreign environment, and host country restrictions on ownership. The intent here is to present an overview of the benefits and drawbacks of each category to enable you to make more intelligent and informed decisions when considering the possibilities open to you on the international scene.

Exporting

Your company may want to begin exporting and take best advantage of selling into markets that may be more responsive than domestic ones. If your productive capacity is not fully utilized, international markets can provide outlets that enable you to get extra mileage out of your plant.

Many firms consider revenues produced by exporting as "found money," because domestic sales and the profit margin have already covered the fixed costs of the plant.

Table 11.1 Comparison of Entry Strategies for Global Markets

Strategy	Definition	Intensity of Commitment	Amount of Investment	Extent of Control	Degree of Profitability
Exporting	Marketing in one country goods produced in another	Typically very limited	Possible investment in inventory	Rather limited, except in the case of exclusive distribution	Moderate, due to transportation cost, import duties, middlemen cost
Licensing	Licensor grants licensee right to use patent, know-how	Own marketing effort precluded until expiration of license	Virtually none	Very restricted; spelled out in license agreement	Fixed royalties dependent on licensee effort
Joint venture	Sharing ownership and control of foreign operation with at least one partner	Generally provide know-how and equity capital portion	Dependent on equity share	Dependent on ownership ratio and power play	Varies according to circumstances
Wholly owned subsidiary	Firm abroad 100% owned by U.S. company	Strong commitment of all kinds of resources	Substantial investment in plant, etc.	Complete control over all phases of operation	Can be highly profitable
Management contract	Managing a foreign facility under contract	Only human resources	Facility not owned by managing firm	Restricted by contract; typically quite limited	Moderate, due to its fee character

Also, your firm may stumble onto the international scene because of excess production capacity and need stopgap measures to bring utilization up to a more desirable level. You may not be serious about continuing export activities, but are attracted by the ratio of considerable sales potential to limited commitment and risk.

At the outset, for instance, you might not be inclined to invest in inventories abroad. Rather, you would want to minimize exposure by initially restricting activities to representation or distribution arrangements in a given country without committing funds for inventory, advertising, and so forth. There is a price to pay, of course, for this lack of initial commitment.

If you leave everything to agents or distributors, you will have very little control over what happens. And with inexperience, costs tend to be somewhat higher than they are otherwise, thus cutting into profit potential. In international trade, cost categories include transportation, import duties, and middleman expenses. The paperwork involved in exporting should not be underestimated, either.

Licensing

In one way, the simplest way to enter international markets is through licensing. In this setup, a licensor grants the right to exploit patents, trademarks, or proprietary technological know-how to a licensee (usually one per country) on an exclusive basis. Thus, without additional investment, your company could benefit from the efforts of others, based on its specialized knowledge and proprietary rights.

Relationships with individual licensees are arranged in licensing agreements. Such agreements generally stipulate the responsibilities of each party, the rights transferred, markets to be served, payments to be made, control procedures, and termination circumstances. And protective clauses relate to the maintenance of proprietary rights, to protection against disclosure of information, and to arbitration or litigation procedures.

On the surface, licensing looks like the ideal way for reaping effortless rewards. You can penetrate overseas markets with virtually no investment. There is no need to make capital outlays and send key personnel abroad, as in other entry strategies. Your licensee is likely to be a firm that is well established in the field and can give maximum support and exposure to your product.

Licensing offers you a source of additional earnings with little risk and minor demands on executive time. It gives you a chance to meet the needs of foreign prospects, overcome trade barriers, build up goodwill, and protect your patents and trademarks through usage. Sometimes, licensor and licensee cross-license each other, thus mutually benefiting from present and future know-how in a field.

Licensors are compensated for granting the license in the form of royalties. The royalty rate depends on the value of the rights being made available, the bargaining power of each party, and the prevailing rate level. The amount of these royalties is, naturally, the direct outcome of the level of effort expended by the licensee.

And this is the crux of the matter — once you have gained a license, you are at the mercy of your licensee. Though your agreement may provide for quality inspections and audits, you really cannot control the day-to-day operations of your licensee and the extent of market development.

Should the licensee's efforts prove unsatisfactory or the international potential of the licensed property grows, a license agreement can turn out to be a stranglehold, effectively restricting you from using your own property and quite possibly creating a strong international competitor. So, be cautious at the outset.

Joint Venture

If you want an active manufacturing presence in a host country transcending the amount of involvement and impact that you can have with exporting or licensing, a joint venture can prove an attractive possibility. In essence, a joint venture means that your firm establishes a subsidiary abroad that is jointly owned with at least one individual or company native to the country in question. This approach may be advisable for a number of reasons:

- A joint venture may provide valuable help in gaining a foothold in a host country
- It may reduce the risk of failure or expropriation
- It provides additional capital or personnel you may lack to expand into this market on your own
- It provides access to a local partner's distribution system or know-how
- The law of the land may prevent setting up wholly owned subsidiaries

In co-owning and co-controlling your common subsidiary, your firm and its overseas partner may share patents, trademarks, and control over manufacturing or marketing. Joint ventures prove to be an excellent vehicle for entering international markets if the local partner has the marketing expertise to complement your firm's technological know-how. A well-established local partner can provide your firm with physical facilities, a labor force, and contacts with businesses and officials, while your company may offer capital, technology, and managerial talent.

The most obvious disadvantage of joint ventures is the reduced control of the foreign co-owner. Points of view may differ as to the policies and practices of the joint venture operation. Differences in culture, language, and business philosophy may be difficult to overcome. While the potential for conflict is substantial, a well-chosen and well-motivated partner could result in great value.

Wholly Owned Subsidiaries

The greatest form of commitment abroad is a subsidiary that is wholly owned by your firm. The underlying idea is that ownership equals control and that complete control is necessary to meet corporate objectives. When demand and the competitive situation justify the substantial investment involved, this strategy can provide substantial benefits to the parent company. Your company may want to manufacture abroad in order to:

■ Capitalize on low-cost labor
■ Avoid high import taxes or quotas
■ Reduce transportation cost
■ Gain access to raw materials
■ Export preferentially to related markets

If your products are labor intensive, you may want to locate plants in low-wage nations or areas, subsequently exporting the finished goods to more developed countries. Some countries and markets have erected high, even prohibitive, import duty barriers in an effort to preserve precious hard currency and foster local industry.

Less developed countries are concerned about possible exploitation of local resources if foreign firms within their borders do not have local partners. Thus, almost without exception, they require joint ownership and no longer permit wholly owned subsidiaries. Increasingly, even in developed nations, firms may insist on taking local partners into their overseas subsidiaries. Doing so avoids criticism and improves their ability to cope with union demands and the complex requirements of the host government.

Management Contract

A management contract involves managing an overseas facility for its owner. It is entered into when the local owner does not possess, and cannot obtain, sufficient management expertise locally to run the facility efficiently.

Such a contract may be connected with the building of a sophisticated new facility, such as an airport or an oil refinery in a less developed country. The general contractor of such a turnkey facility then often provides the talent to run it under a management contract.

Yet management by contract can represent the ultimate humiliation for the contractee when developing countries expropriate major industrial complexes and then ask the former owners to run these facilities under contract. At one time, this happened in the "friendly" takeover of oil producing facilities by the Venezuelan government. Being pragmatic, U.S. firms agreed to manage their former properties in return for special considerations in addition to their management fees.

Summary

You can feel out a selected market through exporting. If you are successful, the need may arise for local production. If you are not ready for direct investment, licensing provides a reasonable substitute. In order not to have to go it alone from the financial and marketing angles, you may instead (or subsequently) choose a joint venture arrangement. Where permitted, wholly owned subsidiaries put you fully in charge. Management contracts offer a solution when a host country seeks your company's expertise, without allowing it to acquire ownership of the managed properties.

Whichever entry strategy your firm chooses to penetrate a foreign market, going global will increase your potential for growth and profit.

PART 12:
THE TEAM APPROACH:
THINKING LIKE A STRATEGIST

Contents	
HELP TOPICS	*Applies to SMP in*

12.1 The Team Approach — Thinking Like a Strategist
12.2 The Roles and Responsibilities of Strategy Teams
    Team Duties
    Team Responsibilities
12.3 Identifying Business-Building Opportunities
	Sections 1
	through 9

12.1 THE TEAM APPROACH — THINKING LIKE A STRATEGIST

This final part of Help Topics concerns people interaction; that is, the mind of the strategist and the human will. These human factors intensify whenever there is a conflict of human wills, whenever there is an effort to grow, expand, or achieve objectives.

The purpose of this section is to show how you can coordinate the diverse talents of individuals into a cohesive force for developing your SMP. Therefore, the focus will be on (1) the role of strategy teams in developing your SMP; (2) broadening the perspective of teams to look at new developments that can be incorporated into the SMP; and (3) guidelines to thinking like strategists.

12.2 THE ROLES AND RESPONSIBILITIES OF STRATEGY TEAMS

The mind of the manager, the human factors, and the people interactions are all key ingredients in organizing the input of market and competitive analyses into your SMP. Now let's overlay that concept by repeating the definition of strategic marketing as a

> *total system of interacting business activities designed to plan, price, promote, and distribute want-satisfying products and ser-vices to household and organizational users at a profit in a competitive environment.*

You can effectively blend people interaction with the marketing con-cept through strategy teams consisting of individuals from all functional areas of the organization (for example, manufacturing, product develop-ment, R&D, finance, distribution, and sales/marketing). These functions may vary in some organizations.

Nonetheless, the key idea is that individuals from those major functions must be present on the strategy team to fulfill the strategic vision (SMP Section 1) and the tactical day-to-day objectives (SMP Section 7) within a competitive environment.

One of the most notable users of strategy teams is Dow Chemical Co. It has employed an organizational structure for over 25 years that permits strategy teams to operate for individual products and markets, and at various levels throughout its worldwide operations. At any given time there may be as many as 40 strategy teams at work within Dow.

These teams have the various designations of Product Management Team (PMT), operating at a product manager level for a product line; Business Management Team (BMT) at the next higher level, dealing with a business unit or major market; and Industry Management Team (IMT), operating on a still broader dimension.

Looking, for example, at the BMT, it is usually chaired by a prod-uct/marketing manager and staffed by individuals representing such func-tional activities as manufacturing, finance, technical management, and marketing/sales. This arrangement not only allows for the dynamics of team members working together, but also defuses traditional adversarial relationships — for example, between marketing and manufacturing.

Team members may change from time to time, and the frequency of meetings may vary with teams. Yet, the key element is that the permanency of the team as part of the organizational structure exists and can be called into action at any time.

In establishing a strategy team in your organization, take the lead in educating the team members to the key corporate concepts and expectations, SMP requirements, and strategy techniques illustrated in this book. Further, brief the members, with the active endorsement of senior management, on the team's roles and responsibilities, which follow.

The strategy team, BMT or PMT — whichever designation you select — is one of the most successful organizational formats for conceiving and delivering innovative and entrepreneurial thinking to the organization. Such a team should be initiated at every operational level by adopting role and responsibility guidelines.

For our purposes, let's designate the team as a BMT and establish its duties and responsibilities.

Team Duties

The BMT serves as a significant functional contributor to the strategic marketing planning process with the following leadership responsibilities:

- Define the business or product strategic direction (SMP Section 1)
- Analyze the environmental, industry, customer, and competitor situations (SMP Sections 1 and 5)
- Develop long- and short-term objectives and strategies (SMP Sections 2 and 7)
- Define product, market, distribution, and quality plans to implement competitive strategies (SMP Sections 3, 4, and 8)

Team Responsibilities

- Create and recommend new or additional products
- Approve all alterations or modifications of a major nature
- Act as a formal communications channel for field product needs
- Plan and implement strategies throughout the product life cycle
- Develop programs to improve market position and profitability
- Identify market or product opportunities in light of changing consumer demands
- Coordinate activities of various functions to achieve short- and long-term objectives
- Coordinate efforts for the interdivisional exchanges of new market or product opportunities
- Develop a SMP

12.3 IDENTIFYING BUSINESS-BUILDING OPPORTUNITIES

A team should enjoy a clear-cut mandate to create marketing opportunities or to tackle competitive threats. More specifically, the team should actively look for opportunities and take action. The following opportunities are presented as examples.

Opportunity 1: Search for opportunities in unserved, poorly served, or emerging market segments.

- ■ *Actions:*
  - Penetrate and expand niches
  - Improve products and services
  - Stretch product lines
  - Position products to the needs of customers and against competitors

Opportunity 2: Identify ways to create new opportunities.

- ■ *Actions:*
  - Seek new product or market niches
  - Participate in new technology, innovations, and manufacturing
  - Pioneer something new or unique

Opportunity 3: Look for opportunities through marketing creativity.

- ■ *Actions:*
  - Promote image through quality, performance, and training
  - Promote creativity in sales promotion, advertising, personal selling, and the Internet

Opportunity 4: Monitor changing behavioral patterns and preferences.

- ■ *Actions:*
  - Practice segmenting markets according to behavioral patterns
  - Identify clusters of customers who might buy or utilize different services for different reasons

Opportunity 5: Learn from competitors and adapt strategies from other industries.

- ■ *Action:* Understand competitors
  - How they conduct business

- What products they sell
- What strategies they pursue
- How they manufacture, distribute, promote, and price
- What are their weaknesses, limitations, and possible vulnerabilities

Opportunity 6: Help your organization develop into an upbeat, customer-driven organization.

- *Action:* Show customers revenue expansion opportunities
  - Reduce returns and complaints from the end user
  - Speed up production and delivery
  - Improve the customer's market position and image
  - Add brand-name value for the customer (where appropriate)
  - Add customer benefits through additional services
  - Create areas of differentiation that gives a customer a competitive advantage
  - Improve a customer's reordering procedures
- *Action:* Show cost-reduction opportunities
  - Cut the customer's purchase costs
  - Reduce the customer's production costs
  - Absorb all or part of a customer's product development function
  - Reduce the customer's delivery costs
  - Lessen the customer's administrative overhead
  - Maximize the customer's working capital

Internalize these guidelines and you will master the essence of Strategic Marketing Planning.

VI

COMPUTER DISK:

*How to Develop
a Strategic Marketing Plan —
A Step-by-Step Guide*

INTRODUCTION

This computer disk offers you a convenient, hands-on format to develop your personalized Strategic Marketing Plan (SMP), based on the planning guidelines and forms used in the accompanying book. That means that you retain the proven planning structure of the SMP, yet you are free to customize the forms by inserting the specific vocabulary and unique issues related to your industry and company.

You can even add special forms required by your organization or insert any of the commercially available spreadsheet programs, thereby making the SMP a permanent part of your management operating system. Otherwise, use the guidelines suggested in the book, which is appropriate for most organizations.

You can count on substantial assistance as you develop your SMP. For instance, to hone your planning skills and improve the quality of the plan you submit to management or to an outside financial institution for funding, you can refer to the following chapters of the book:

Chapter 1, *The Strategic Marketing Plan: Strategic Section,* illustrates through actual case examples how to develop the visionary 3- to 5-year strategic section of the SMP.

Chapter 2, *The Strategic Marketing Plan: Tactical Section,* describes how to develop a realistic 1-year tactical section of the SMP, also using a real case example to illustrate each planning guideline.

Chapter 3, *Marketing Problem Solver: the Strategic Marketing Plan in Action,* shows how successful companies solved severe competitive problems and won. After each example, references are made to those sections of the SMP that address the specific problem.

Chapter 4, *Checklists for Developing Competitive Strategies,* includes numerous forms to help you evaluate the potential of a market and develop competitive marketing strategies. It is particularly valuable in adding greater precision to your SMP and improving the overall performance of your company.

Chapter 5, *Help Topics,* provides you with a comprehensive reference on most subjects related to developing your SMP.

OVERVIEW OF THE STRATEGIC MARKETING PLAN (STRATEGIC SECTION)

You can obtain optimum results for your SMP by following the process diagrammed in Figure 6.1. As you examine the flowchart, notice that the top row of boxes represents the *strategic* portion of the plan and covers a 3- to 5-year time frame.

The second row of boxes displays the *tactical* 1-year marketing plan. It is the merging of the strategic plan and the marketing plan into one unified SMP that makes it a complete format and an operational management tool.

You will find that following the SMP process will add an organized and disciplined approach to your thinking. Yet the process in no way confines your thinking or creativity. Instead, it enhances your inventiveness, extends your strategy vision, and elevates the creative process. In

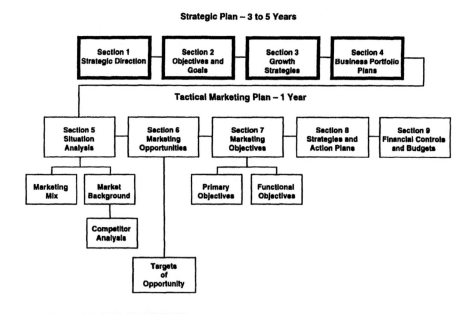

Figure 6.1 Strategic Marketing Plan

turn, the strategy vision results in providing you with a choice of revenue-building opportunities expressed through markets, products, and services.

THE STRATEGIC PLAN: LOOKING FORWARD 3 TO 5 YEARS

The *Strategic* portion of the SMP is defined as the managerial process for developing and maintaining a strategic fit between the organization and changing market opportunities. It relies on developing the following sections: (1) a strategic direction or mission statement, (2) objectives and goals, (3) a growth strategy, and (4) business portfolio plans.

SECTION 1: STRATEGIC DIRECTION

The first box, Section 1, *Strategic Direction,* allows you to visualize the long-term direction of your company, division, product, or service.

Planning Guidelines

The first step is to use the following questions to provide an organized approach to developing a Strategic Direction. Answering the questions will help you shape the ideal vision of what your company, business unit, or product/service will look like over the next 3 to 5 years.

More precisely, it should echo your (or your team's) long-range outlook, as long as it conforms with overall corporate objectives and policies. To develop your strategic direction, fill in your answers to the following six questions.

1. What are your firm's distinctive areas of expertise? This question refers to your organization's (or business unit's) competencies. You can answer by evaluating the following:
   - Relative competitive strengths of your product or service based on customer satisfaction, profitability, and market share
   - Relationships with distributors and/or end-use customers
   - Existing production capabilities
   - Size of your sales force
   - Financial strength
   - R&D expenditures
   - Amount of customer or technical service provided
   Fill in:

2. What business should your frim be in over the next 3 to 5 years? How will it differ from what exists today?
    Fill in:

3. What segments or categories of customers will you serve?
    Fill in:

4. What additional functions are you likely to fulfill for customers as you see the market evolve?
    Fill in:

5. What new technologies will you require to satisfy future customer/market needs?
    Fill in:

6. What changes are taking place in markets, consumer behavior, competition, environmental issues, culture, and the economy that will impact your company?
    Fill in:

Now compress your answers to the above six questions into one statement that would represent a realistic Strategic Direction for your product, business unit, or company. (See Chapter 1 for an example of how a Strategic Direction is written.)

Fill in:

SECTION 2: OBJECTIVES AND GOALS

Planning Guidelines

State your objectives and goals both quantitatively and nonquantitatively (the second box in the top row in Figure 6.1). Your primary guideline: take a strategic focus covering a time frame of from 3 to 5 years. That means, look again at how you defined your Strategic Direction, so that you can develop objectives that will have the broadest impact on the growth of your business.

Quantitative Objectives

Indicate, in precise statements, major performance expectations such as sales growth ($/units), market share, return on investment, profit, and any other quantitative objectives required by your management.

With the longer time frame of 3 to 5 years, your objectives are generally broad and relate to the total business or to a few major segments. (In the tactical portion of the SMP these objectives will be more specific for each product and market.)

Fill in:

Nonquantitative Objectives

Think of nonquantitative objectives as setting a foundation from which to build on to your organization's existing strengths, as well as to eliminate any internal weaknesses.

Use the following examples to trigger objectives for your business. Above all, keep your objectives specific, actionable, realistic, and focused on achieving a sustainable competitive advantage.

■ Upgrading distribution channels
■ Expanding secondary distribution
■ Consolidating an industry or segment position
■ Building "specialty product" penetration
■ Establishing or improving marketing intelligence systems
■ Focusing training actions
■ Launching new and repositioning old products
■ Upgrading field services
■ Improving marketing mix management

Fill in:

SECTION 3: GROWTH STRATEGIES

Planning Guidelines

This section outlines the process you can use to secure your objectives and goals. Think of *strategies* as actions to achieve your longer-term objectives; *tactics* as actions to achieve shorter-term objectives.

Since this time frame of this section covers 3 to 5 years, strategies are indicated here. The 1-year portion, illustrated later in the plan, identifies tactics.

In practice, where you have developed broad-based, long-term objectives you should list multiple strategies for each objective. In instances where you find it difficult to apply specific strategies, it is appropriate to use general strategy statements.

Tip: how you write strategies can vary according to your individual or team's style. For example, you have the option of merging the objectives and strategies sections by restating each objective from Section 2 followed by a listing of corresponding strategies. Still another option is to write a general strategy statement followed by a detailed listing of specific objectives and strategies. (See Chapter 1 for examples.)

Overall, your thinking about strategies boils down to actions related to the following:

- Growth and mature markets
- Long-term brand or product positioning
- Product quality
- Market share growth potential
- Distribution channel options
- Product, price, and promotion mix
- Spending strategies
- Specific marketing, sales, R&D, and manufacturing strengths to be exploited

Fill in:

SECTION 4: BUSINESS PORTFOLIO PLAN

Planning Guidelines

The business portfolio includes listings of *existing* products and markets and *new* products and markets. Following a logical progression, it is based on the strategic direction, objectives and goals, and growth strategies outlined in previous sections.

Tip: your strategic direction should mirror the content of your portfolio. That is, the broader the dimension of your strategic direction, the more expansive the range of products and markets in the portfolio. Conversely, the narrower the dimension of your strategic direction, the more limited the content of products and markets.

Use the following format and guidelines to develop your own business portfolio:

Existing Products/Existing Markets (Market Penetration)

List those *existing* products you currently offer to *existing* customers or market segments. In an appendix of the SMP, you can document sales, profits, and market share data. From such information you can determine if your level of penetration is adequate and if possibilities exist for further growth.

After identifying new opportunities, it may be necessary for you to revisit Section 3 (Growth Strategies) and list actions you would take to implement the opportunities.

Fill in:

New Products/Existing Markets (Product Development)

Use this section to extend your thinking and list potential *new* products you can offer to *existing* markets. Again, recall the guideline that the broader the dimension of your Strategic Direction the broader the possibilities for the content of your portfolio.

Fill in:

Existing Products/New Markets (Market Development)

Now list your *existing* products into *new* markets. Explore possibilities for market development by identifying emerging, neglected, or poorly served segments in which existing products can be utilized.

Fill in:

New Products/New Markets (Diversification)

This portion of the business portfolio is visionary, since it involves developing *new* products to meet the needs of *new* and yet-untapped markets. Consider new technologies, global markets, and potential strategic alliances to provide input into this section.

Once again, interpret your Strategic Direction in its broadest context. Do not seek diversification for its own sake. Rather, the whole purpose of the exercise is for you to develop an organized framework for meaningful expansion.

The grid in Figure 6.2 is a useful format to fill in your business portfolio of products and markets, both existing and new.

	Existing Products	**New Products**
Existing Markets	Market Penetration	Product Development
New Markets	Market Development	Diversification

Figure 6.2   Business Portfolio Plan

Fill in:

The Business Portfolio completes the strategic portion of the SMP. Now you are ready to proceed to the tactical 1-year marketing plan.

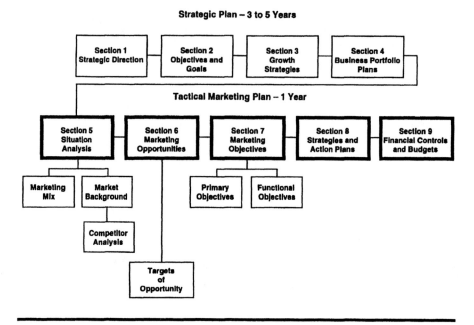

Figure 6.3   Strategic Marketing Plan

THE STRATEGIC MARKETING PLAN (TACTICAL SECTION)

Overview

The tactical marketing plan, the second row of boxes designated as Sections 5 through 9 in Figure 6.3, is not a stand-alone plan. It is an integral part of the total SMP.

Where commonalties exist among products and markets, one marketing plan can work as long as you make the appropriate changes in such areas as the sales force and the communications mix (advertising, sales promotion, and publicity). Where you face substantial differences in the character of your product and markets, then develop separate tactical plans.

Tip: avoid the temptation to develop a plan for a business, division, or product line by jumping into the middle of the SMP and beginning the process with the tactical 1-year marketing plan.

There are no short cuts. Reason: input to the Tactical Marketing Plan flows from two directions: (1) from the strategic portion of the SMP (top row) containing the strategic direction, objectives, strategies, and business portfolio; (2) from the situation analysis (second row), which progresses to opportunities, annual objectives, tactics, and budgets. Also, the thought process that went into the strategic portion of the plan now flows down to feed the shorter-term, action-oriented marketing plan.

SECTION 5: SITUATION ANALYSIS

The following three-part situation analysis details the past and current situations of your business:

Part I: Marketing Mix (product, price, distribution, and promotion)
Part II: Competitor Analysis
Part III: Market Background

The purpose of the Situation Analysis is to define your business in a factual and objective manner. Compile historical data for a period of at least 3 years. Doing so provides an excellent perspective about where your company has been, where it is now, and where you want it to go as defined in your Strategic Direction (Section 1).

Planning Guidelines

Part I: Marketing Mix — Product

Objectively describe the performance of your product or service by:

- Sales history, profitability, share of market, and other required financial data; where appropriate, you can graphically chart sales history with spreadsheets or your company's forms
Fill in:

- Current position in the industry related to market share, reputation, product life cycle (introduction, growth, maturity, or decline), and competition
Fill in:

■ Future trends related to environment, industry, customer, and competitive factors that may affect the position of your product
Fill in:

■ Intended purpose of your product in terms of its applications or uniqueness
Fill in:

■ Features and benefits of your product as related to quality, performance, safety, convenience, or other factors important to customers
Fill in:

■ Other pertinent product information such as expected product improvements and additional product characteristics (size, model, price, packaging); recent features that enhance the position of your product; competitive trends in features, benefits, technological changes; and changes that would add superior value to the product and provide a competitive advantage
Fill in:

Part I: Marketing Mix — Pricing

History of pricing

Examine the history of pricing policies for each market segment and/or distribution channel; consider their impact on the market position of your product.

Fill in:

Future Pricing Trends

Predict pricing trends as they pertain to product specification changes (including formulation and design), financial constraints, and expected market changes (trade/consumer attitudes, and competitive responses to price changes).
Fill in:

Part I: Marketing Mix — Distribution Channels and Methods

Current Channels

Describe your current distribution channels. Identify the functions performed for each stage in the distribution system (distributor, dealer, direct, E-commerce) and indicate levels of performance (sales volume, profitability, and percentage of business increases).

Where appropriate, analyze your physical distribution system, such as warehouse locations, inventory systems, or just-in-time delivery procedures.
Fill in:

Effectiveness of Coverage

Characterize the effectiveness of coverage of current channels by the programs and services provided.

Comment on effectiveness of distribution systems (distributors, dealers, direct). Specify the key activities performed at each point and indicate any areas that require corrective action. Also comment on the impact of future trends in distribution channels and methods, such as E-commerce.

Fill in:

Special Functions

Indicate special functions performed by your company's sales force for a particular distribution channel and what effect it had on the targeted market segments. Also include your distributors' sales forces, if applicable. Comment, too, on such approaches as "push" strategy (through distributors) or "pull" strategy (through consumers).

Fill in:

Target Accounts

List target accounts and their level of performance related to quantity and dollars. Add comments related to special needs of any account.

Fill in:

Future Trends

Indicate future trends in distribution methods and channels. Project what growth is expected in each major market segment. Also identify how this growth will affect your need for different distribution channels or methods of physical distribution.

Fill in:

Part I: Marketing Mix — Advertising and Sales Promotion

Analyze your advertising and sales promotion directed at each segment of the market or distribution channel based on the following elements: advertising dollar expenditures, creative strategy, media, trade promotions (dollars and type), consumer promotions (dollars and type), and other forms of promotion unique to your industry.

Fill in:

Competitive Trends

Identify and evaluate competitive trends in the same categories as above. Your advertising agency (or advertising department) and the sales force may prove helpful in providing this information.

Fill in:

Strategies

Identify your company's past and current advertising and sales promotion strategies by product and market segment and describe trends in these areas.

Fill in:

Other Support Strategies

Identify other support programs (publicity, educational, professional, trade shows, literature, films/videos, the Internet) that you have used and evaluate their effectiveness.

Fill in:

Planning Guidelines

Part II: Competitor Analysis

Market Share

List all your competitors in descending-size order along with their sales and market shares. Include your company's ranking within the listing. Show at least three competitors (more if the information is meaningful).
   Fill in:

Competitors' Strengths and Weaknesses

Identify each competitor's strengths and weaknesses related to such factors as product quality, distribution, pricing, promotion, management leadership, and financial condition. Also indicate any significant trends that would signal unsettling market situations, such as aggressiveness in growing market share or excessive discounting to maintain market position.

Attempt to make your competitive analysis as comprehensive as possible. The more competitive intelligence you gather, the more strategy options you have open to you. (To assist you in developing a quality analysis, go to Chapter 4: Checklists for Developing Competitive Strategies.)
   Fill in:

Product Competitiveness

Identify competitive pricing strategies, price lines, and price discounts, if any. Identify those competitors firmly entrenched in low-price segments of the market, those at the high end of the market, or competitors that are low-cost producers.
   Fill in:

Product Features and Benefits

Compare the specific product features and benefits with those of competitive products. In particular, focus on product quality, design factors, and performance. Evaluate price/value relationships for each, discuss customer preferences (if available), and identify unique product innovations.

Fill in:

Advertising Effectiveness

Identify competitive spending levels and their effectiveness, as measured by awareness levels, competitive copy test scores, and reach/frequency levels (if available). Such measurements are conducted through formal advertising research conducted by your advertising agency, independent marketing research firms, or publications. Where no reliable quantitative research exists, use informal observation or rough measurements of advertising frequency and type.

Fill in:

Effectiveness of Distribution Methods

Compare competitive distribution strengths and weaknesses. Address differences in market penetration, market coverage, delivery time, and physical movement of the product by regions or territories. Also identify major accounts where competitors' sales are weak or strong.

Fill in:

Packaging

Compare the package performance, innovation, and preference of competitive products. Also review size, shape, function, convenience of handling, ease of storage, and shipping.
Fill in:

Trade/Consumer Attitudes

Review both trade (distributor or dealer) and consumer attitudes toward product quality, customer/technical service, company image, and company performance.
Fill in:

Competitive Share of Market Trends

While share of market was previously included as a way of determining overall performance, the intent here is to specify trends in market share gains by individual products, as well as by market segments. Further, you must identify where each competitor is making a major commitment and where it may be relinquishing control by product and segment.
Fill in:

Sales Force Effectiveness and Market Coverage

Review effectiveness as it relates to sales, service, frequency of contact, and problem-solving capabilities by competitor and by market segment. Look to all sales force performance within the distribution channel. For example, if you are a manufacturer, look at your distributors' market coverage. Then examine distributors' coverage of *their* customers, which could be dealers and/or end users.

Fill in:

Planning Guidelines

Part III: Market Background

This last part of the situation analysis focuses on the demographic and behavioral factors of your market. Doing so helps you determine market size and customer preferences (both trade and consumer) in a changing competitive environment.

You can derive data from primary market research (market segmentation studies, awareness levels, and usage studies) or from secondary sources (trade and governmental reports). See extensive information on this subject in Chapter 5, Help Topics.

If you give careful attention to compiling accurate information, you will benefit from reliable input for developing the following parts of the SMP: Section 6: Opportunities, Section 7: Objectives, and Section 8: Strategies/Tactics.

This information also highlights any gaps in knowledge about markets and customers and thereby helps you determine what additional market intelligence is needed to make more effective decisions.

The following categories are considered part of the market background.

Customer Profile

Define the profile of present and potential end-use customers that you (or your distributors) serve. Your intent is to look further down the distribution channel and view the end-use consumer. Examine the following factors:

■ The Market Segments Distributors/Dealers Serve
   Address this question from your distributors' point of view.
Fill in:

- Distributors' Overall Sales

  Concentrate on classifying the key customers that represent the majority of sales.

  Fill in:

- Other Classifications

  Profile your customers by such additional factors as type of products used, level of sophistication, price sensitivity, and service. Also indicate any target accounts that you can reach directly, thereby bypassing the distributor.

  Fill in:

- Frequency and Magnitude of Products Used

  Define customer purchases by frequency, volume, and seasonality of purchase. Additional information might include customer inventory levels, retail stocking policies, and volume discounts. Also look at consumer buying behavior related to price, point of-purchase influences, or coupons.

  Fill in:

- Geographic Aspects of Products Used

  Define customer purchases regionally or territorially (both trade and consumer). Segment buyers by specific geographic area (e.g., rural, urban) or by other factors relevant to your industry.

Fill in:

■ Market Characteristics

Assess the demographic, psychographic (life-style), and other relevant characteristics of your customers. Also examine levels of product technology in use; purchase patterns and any distinctive individual or group behavioral styles; and attitudes toward the company's products, services, quality, and image.

Fill in:

■ Decision Maker

Define who makes the buying decisions and when and where they are made. Note the various individuals or departments that may influence the decision.

Fill in:

■ Customer Motivations

Identify the key motivations that drive your customers to buy the product. Why do they select one manufacturer (or service provider) over another? Customers may buy your product because of quality, performance, image, technical/customer service, convenience, location, delivery, access to upper-level management, friendship, or peer pressure.

Fill in:

■ Customer Awareness

Define the level of consumer awareness of your products. To what extent do they:
- Recognize a need for your type of product?
- Identify your product, brand, or company as a possible supplier?
- Associate your product, brand, or company with desirable features?

Fill in:

■ Segment Trends

Define the trends in the size and character of the various segments or niches. (A segment is a portion of an entire market; a niche is part of a segment.) A segment should be considered if it is accessible, measurable, potentially profitable, and has long-term growth potential.

Segmenting a market also serves as an offensive strategy to identify emerging, neglected, or poorly served markets that can catapult you to further sales growth.

You can also consider segments as a defensive strategy to prevent inroads of a potential competitor through an unattended market segment.

Fill in:

■ Other Comments/Critical Issues

Add general comments that expand your knowledge of the market and customer base. Also identify any critical issues that have surfaced as a result of conducting the situation analysis — ones that should be singled out for special attention.

Fill in:

SECTION 6: MARKETING OPPORTUNITIES

Planning Guidelines

In this section, you examine marketing strengths, weaknesses, and options. Opportunities will begin to emerge as you consider the variety of alternatives.

Try to avoid restricted thinking. Take your time and brainstorm. Dig for opportunities with other members of your planning team. If one doesn't exist, then put together a team representing different functional areas of the business (or persuade senior management to approve its formation).

Consider all possibilities for expanding existing market coverage and laying the groundwork for entering new markets. Also consider opportunities related to your competition. For instance, offensively, which competitors can you displace from which market segments? Defensively, which competitors can you deny entry into your market?

As you go through this section, revisit your strategic portion of the SMP (top row of boxes in Figure 6.1). While that portion represents a 3- to 5-year period, work must begin at some point to activate the strategic direction, objectives, growth strategies, and business portfolio sections.

Further, you should refer to the situation analysis in the last section, specifically the competitive analysis, for voids or weaknesses which could represent opportunities.

Note the two-directional flow used to create opportunities: (1) the visionary thinking you used to shape the strategic portion of the SMP now flows down to focus on 1-year opportunities, and (2) the situation analysis that exposes voids and weaknesses also represents opportunities.

Now review the following screening process to identify your major opportunities and challenges. Once you identify and prioritize the opportunities, convert them into objectives and tactics, which are the topics of the next two sections of the SMP.

Present Markets

Identify the best opportunities for expanding present markets through:

- Cultivating new business and new users
- Displacing competition
- Increasing product usage or services by present customers
- Redefining market segments
- Reformulating or repackaging the product
- Identifying new uses (applications) for the product

- Repositioning the product to create a more favorable perception by consumers and to develop a competitive advantage over rival products
- Expanding into new or unserved market niches

Fill in:

Customers/Buyers

Identify the best opportunities for expanding your customer base through:

- Improving or expanding distribution channels
- Product pricing including discounts, rebates, volume purchases, and allowances
- Product promotion covering advertising, sales promotion, and publicity — including the promotional activities of the sales force
- Enhancing customer service, including technical support
- Trade buying practices, identifying where the buying power is focused or has shifted (e.g., from manufacturer to distributor or to end user)

Fill in:

Growth Markets

Identify the major product growth markets in key areas (geographic locations) and specify which markets represent the greatest long-term potential.

Fill in:

Product and Service Development and Innovation

Identify the immediate and long-range opportunities for product development and innovation through:

- Adding new products to the line
- Diversifying into new or related products, product lines, and/or new items or features
- Modifying and altering products
- Improving packaging
- Establishing new value-added or customer services

Fill in:

Targets of Opportunity

List any areas outside your current market segment or product line not included in the above categories that you would like to explore. Be innovative and entrepreneurial in your thinking. These areas are opportunistic. Therefore, due to their innovative and risky characteristics, they are isolated from the other opportunities. Those you select for special attention are placed in a separate part of the objectives section of the SMP.

Fill in:

SECTION 7: MARKETING OBJECTIVES

At this point, you have reported relevant factual data in Section 5: Situation Analysis, and you have interpreted their meaning and consequences to your product line in Section 6: Opportunities. You must now set the objectives you want to achieve during the current planning cycle — generally defined as a 12-month period.

Once again, you will find it useful to review Sections 5 and 6. Also, it will help to review the strategic portion of the plan (top row of boxes in Figure 6.1). You want to be certain that actions related to your long-range strategic direction, objectives, and strategies are incorporated into your tactical 1-year objectives.

This section consists of three parts:

- *Assumptions:* projections about future conditions and trends
- *Primary objectives:* quantitative measurements related to your responsibility, including targets of opportunity
- *Functional objectives:* operational goals for various parts of the business

Planning Guidelines

Assumptions

For objectives to be realistic and achievable, you must first generate assumptions and projections about future conditions and trends. List only those major assumptions that will affect your business for the planning year at it relates to the following:

- Economic assumptions: related to Gross Domestic Product (GDP), local economics, industrial production, plant and equipment expenditures, consumer expenditures, and changes in customer needs. Also document market size, growth rate, costs, and trends in major market segments.

Fill in:

- Technological assumptions: include depth of research and development efforts, likelihood of technological breakthroughs, availability of raw materials, and plant capacity.

Fill in:

■ Sociopolitical assumptions: indicate prospective legislation, political tensions, tax outlook, population patterns, educational factors, and changes in customer habits.

Fill in:

■ Competitive assumptions: identify activities of existing competitors, inroads of new competitors, and changes in trade practices.

Fill in:

Planning Guidelines

Primary Objectives

Focus on the primary financial objectives that your organization requires. Also include targets of opportunity that you initially identified as innovative and entrepreneurial in Section 6.

Where there are multiple objectives you may find it helpful to rank them in priority order. Be sure to quantify expected results where possible. You can separate your objectives into the following categories:

■ Primary objectives
Current and projected sales, profits, market share, and return on investment (use Table 6.1, a form provided by your organization, or any spreadsheet software)

Fill in:

Table 6.1 Primary Objectives

Product Group Breakdown	Current				Projected			
	Sales ($)	Units	Margins	Share of Market	Sales ($)	Units	Margins	Share of Market
Product A								
Product B								
Product C								
Product D								
Other financial measures								

■ Targets of opportunity objectives
    Innovations in such areas as markets, products, pricing, promotions, and distribution
Fill in:

■ Functional objectives; product and nonproduct objectives

Planning Guidelines

Functional Objectives

State the functional objectives relating to both product and nonproduct issues in each of the following categories (you can alter the list of objectives to fit your business and industry):

Product Objectives

■ Quality
    Identify quality objectives that would achieve a competitive advantage by exceeding industry standards in some or all segments of your market.
Fill in:

■ Development
    Deal with new technology through internal R&D, licensing, or joint ventures.
Fill in:

■ Modification

Deliver major or minor product changes through reformulation or engineering.

Fill in:

■ Differentiation

Enhance competitive position through function, design, or any other changes that can differentiate a product or service.

Fill in:

■ Diversification

Transfer technology or use the actual product in new applications, or diversify into new geographic areas, such as developing countries.

Fill in:

■ Deletion

Remove a product from the line due to unsatisfactory performance, or keep it in the line if the product serves some strategic purpose, such as presenting your company to the market as a full-line supplier.

Fill in:

- Segmentation

    Create line extensions (adding product varieties) to reach new market niches or defend against an incoming competitor in an existing market segment.

Fill in:

- Pricing

    Include list prices, volume discounts, and promotional rebates.

Fill in:

- Promotion

    Develop sales force support, sales promotion, advertising, and publicity to the trade and consumers.

Fill in:

- Distribution channel

    Add new distributors to increase geographic coverage, develop programs or services to solidify relationships with the trade, remove distributors or dealers from the channel, or maintain direct contact with the end user.

Fill in:

- Physical distribution

     Identify logistical factors that would include order entry to the physical movement of a product through the channel and eventual delivery to the end user.

Fill in:

- Packaging

     Use functional design and/or decorative considerations for brand identification.

Fill in:

- Service

     Broaden the range of services, from providing customers access to key executives in your firm to providing on-site technical assistance.

Fill in:

- Other

     Indicate other objectives as suggested in Targets of Opportunities.

Fill in:

Nonproduct Objectives

Although most activities eventually relate to the product or service, some are support functions which you may or may not influence. How much clout you can exert depends on the functions represented on your planning team.

- Targeted Accounts

    Indicate those customers with whom you can develop special relationships through customized products, distribution or warehousing, value-added services, or participation in quality improvement programs.

Fill in:

- Manufacturing

    Identify special activities that would provide a competitive advantage, such as offering small production runs to accommodate the changing needs of customers and reduce inventory levels.

Fill in:

- Marketing research

    Cite any customer studies that identify key buying factors and include competitive intelligence.

Fill in:

■ Credit

   Include any programs that use credit and finance as a value-added component for a product offering, such as rendering financial advice or providing financial assistance to customers in certain situations.

Fill in:

■ Technical sales activities

   Include any support activities, such as 24-hour hot-line telephone assistance that offers on-site consultation to solve customers' problems.

Fill in:

■ R&D

   Indicate internal research and development projects as well as joint ventures that would complement the Strategic Direction identified in Section I of the SMP.

Fill in:

■ Training

   List internal training programs as well as external distributor and end-user programs.

Fill in:

- Human resource development

    Identify specialized skills and levels of performance required by those individuals who would make the SMP operational.

Fill in:

Other

    Include specialized activities that may be unique to your organization.

Fill in:

SECTION 8: STRATEGIES AND ACTION PLANS

Strategy is the art of coordinating the means (money, human resources, materials) to achieve the ends (profits, customer satisfaction, growth) as defined by company policy, strategic direction, and objectives.

In this section, strategies have to be identified and put into action. You must assign responsibilities, set schedules, establish budgets, and determine checkpoints. Make sure that the members of the planning team actively participate in this section. They are the ones who have to implement the strategies.

This section, then, is the focal point of the SMP. All the previous work was done for one reason and one reason only: to develop strategies and tactics. To refine the definition further: strategies and tactics are actions to achieve objectives. Strategies aim to fulfill longer-term objectives; tactics aim to reach shorter-term objectives.

Planning Guidelines

Restate the functional product and nonproduct objectives from Section 7 and link them to the strategies and tactics you will use to reach each objective.

One of the reasons for restating the objectives is to clarify the frequent misunderstanding between objectives and strategies. Objectives are *what* you want to accomplish; strategies are actions that indicate *how* you intend to achieve your objectives.

If you state an objective and don't have a related strategy, you may not have an objective. Instead, the statement may be an action for some other objective.

Fill in:

Planning Guidelines

Summary Strategy

Summarize the basic strategies for achieving your primary objectives. Also include alternative and contingency plans should situations arise to prevent you from reaching your objectives. Be certain, however, that such alternatives relate to the overall SMP.

As you develop your final strategy statement, use the following strategic issues as a checklist to determine its completeness:

- Changes needed to the product or package
- Changes needed to prices, discounts, or long-term contracts
- Changes needed to advertising strategy, such as the selection of features and benefits, or copy themes to special groups
- Changes needed in media plan
- Promotional strategies related to private-label products; dealer and/or distributor, consumer, and sales force incentives

Fill in:

SECTION 9: FINANCIAL CONTROLS AND BUDGETS

Planning Guidelines

Having completed the strategy phase of your SMP, you must decide how you will monitor its execution. Therefore, before implementing it, you have to develop procedures for both control (comparing actual and planned figures) and review (deciding whether planned figures should be adjusted or other corrective measures taken).

This final section incorporates your operating budget. If your organization has reporting procedures, you should incorporate them within this section.

Included below are examples of additional reports or data sheets designed to monitor progress at key checkpoints of the plan and to permit either major shifts in strategies or simple midcourse corrections:

- Forecast models
- Sales by channel of distribution
    - Inventory or out-of-stock reports
    - Average selling price (including discounts, rebates, or allowances) by distribution channel and customer outlet
- Profit and loss statements by product
- Direct product budgets
- R&D expenses
- Administrative budget
- Spending by quarter

As an overall guideline — regardless of the forms you use — make certain that the system serves as a reliable feedback mechanism. Your interest is in maintaining explicit and timely control so you can react swiftly to impending problems. Further, it should serve as a procedure for reviewing schedules and strategies.

Finally, the system could provide an upward flow of fresh market information which, in turn, could impact on broad policy revisions at the highest levels of the organization.

The only other part left in your SMP is an optional appendix. Your appendix should include the following items: copies of advertising campaigns for your product as well as those of your competitors, market data from market research, additional data on competitors' market strategies and pricing schedules, and details about product features and benefits.

INDEX